Beauty Bites Beast

Awakening the Warrior Within Women and Girls

To Dawn – Happy Birthday! Read this in good health

Beauty Bites Beast

Awakening the Warrior Within Women and Girls

Ellen Snortland

Trilogy Books
Pasadena, California

For information, write to Trilogy Books, 3579 E. Foothill Blvd., #236, Pasadena, CA 91107, or e-mail 72274.44@CompuServe.com.

Cover Design: J. Stevens Art & Design

Publisher's Cataloging in Publication

Snortland, Ellen.

Beauty bites beast : awakening the warrior within women and girls / by Ellen Snortland. -- 1st ed.

p. cm.

Includes bibliographical references.

ISBN: 1-891290-00-2

1. Feminist theory. 2. Assertiveness in women. 3. Self-defense for women--Psychological aspects. 4. Women (Psychology) 5. Women, Crimes against--Prevention. I. Title.

HQ1206.S66 1998 305.4'2

QBI98-122

Library of Congress Catalog Card Number: 98-60024

For my Mom and Dad
with thanks for their abiding commitment
to justice for the underdog

Acknowledgements

I am forever grateful to my immediate family, Barbara and Arnold Snortland and my sisters Alane Hohenberg and Mary Snortland, whose support truly makes everything I do possible. I am indebted to Beatriz Gandara and her family for their love, inspiration and loyalty. I couldn't have written this book without them. Thank you to Gregory Dowden and his family for the support they gave me over the years. Also, Lilia Mathieu and Ofelia Hutchison generously provided office space so I could complete my work. And although they couldn't care less for a formal thank you, my dogs have been in my heart and at my feet for the entire project.

I give special thanks to Tristine Rainer. It was her initial belief in this book that gave me the courage to go forward. Thank you to Betsy Amster for her invaluable assistance. My enduring thanks to Keven and Jim Bellows, kind and generous people who probably wouldn't even know me if they saw me on the street, but who helped me launch my writing career. I also want to thank Gavin de Becker and John Stoltenberg for their continued professional inspiration and guidance. Thank you to Laura Bellotti for her editing skills.

I can't thank all the folks in the full-impact, full-force self-defense community enough for their dedication, persistence and kindness. I especially want to thank all of the male instructors for the generosity of spirit and strength it takes to teach women how to fight. I particularly want to thank Mark Morris, Johnny Albano, Rondell Dodson and Randy Mamiaro for their encouragement and friendship. Please refer to my Epilogue for my express gratitude to female instructors.

I want to thank Marge Wood and Jim Laris for their kindness, patience and belief in my writing. Special thanks go to old and dear friends who have cheered me up and on for years: Sonja Staley, Susan Hammond, Kathryn Gravdal, Ken Kuta, Dianne Miller, Susie Johnson, Mary Noel, April Allen-Fritz, Linda Jenkins, Gary Kress, Georgia Bragg, Julie Engelman, Jennie Tomao, Janice Flynn, Ronda Ginsberg, Geanne Frank, Christopher Bradley, Peg Wills, Linda Morley, Kimberly Ward, the Larsens, June August, Jay Zorn, Larold Reghun, Rob Newman, Tina Levine, Anne La Borde, Zita, and Mary Migliorelli. They all have encouraged and believed in my writing.

A special thanks to Dr. Betty Brooks for her unyielding vision of women's liberation through self-defense and plain human decency.

Thank you to Susan Gegenhuber at the Pasadena Public Library for coming through for me in a pinch.

Table of Contents

FOREWORD

Gavin de Becker, author of the national best-seller, *The Gift of Fear: Survival Signals That Protect Us From Violence* i

PROLOGUE vii

CHAPTER 1

The Vagabond in the Castle Cellar 1

CHAPTER 2

The Awakening Kiss of Knowledge 9

CHAPTER 3

Sleeping Beauties Awake: Before and After the Self-Defense Class 19

CHAPTER 4

Why Beauty Sleeps — The Spells of Home and Hearth 31

CHAPTER 5

The Sleeping Potions of Religion and Science 43

CHAPTER 6

The Rules of the Realm of Men 55

CHAPTER 7

Veiled Villainies — Covert Verbal Attacks 65

CHAPTER 8

Awakening the Word Warrior — Defending Our Intellects and Ideas 77

CHAPTER 9

The Queen is Not Amused — Commanding Respect With Verbal Self-Defense 89

CHAPTER 10

A Woman's Home is Her Castle, The World Her Playground . . . 101

CHAPTER 11

Bitches, Battle Axes and Boadiceas 111

CHAPTER 12

The Magic Potion of Fighting Spirit 121

CHAPTER 13

Beauty's Battle Tales — Self-Defense Success Stories 131

CHAPTER 14

Knights We Know — The Good, The Bad, The Clueless 139

CHAPTER 15

The King's Messenger and The Village Crier — News and History 153

CHAPTER 16

The King's Entertainment — Film, TV, Music, and Fashion 163

CHAPTER 17

The Round Table — Think Globally, Act Locally 175

EPILOGUE 183

APPENDIX:

Most commonly asked questions 185

Resources for Violence Prediction, Prevention and Healing from Violence 193

Recommended Reading List 195

Foreword

Imagine we are designing a culture. We gathered together a committee of like-minded people (all men, of course, for it is men who design such things). Since these guys were already in charge, it would seem best to keep it that way, so one step would be the inculcation of a few rules. First and foremost, women will serve men; they will fear men; and they will need men. The penalty for disobedience will follow a sliding scale: an offending woman might be insulted, branded as a bitch, ostracized, or even killed. Of course, the patriarchy won't be without heart. WE will protect our women from other men — that only makes sense; they are, after all, our women.

We'll have to raise the girls believing that they need our protection — not an easy task given that every one of them is born with a rather remarkable self-defense system of her own. Each is an animal of nature, armed with dexterity, acute senses, strength, agility, intellect, guile, cleverness, and fantastic intuition. But we will tell them that they alone, in all of nature, are utterly defenseless, particularly against angry men. This will save a lot of grief all around, and the women will walk quietly along a path of eggshells, ever watchful not to anger any man.

A few of them, of course, will test the rules, and they'll need to experience the consequences of non-compliance. They will be beaten, raped, or killed, or just scared half to death, and their stories will be told through local news, movies, television shows, books and newspapers. The message will always be the same: "They shouldn't have done whatever they did that got some man so angry." The consequences suffered by the few will serve the many by reminding them that compliance is safer than resistance.

If some aberration occurs, and a woman finds the nuclear code for that remarkable defense system and elects to use it, perhaps even to show a man some consequences, that story will not be widely told. It would only encourage more trouble.

But what's this: Ellen Snortland has written a book that says the status quo is based on a lie? Women can protect themselves? Women should protect themselves? Women don't need men to guard them? This could change everything, upset the whole natural order of things.

Or would it restore the natural order of things?

*** *** ***

Our culture's dismantling of the defenses of women didn't happen the way I described, of course, but it did happen. However complex the actual reasons, the result is so simple that we rarely even question it: millions of women do not know that they can protect themselves, that they are dangerous creatures of nature. Millions more would never consider undertaking the most male of pastimes: delivering consequences to deter unwanted behavior.

But here's a fact: men are not supermen. WE have weaknesses just like every other creature — our eyes, for example. Another vulnerability is more famous. The acute pain we suffer from the much-unwanted kick to the groin is, as writer Carrie Fisher reminds men, "what you get for being foolish enough to wear your sex organs on the outside." I've noted only two vulnerabilities (more accurately, four vulnerabilities), but Ellen Snortland reveals the rest.

I recall taking an after-dinner walk with my then-girlfriend, who was an assistant instructor of Impact Personal Safety, the full-force, full-contact self defense training. A man approached us from the shadows and demanded some money. He was slightly more assertive than a street beggar, and slightly less threatening than an armed robber. He was angry even before we declined to stop walking, and he quickly stood in our path to raise the stakes of his request for financial assistance.

This man was sober, serious, and sane. He was intently focused on me, paying no attention to the woman at my side. I looked at him and thought: "Man, if you don't change your plans, you are about to get a life-changing lesson, because while you're evaluating which one of us men will prevail if I resist you, that woman you are disregarding is going to kick your ass . . . badly."

He must have seen a confidence in my eyes that is usually displayed by men who are not alone. "You see," I telegraphed, "This woman is not some prize I'm guarding — she is another soldier in my army, the superior fighter, in fact, because you have offered her the element of surprise. But don't concern yourself with figuring out what secret weapon makes me so unafraid of you. Best to spend your time retreating."

And that's exactly what he did, saving himself one of those humiliating experiences that Impact graduates deliver to unsuspecting bullies and criminals from time to time.

Do I advocate that women march about, staring men down, unafraid of a fight, provoking anger just by the look in their eyes? No, that job is already taken by plenty of men. But I do endorse, with every syllable I write here, that women learn the code of violence, and accept that they too have a stunningly powerful resource within them.

Occasionally, I encounter a timid soul who says, "I could never be violent," but she invariably adds a telling caveat: "Unless a person tried to hurt someone I love." So, the resource of violence is in us all; the only thing that changes is the justification for letting it out. Women can justifiably awaken that warrior within and let her do the job that nature gave her. All these warriors, in women and in men, have been dispatched with one clear order: protect the self. We cannot really expect half the population to disobey nature, even if that would occasionally serve the other half.

And yet some people expect precisely that. For example, they teach their sons that when a woman says, "No," that's not what she means. Thus the word "No" is far too frequently the beginning of a negotiation instead of the end of a discussion. In focusing on the verbal as well as physical self-defense methods, Ellen Snortland teaches a new lesson about the word "No." She shows that speaking it explicitly and with conviction is not unfeminine or rude.

When I encounter people hung up on the rudeness issue, (and there are many), I imagine this conversation after a stranger is told "No" by a woman he has approached:

MAN: What a bitch. What's your problem, lady? I was just trying to offer a little help to a pretty woman. What are you so paranoid about?

WOMAN: You're right. I shouldn't be wary. I'm overreacting about nothing. I mean, just because a man makes an unsolicited and persistent approach in an underground parking lot in a society where crimes against women have risen four times faster than the general crime rate, and three out of four women still suffer a violent crime; and just because I've personally heard horror stories from every female friend I've ever had; and just because I have to consider where I park, where I walk, whom I talk to, and whom I date in the context of whether someone will kill me or rape me or scare me half to death; and just because several times a week someone makes an inappropriate remark, stares at me, harasses me, follows me, or drives alongside my car pacing me; and just because I have to deal with the apartment manager who gives me the creeps for reasons I haven't figured out, yet I can tell by the way he looks at me that given an opportunity he'd do something that would get us both on the evening news; and just because these are life-and-death issues most men know nothing about so that I'm made to feel foolish for being cautious even though I live at the center of a swirl of possible hazards DOESN'T MEAN A WOMAN SHOULD BE WARY OF A STRANGER WHO IGNORES THE WORD 'NO.'"

Whether or not men can relate to it or believe it or accept it, many women live with a constant wariness. Their lives are literally on the line in ways men just don't experience. To learn this first-hand, ask some man you know, "When is the last time you were concerned or afraid that another person would harm you?" Many men cannot recall an incident within years. Ask a woman the same question and most will give you a recent example or say, "Last night," "Today," or even "Every day."

Still, women expressing concerns about safety are frequently the subject of critical comments from the men in their lives. I have a message for women who feel forced to defend their safety concerns: tell Mister I-Know-Everything-About-Danger that he has nothing to contribute to the topic of your personal security. Tell him that your survival instinct is a gift from nature that knows a lot more about your safety than he does. And tell him that nature does not requires his approval.

*** *** ***

The Impact training Ellen Snortland writes about brings many gifts, the most profound of which is the permanent, visible, quantifiable change that graduates experience. It comes from learning — deep in their cells— that no creature in nature is defenseless, that no person was put here just to be a victim or a frightened victim-in-waiting. I have several dear friends who went into Impact training with a hesitation about life, and came out with a new certainty. They are safer — they know it and they show it — but they are also less tentative, more confident, and above all, less afraid. A great truth has been revealed to them: The emperor has no armor; he has just flesh and blood.

Reading the stories in *Beauty Bites Beast*, stories of women who prevailed against male attackers, I found the only text I've ever read that balances our sad statistics: American women visit emergency rooms for injuries caused by their husbands or boyfriends more often than for injuries caused by car accidents, robberies, and rapes combined. And those going to the hospital are, in a sense, the lucky ones, for a woman is killed every two hours by a husband or boyfriend. Within this minute, as you read these words, another woman will be raped. What do we do about this? Tougher laws? More police? Longer prison terms for these awful men who attack the defenseless?

No, says Ellen Snortland, we stop buying into the myth of defenselessness. I am proud to stand with her, shoulder to shoulder, and add my voice to that message. I hope it helps to awaken some of the "sleeping beauties" she so eloquently calls out to. I also hope the men they accept as princes in their lives will be selected not because they offer protection, but because they behave the way princes ought to behave.

Bless you, Ellen, for telling your story, for writing an original and powerful book, and for showing that the warriors are just as feminine as the women waiting for the male soldiers to come back home.

Gavin de Becker

Prologue

When I told a friend that I was writing a book about self-defense, she asked, "Is it a 'How-to' book?" I thought a bit and said, "No, actually, it is a 'How come?' book." How come if women are just as intelligent as men, and are seeking liberation, so many of us consciously and unconsciously delegate our personal physical safety to the men in our lives? Is the vestigial dream of romantic rescue still that strong, even when we know our men are not with us all the time?

How come the females of every other species on the planet are fierce, regardless of size, and are the ones who train their offspring, male and female, in defense and hunting? How come most women wouldn't ever think of themselves as potentially dangerous toward an assailant? So this is a "How come" or "What's up" book about self-defense — a call to universal education, for women and children.

When I completed my first full-force class where I learned how to fight back against violence, I could not believe the shift I had in consciousness. Everyone in my class was as enthusiastic as I was. We all concurred that every woman, every girl should know how to do what we'd just learned. But as I went out and encouraged friends and loved ones to take the class, I ran into enormous resistance — resistance in the form of denial, procrastination and disbelief. I too had for years thought, "I really should take a self-defense class," but I always put it on the back burner. I, like most women, had to have an incident happen to give me the push into actually signing up for a class.

As I started to actively "proselytize" for women to take self-defense, I started hearing a constant refrain, "Well, what are the statistics?" It was as if there were a magic number that, when hit, would prove to the woman that her luck would finally run out. I realized women were playing the numbers, a rather sophisticated form of "It'll never happen to me." It was actually, "I have a one out of three chance of not being attacked." Well, ladies, sisters, daughters, mothers, friends, grandmas, the numbers are bad enough already. Anyone being attacked just by virtue of their gender, color, religious affiliation, sexual orientation, is enough. It's time for women to say enough is enough when it comes to violence.

Back to "How come?" How come so many women fail to learn how to protect themselves? How come so many of us are unwilling to be dependent on men for financial support but are so willing to be dependent in terms of our own safety? It doesn't make sense. How come so many are so willing to let the foxes guard the hen houses? It seems that physical safety, freedom to be in the world without fear of attack, is one of the last bastions of women's independence.

Once I learned how to defend myself I was able to see a parallel between physical self-defense and swimming. Swimming is physical self-defense too. The only difference really is that self-defense concerns people safety rather than water safety. Water rages out of control just as some people do.

I want to tell you about two incidents which took place when I was 18 years old. These events form part of the foundation upon which I have built my passionate belief in the need to acquire life-saving skills. On June 9th, the life-saving skill which saved my life and the lives of my mother and father was swimming. Two days later I had an encounter with a man that scared me more than a flood that had killed many people. Later in my life I was to realize how closely the events of that day mirrored the circumstances of millions of women throughout the world who have the choice, but don't know it, of defending themselves against the impending "disaster" of physical attack by another human.

On June 9, 1972, I was home in Rapid City, South Dakota, on vacation from college in California. The Black Hills of South Dakota are gorgeous and this particular spring had been really wet, so the hills were lush. I was golfing with my parents on that lovely afternoon when we noticed that there was something odd about the atmosphere. My Dad likened it to the feeling before a tornado. I called it "electric" or "yellow." If yellow has a smell, that's what it was like. The dogs in the neighborhood barked incessantly.

We went home and I talked my Mom into going into town to see a play. It was merely drizzling as we drove into the downtown area from our semi-rural, creek-side home. We were turned away at the box office because someone in the cast had called to say that they couldn't get into town due to a bridge going out in the Black Hills. Amateurs, I thought.

On the drive home, I repented my harsh judgement of the actor who couldn't get into town for the play. The water was pouring down in sheets. I was terrified, and for such a cocky young woman, I was quite willing to listen to my instincts.

I pulled over to the side of the road and told Mom that I wanted to call Dad and have him meet us at a friend's house. I did not want to go home. I didn't want him to be there either. I had nothing logical to point to, just a gut feeling of danger — big, big danger. All my senses had been on overload since the air had turned "yellow" that afternoon, but the deluge was all I needed to go on "red alert." My Mom wanted to get home. I let her talk me out of calling Dad.

The first thing I did when we got home was try to convince my Dad that we should leave. Wouldn't he just humor me, I begged? If I'm wrong that would be OK, but I just had a very bad feeling about the rain. There was nothing I could say that would move him. He watched TV as if nothing was happening.

I went down to the creek and noticed that it was coming up quickly. Then I saw dead livestock in the water. Dad started to get a bit concerned but declared that we wouldn't do anything but stay. My memory of this evening is one of enormous frustration. I felt like Cassandra, daughter of Hecuba and Priam. Apollo loved Cassandra and gave her the gift of prophecy. When she spurned Apollo, he turned her gift of prophecy into a source of suffering, for she was doomed to never be listened to or believed.

I remember running around, checking the creek, reporting back, trying to get some action. The action I wanted was to get the hell out. My parents were accustomed to my theatrics, I was a drama student after all, but looking back more than twenty-five years now I have a different interpretation of what actually went on that night. More about the analysis later.

As the water got higher and higher, I got calmer and calmer. I realized that I needed to pull myself together if anyone was going to listen to me at all. I convinced Mom that it wouldn't hurt anything if we were to retrieve her cedar hope chest (full of precious memorabilia, including her wedding dress) out of the storage room on the first floor. As Mom and I located the chest, some neighbors stopped by to see if we needed any help. As they grabbed the chest the storage room door burst open and the Rapid City Creek, now turned into the Rapid City "River," surged in. We had a hard time getting back upstairs but Dad helped us up. Finally, my parents listened to me about getting out of our house. We went outside into the wet nightmare that was our idyllic little neighborhood.

Cars were floating by, people were screaming. Trees, debris, you name it, everything was rushing by in water that had enormous force. My parents didn't know how to swim. They had never learned. I was a very strong swimmer so I assured them that I could handle the water and could help them handle it too. They just had to stay with me and not get separated, and we'd try to make it to higher ground.

With my parents on either side of me, we plunged into water that was crotch high. We got about 20 yards away from the house and the water was rising so quickly that it soon became painfully apparent that we were not going to make it. My folks were zombie-like, thank God. If they'd been panicking like some people do when they don't know how to swim, we would have been up, excuse the expression, shit creek. In a matter of minutes the water was chest high. Still in the middle, hanging on to both of my parents for dear life, I got myself and them back to the house safely.

Unbelievable as it was, we had to get up to the attic of our two-story home. We pulled my Mom's sewing machine into the hallway, stood on it and got up into the storage area. I was not wild about being up there because there was no way to get out. There were no windows and I couldn't see anything that I could use to break through. We had a couple of candles and I remember quoting Federico Garcia Lorca's characters, "Poncia" and the generic "servant." I had just been in a production of "The House of Bernarda Alba." I played two parts on that dark night.

Poncia: When you're powerless against the sea, it's easier to turn your back on it and not look at it.

Servant: She's so proud! She herself pulls the blindfold over her eyes.

Poncia: I can do nothing. I tried to head things off, but now they frighten me too much. You feel this silence? In each room, there's a thunderstorm, and the day it breaks, it will sweep all of us along with it. But I've said what I had to say.

Now there's a cheery play. I don't remember my parents saying a word. My poor parents. They were in shock and I was quoting a morbid Spanish play about turning your back on danger and being swept away. I couldn't stand the silence. We were flying blind. We didn't know what was going on outside our attic shelter. My family never was chatty and we weren't about to become so in an attic while we contemplated the possible end of our lives. The suspense was unnerving. I prepared mentally to die and entertained frightening scenarios.

What if I hadn't been there and Mom and Dad had stayed inside until the last minute and then gone into the water and been swept off their feet, unable to swim? What if, what if, what if? I knew that I wasn't one hundred percent able to handle raging water, but I also knew I had a fighting chance. They wouldn't have. I mulled over how awful the rain and creek had turned in such a short span of time.

The water suddenly went down very quickly. It was almost as if a toilet had flushed. We learned later that the dam below us had broken. Once the water receded, we climbed out of the attic. We then separated and went to our respective bedrooms. I found paper and wrote down everything I could until daybreak.

We woke to such utter devastation my heart broke. My buddy from grade school was outside looking for his mother's body. Neighbors' houses were gone from their footings and had crashed downstream. My Dad's car was sticking straight up, front end to the sky. Our other two cars were gone along with their carports. I heard they found four bodies in our yard later on. Our neighborhood had been one of the hardest hit. We were among the few people in our little community to make it out alive. It was one of the worst flood disasters in U.S. history. Overall, the death toll reached 238.

We had survived against terrible odds. I believe my respect for the force of water and my knowledge from Red Cross swimming classes saved us. While I certainly felt fear, I never panicked or froze, and was constantly assessing and making adjustments to our situation. Had I been alone, I would have left, but leaving my parents was not an option. I never once thought that our situation was impossible.

On to the second related yet separate incident: Our neighborhood was declared a flood plain, and we were barred from going back in for a few days. Finally, we were let back in and we attempted to clean up our house. We wiped down wallpapers, uprighted the refrigerator, got rotting food out of the freezer, and hosed off as much as we could. We also started the daunting task of cleaning our floors.

I was on my hands and knees washing the formerly white-painted wood floor in our sun room one morning the day before I was to go back to California. It was hard work consisting of scraping, picking, wiping, and mopping square foot by square foot. Although it was back-breaking work, it helped keep my mind occupied. My parents were gone with a load of salvaged items.

I felt the back of my neck bristle. I turned around and saw that a National Guard guy had walked into our house unannounced, and very quietly had made his way to where I was scrubbing.

My heart leapt into my throat. It's amazing how apt many of the clichés are in times of stress. He kept staring at me. Finally, he broke the silence with, "Are you alone?"

I froze. My mind stopped. I finally answered that my parents would be back any minute. He said, "You're real cute."

I replied, "Excuse me, but I've got a lot of work to do here."

"You don't need to be rude," he said. Can you imagine? Here I am in a position of trying to salvage our home and this guy is hitting on me — or contemplating more than that.

"I don't mean to be rude," I answered, "I just have a lot to do," whereupon he turned on his heel and left.

My heart was pounding so hard I thought it would burst out of my chest. I was shaking terribly. I could barely stand it until my parents got back, but I didn't tell them what had happened because nothing *had* happened.

The Guardsman definitely had more than National Guarding on his mind. It was a perfect setup for an assault. He was sizing me and the situation up. I can't prove anything, and I'll never really know what his intentions were. I just know that he did nothing to make me feel safe or protected. Rather, I felt that he was a predator who ultimately decided that his chances of overtaking his prey weren't very good.

I was scared to death of a man when I'd just confronted a killer flood with relative calm. How ironic it would have been for me to have survived a life-threatening flood only to be assaulted by a domestic soldier. Given that I didn't know anything then about fighting off a man, I had nightmares about that guy for years. The nightmare was that I froze, that the Guardsman jumped me and I couldn't scream, couldn't move, in effect, couldn't "swim." I muse now that if I'd had the same level of training in self-defense that I had in swimming I could have told the guy off and then, perhaps, reported him. I had no such skills at that time in my life. How unfortunate, because now I know that physical self-defense is no harder, nor any more foreign, than learning how to swim.

Because my parents lacked basic swimming skills, they would have had little chance of surviving the flood had I (or someone else who knew water safety) not been there. They were not only unable to swim to safety on their own, they were also unable to accurately assess the danger of the coming flood due to their unfamiliarity with bodies of water. To their great credit, however, they had insisted that I learn how to swim at a very young age. Because I had learned how to swim, swam competitively, and had taken Red Cross life-saving training, I was always extremely comfortable in and around water. Although the flood terrified me, the terror was empowering, not paralyzing. I was able to use my skills to accurately assess the impending danger and to negotiate the water safely with my parents.

A non-swimmer must, by necessity, always be afraid around any water. They can never relax or feel "free" around it, because it's always a potential threat. To cope, people with deep fears of the unknown must be in denial about their vulnerability, whether they are afraid of water or of men. Those who lack self-defense skills must always be afraid — of giving off the wrong "signals" to the wrong people, of strange men or men in general, of traveling alone, driving or walking alone at night, of being confronted at any time in any place by a potentially dangerous person, including a National Guardsman with possibly bad intentions.

Although swimming is natural to most people, it still must be taught. Swimming is not only a skill that can save one's own life, but is a skill that can be used to benefit others who are in trouble in the water.

Many women turn their back on the possibility of violence. If they can't see it, it won't happen. Some women are unconscious to even being afraid of assault. It's as if they've been around water, to stretch the swimming parallel further, and cope through hoping that they don't get into anything too deep. They are basically counting on the water behaving itself. Or they avoid many situations, thereby also missing out on a lot of living that's available to men.

While avoidance is certainly a strategy, it's a poor one if it's the only one you have. One can only strategize when one knows the possibilities available, whether it's in sports, career moves or warfare. Too many women are unable to strategize effectively about dangerous human situations because they've remained ignorant about the subject.

Violence that kills or maims can be as preventable as water injury or drownings. What if you heard of a country where six thousand of its citizens drowned every year, and where 500,000 citizens come very close to drowning? "Damn, why don't those people learn how to swim?" you would say. You would say that because you are not burdened by an erroneous belief that some people simply cannot or should not learn to swim. Sadly, most human beings are still burdened with the belief that it's impossible for women to defend themselves or others when confronted with violence. The purpose of this book is to convince you of just how wrong that belief is — and to inspire you to become a "beauty" who fearlessly "bites back" when your safety, or that of a loved one, is threatened.

I am not afraid of the water, and today I am not afraid to be out in the world and to fight back if I need to. I want each of you to experience the sense of freedom that I feel knowing I have the skills to defend myself. While I hope I am never in the position to have to swim for my life again — or fight off an assailant in a dark alley —

knowing that I can do either of these things if I have to enables me to live a freer, more relaxed life. And that is the kind of freedom I promise you will enjoy once you make the decision to "bite back." My fondest dream is that each woman learns the self-defense skills she needs to keep herself safe. If enough of us do that, if a critical mass of us knows the basics of self-protection, the rate of completed crimes will go down.

You may be surprised that I make fun and have fun with a serious topic: the physical safety of women and kids. That's not because the topic is funny. Humor is a form of self-defense and self-repair. Laughter is empowering and encouraging.

Beauty Bites Beast is an unabashed recommendation for full-force, full-contact self-defense, where a female and male team of co-instructors teach women realistic physical self-defense. Another feature of this form of instruction is that the male instructor is padded from head to foot so that the students can engage in as realistic a "fight" as possible. These classes have been around for more than twenty years and are given by groups like the Impact Foundation, Impact Personal Safety, FullPower and PrePare, Inc., and other organizations all related to the original organization called Model Mugging. However, any self-defense is useful and I don't put other forms down.

I must point to the many self-defense advocates and instructors who are working, often at great sacrifice, to bring what they know to women and children in their communities. I stand with many who have felt and believed in what I advocate long before I wrote *Beauty Bites Beast*. I honor them as warriors. And yet too many women keep putting off getting into a class. I wanted to see what I could do to remedy that unfortunate situation. Thus, this book.

I also wanted to find out more about my own and my "sisters'" resistance to learning the skills that ultimately completely altered my experience of the world. This is a book that explores my belief that *women must reclaim their natural ability to be physically dangerous in order to achieve true freedom.*

What I dream of accomplishing in my lifetime, along with the others within my self-defense community, is making effective, full-force self-defense classes taught by qualified, ethical instructors available to anyone who wants them, gentle men included. I'd like these classes to be available in schools, at all levels, just as a matter of course. I'd like corporations and unions to provide classes for their employees and members.

I believe that women and girls have been bamboozled into believing that they don't have a warrior within. I am here to say that's ludicrous and to help wake up that warrior. Wake her up; no more hitting the snooze button. She's there, she's strong, and she's ready to protect you if you'll give her the chance.

Ellen Snortland
Baja, Mexico, October 23, 1997

1

The Vagabond in the Castle Cellar

Frequent encounters with DANGER are a part of life. Beyond making you inwardly strong, familiarity with DANGER, like the near brush of death, can instill in you a profound awareness of the life force and the mysterious nature of the cosmos. Such heightened awareness can bring new meaning, determination, and richness into your life.

THE I CHING, HEXAGRAM 29, R.L. WING

Los Angeles, 1990—The knife-wielding man hiding in our basement must have frozen in fear when he heard our cars in the driveway. It was midnight. Oblivious to any danger, we'd driven to dinner in Westwood in separate cars and had come home in separate cars. That's what many of us do in L.A. because of busy schedules and long distances.

My husband parked first. When I shut the car off, I looked out my window and saw my husband's face as he leaned toward my car door. I jumped. He looked alarmed. I opened the door and he immediately shut it. He told me to stay in the car with our dog. Little did I know that this evening would change the course of my life.

I said, "Why should I stay in the car?" He put his finger to his lips and whispered, "I think there's someone in the house. Look over at the door. There's a brick next to it and the window is broken." I looked over and instantly, my heart was beating not only in my chest cavity but all over, in my throat, down to my toes. He turned and went into the house.

I was too ignorant and too frozen to know any better. I didn't stop him from going into a dark Victorian mansion at midnight with a possibly violent person inside. He was the man, my prince, wasn't he? Wasn't it my job as the woman, the princess, to stay safe, to sit beautifully, be protected and rescued while he put himself at risk?

I just sat in the car, waiting for him to come back out. I waited. I waited some more. My dog started whining because she had to pee. She'd waited in the car long enough. She brought me back to the present.

Breaking the princess mold, I couldn't wait any longer. He'd been in there too long. Finally, I decided to go inside the house. I approached the side door and as I stepped over the threshold, a black man with a navy blue knit cap bounded up the basement stairs, squared off with me in the doorway, and held his arm up high over his head with a knife ready to come down on me.

I screamed bloody murder, and later would come to understand why that clichéd phrase had become a cliché. My scream was powerful enough to startle him. He yelped, turned, and ran down our urban driveway lined by cinder blocks with barbed wire on top. I saw lights switch on in the tenement apartment building next door. I heard the clatter of the knife as he dropped it on the cement. In seconds he was gone. My bone-rattling scream, the only self-defense I "knew," had worked.

Just as I saw his back turn the corner at the bottom of our driveway, my husband came running out of the house to see, God knew what. He could have found me dead in a pool of blood for all he knew. Instead, he found me where I'd slumped to the ground in relief and abject terror. I couldn't stop shaking. I then sobbed uncontrollably. It was as if all my emotions went to the foreground and had me by my neck, strangling me. I couldn't breathe. My husband was frozen with disbelief. He got me into the house and managed to call the cops.

We waited for 30 minutes before the officers arrived. We always had to deal with other white people being amazed that we lived in that neighborhood in the first place and this was no exception. The cops pronounced how lucky I was. They went down into the basement and discovered that the man had been stealing food from our freezer. My heart ached when I heard that. I was racked with all sorts of emotions — fear, relief, gratefulness and now, guilt. I would have given the guy the food.

The knife retrieved from the driveway was a plain kitchen knife, the size that's used for carving. Not expensive, it bent easily. The officers took it as evidence once they'd asked me questions. I described the man. I went through the incident, step by step. I remembered our dog was still in the car and retrieved and relieved her.

I described the scream which I now realized was an ear-buster. As I finally calmed down, I started to joke around and told the police that they should check the local hospitals for any African American male between 30 and 40, 140 lbs., 5'8", a ruptured ear drum, and we'd have our guy.

They left and, while they'd done their job, I found the experience to be disempowering. They were resigned. I felt helpless in the face of urban crime and violence. The officers were polite, but skeptical that they'd ever find the guy. I kept thinking how lucky I was that it hadn't been worse. I also felt sick to my stomach. My throat was dry and raspy and I started to obsess. Imagine if he'd cut me . . . imagine if he'd hit me in the chest with the knife, or the throat, or the stomach.

My obsessing continued. What could have happened? I was outraged that I didn't know how to do anything but scream for God's sakes. What was up with that? Here I was, an intelligent, educated, physically fit, grown-up woman. I had been independent and a risk-taker for most of my life. And the only thing I knew how to do in the face of violence was scream? How weird. How utterly weird. As with many women who procrastinate about learning self-protection, it wasn't until that night, when I came face-to-face with a crime, that I became determined to take a self-defense class.

I would soon find that most women come to self-defense because of an actual violent incident that scared them into action. What a costly mistake, penny wise, pound foolish. Most women finally get angry enough to do something only after something happens to them. That night I didn't realize that my attitude was a cultural phenomenon and not a personal character flaw.

My husband stayed up with me while I ranted. He promised that he would give me a self-defense class for my birthday. Any one I wanted. How would I find one? We didn't really know where to start except for the yellow pages, which we took out that night. There were barely any entries. Funny, we thought, there's so much violent crime, one would think that the city of Los Angeles would be crawling with self-defense classes. Later we were to find that had we looked under the martial arts, we would have found more entries.

I didn't sleep that night. I kept replaying the scene in my mind. The man's arm loomed over me with the knife's blade catching the reflection of the driveway light we had on a motion detector. Why had I frozen? Why did I scream? What would I have done had he moved toward me? I couldn't come up with answers. My worst nightmare, that I would freeze in the moment of a dangerous encounter, had materialized 90%. My 100% nightmare which most women have, was that I would be too frozen to even scream. I had managed to scream. Why? Was it because screaming is natural?

My curiosity kicked in. In the following months I would become relentless in my efforts to understand my reaction to the knife wielding guy. I didn't know that I was beginning an investigative journey that would lead to my belief that self-defense is as important to a woman's well-being as other forms of independence. I had no idea then that I would soon adamantly conclude that self-defense is a major key to world-wide women's liberation, as well as an answer to the age-old question of how to vanquish violence without violence.

After that night, I came up with some theories about violence and about women that I'd never had before. I started to think that perhaps the reason I could scream was because I had seen other women scream in the movies. I had never seen my mother or sisters, friends, or relatives scream in real life. But I had seen it on the screen, large and small. Hmmm. Interesting. I'd never wondered, for instance, if men scream. Was screaming only the province of women? If so, why?

When I went to work the next day, I decided that I would produce a segment about self-defense for the talk show I worked for. The process of producing a talk show segment starts with an idea and then the proverbial "pitch." I had to pitch the idea in a meeting with my supervising producer.

To say I disliked my supervising producer is to be mild. I hid my disregard from him, and since he was so self-centered he probably didn't know how little I thought of him and his take on life. He was arrogant, and deigned to know "what the women of America want" from television. When I pitched the idea of a segment on self-defense, he scoffed.

"It's overdone, overworked, women don't want to see another thing about self-defense on a daytime talk show." I did not get the go-ahead. Funny, I thought. I don't know anything about self-defense. Maybe it was because I didn't watch daytime, morning or nighttime talk shows. Maybe I was the only dufus in America who didn't know anything about self-defense for women. The week prior to that he'd jeered at my suggestion that we book Rosa Parks. "Rosa Parks? No one cares about Rosa Parks, she's history." Precisely.

Dejected, I went back to my co-segment producers, mostly women and relatively diverse racially, all well-educated, and asked them if they knew what to do if someone attacked them. Nope. Not a soul did. Maybe it was because, they, like me, worked during the day and hadn't been watching talk shows, just producing them. I ran by them the scenario that had happened the night before, and they were amazed that I had even been able to scream.

Interesting that my supervisor thought self-defense was so passé. Over the next week or so, self-defense became my passion, not from the point of view of someone who knew anything about it, but from someone who had no clue about any of it. None of my friends knew what to do. I asked women everywhere I went, every time I spoke with a woman on the phone. They were stumped.

My informal self-defense survey convinced me I must do a self-defense segment, but I had to find a new angle to pitch to my producer. I went to the research staff and asked them to pull up anything they could find in a computer search on self-defense and to give me anything they came up with. We were hooked up to a vast network of computer research where one could enter any subject and virtually access whatever was written or produced on the topic.

The self-defense program that popped up most frequently was something called "Model Mugging." It had testimonials from enthusiastic women of all backgrounds who consistently said that it completely altered their lives. What a service — product — whatever Model Mugging was.

Then I found my hook. They used men dressed up in padding so that women could rehearse fighting back under the most realistic conditions possible without hurting anyone. Made sense to me. It was like driver's ed, driving a real car instead of a stationary one.

Concurrently I continued to ask questions that my mind had never formulated prior to my "incident." How did we learn how to defend ourselves as children? What do we learn as children? Why are we so ignorant as adults, and voila! It occurred to me to call the L.A. Chapter of Model Mugging to find out if they taught children's self-defense.

"Yes, we do. We're affiliated with a woman in northern California who teaches KIDPOWER, a child's version of Model Mugging." They gave me the phone number for Irene van der Zande.

Ms. van der Zande, a self-defense instructor and co-founder of KIDPOWER, started her journey in self-defense when she was confronted by a ranting, raving man who rushed her and her troop of Girl Scouts. He ran at them yelling, "I want one of the girls for my bride!" In the nick of time, a man stepped in and prevented an attack. Irene vowed never to feel so helpless again, got herself trained in full-force self-defense, and went on to create classes that are age-appropriate for girls and boys.

I asked the normal questions when I first reached Irene.

"Don't you terrify the kids when you teach them how to defend themselves?"

"What makes you think that they're not already frightened?" she asked.

"What do you mean?"

"How would you have felt when you were little seeing missing children staring at you from the milk cartons on your breakfast table and not having any idea of what to do in case an adult attempted to hurt or take you?" she queried.

"But isn't it awful, isn't it sad, for kids to have to confront violence so early?" I asked.

Van der Zande had been an activist in this field for years and had dealt with her share of grief in the face of a lot of woman- and child-directed violence. She agreed, "Yes, a lot of adults get sad about their kids confronting violence, but let me tell you a story. My daughter helped me gain perspective.

"One evening, I came home and was particularly emotional about the level of violence in the world. I was full of regret that my daughter would have to grow up and deal with it too. I held her and cried. My daughter, wise beyond her years, comforted me and said, 'Mommy, don't cry. If we lived in dinosaur days, we'd have to worry about being eaten.'"

That logic sold me. Van der Zande's daughter was right, and I had never thought about that either. Here we are, continuously confronted with the possibility of violence but very rarely provided with any answers regarding what to do about it. Another new thought. It seemed that the logical thing to do would be to prepare for violence, not because it was supposed to happen but *in case* it happened — like fire, or earthquake or other natural disasters. I told Irene I'd call her back after I spoke with my supervising producer.

I pitched the idea of kids' self-defense to my producer, fully expecting that he'd see how wonderful that would be. It would be perfect television I told him, action, pathos, little kids. There would be "take home" information that parents could use to keep their kids safe.

His reaction was extremely negative. He yelled at me, "No one wants to see a little kid hit a grown man!" I had described how Model Mugging used huge mock or "model" assailants who were actually instructors dressed from head to foot in armor and who would allow the pupil to hit them without worry of actually injuring the attacker.

"NO! Get off the self-defense thing, would you?" he yelled.

He made me even more determined to do a self-defense segment because I had inadvertently tapped into an area of complete ignorance in my own life, and apparently others' as well. There weren't many things that I didn't at least have a glimmer of knowledge about. I read a lot, I was culturally literate, I'd passed the California bar exam and had traveled a lot, and yet I knew nothing about defending myself. Hmmm. Curiouser, and curiouser, I felt like a pit bull with my teeth sunk into something that mattered.

My producer's reaction made no sense to me. Why was he so adamant? Why was he so convinced that women had had it up to their eyebrows in information about self-defense when clearly, at least in my informal yet extensive survey, the opposite was true? I proceeded to embark on a career move which would eventually cost me my well-paying job. I decided to go over my supervising producer's head to an executive whom I felt could relate to my quest.

She was a dynamic, ambitious woman who had risen in the corporate ranks of the entertainment company I worked for. I went into her office with great humility. I told her that I must have done a terrible job at pitching the segment idea about children's self-defense and that was why my supervisor had nixed it. (By the way, I happen to be a great pitcher when I'm passionate about something.) I couldn't really go into what a jerk I thought my supervisor was so I had to blame my ineptitude.

I started to explain more about KIDPOWER, and she stopped me short because I'd already sold her on the idea. Yes, she agreed that it would be fantastic. She'd never heard of anything like Model Mugging either except for some martial arts studios that taught kids. She'd talk to my supervisor. Sure enough, he smiled and nodded and oozed enthusiasm when she spoke to him about KIDPOWER. I saw him look over at me and give me a dirty look. I knew he would eventually get back at me.

I flew Irene van der Zande in from Santa Cruz so she could conduct a ten-minute segment on KIDPOWER. Ms. van der Zande brought boys and girls who had already graduated from KIDPOWER into the studio where we had an audience. The hosts interviewed her first asking the questions that I had provided them: "Doesn't it scare children more to learn self-defense? Does it make them into bullies? Wouldn't fighting back anger the assailant more and put them in more danger?" "No, no and probably not," Irene said, as she explained her answers in the steak part of her presentation.

But then came the sizzle part of the segment. The padded assailant lumbered out without his helmet. Al Potash, a kindly instructor with helmet off, he became a parent's worst nightmare with the helmet on. Irene directed the children through striking techniques designed to make the "mugger" let them go, so that they could run to safety. Everyone on staff and in the audience loved it.

Watching the children have tools and use them in order to save their own lives generated grief, relief and anger for all of us, staff and audience. As I watched, I realized how bereft my own childhood had been of practical knowledge in danger management. I was proud and envious of the kids for having the training they had. The segment was over in a flash.

In fact, it had turned out to be great television. The producer came over to me and congratulated me. It was exciting, it was evocative, timely, and provocative, she said. It made us ask questions of ourselves. It made us sad to think of how we'd grown up not having to have classes, or plain street smarts (white middle-class people at any rate) and how sad it was that we were having to train our children to protect themselves in case we couldn't be there for them.

My triumph, however, was short-lived. I saw my supervisor speaking animatedly with people who were congratulating him on the KIDPOWER segment. Had he had any style or grace, it would have been a perfect time to toot my horn. He ignored me. I was later laid off when the show moved to another location. I was not surprised.

What did surprise me was how I could not shake the KIDPOWER segment in my own life. I kept wondering how life might have been different had I been taught how to defend myself at the age that those kids had. Would I have traveled more? Would I have seen the world differently? Would my relationships with men have taken a different track? For better, or for worse?

I also took the next step in self-defense and made the commitment to take a class myself. I immediately called the L.A. Chapter of Model Mugging, which was, I was informed, making a name change to Impact Personal Safety, to register in the next possible class. I couldn't wait. And yet, I had a deep dread that I would come to understand better as time went on.

I called a dear friend and insisted that she take it with me. It was in that phone call that she reminded me that she had once called me and told me to look at the television because Model Mugging was being featured on a local TV talk show and I should see it. I had said, "Yeah, yeah, I will," and then promptly forgot it. She'd known about it for a year and had figured she should take it. She simply could not get motivated and something else was always more pressing. That would become a recurring theme I'd hear from women in years ahead.

I finally manipulated her into doing it with me. Why wait, I prodded. I used guilt, logic, humor, and fear. I wouldn't take no for an answer. I reminded her that she'd already had violence in her life, why did she put it off? If not now, when? She'd proved she could wait a long time already. In fact, we all had "A's" in waiting. Now was the time to work on some other skills.

We walked into that first class as ladies-in-waiting and walked out warriors-in-awakening.

2

The Awakening Kiss of Knowledge

I'm just a girl who cain't say 'No', I'm in a terrible fix!

LYRIC BY OSCAR HAMMERSTEIN
FOR THE AMERICAN MUSICAL, "OKLAHOMA!"

Fighting beasts, physical and metaphorical, is an idea that, as a white, middle-class woman, I didn't wrestle with until mid-life. And then it was accidentally, because of the man in our basement who attempted a non-sexual crime. He was simply an armed thief. What did I know about confronting criminals? Nothing. What was I about to learn about my birthright to fight back? Everything. I simply didn't know that I had a warrior asleep within me.

Beauty, its attainment and preservation, is the most frequent challenge that white, middle-class American girls are given. A big chunk of our economy is built on girls and women having enough beauty. And since we are held up in our shrinking global village as the females to emulate, our sisters of all colors around the world are inundated with our beauty battles, victories and losses.

The beasts we fight are zits, pounds, aging and unruly hair. World problems? What world? Feminism? Sorry, I shave my pits. Violence? What violence? Except, why did that girl have bruises? Oh, she fell down the stairs. And Candy, well, you know, she did wear such short skirts, it's no wonder that some boy might go too far. Wasn't it a shame that Sally was raped? She shouldn't have been out so late.

I was raised to believe that there was no reason for me to confront or fight, that fighting was not my domain; I was to leave the beasts to the prince and concentrate on the beauty of myself and his castle. I was taught that because of my erstwhile physical delicacy and, therefore, inferiority, I was not really able to fight. My fighting back would be impossible, futile, and fatal. These beliefs were not exactly beliefs.

"Belief" per se is too conscious. I didn't even give it thought. I subscribed thoughtlessly to fairy tales, bible stories, and social rules that stripped me of survival skills.

The fact that men were supposed to take care of me, of us, simply because we were women, was just so — something that didn't require thought or belief. Men were supposed to be the caretakers of both women and children just as women have been the traditional caretakers of children. The ideal relationship was a father who worked outside the home, and a mother who stayed home and took care of the house and kids. He was supposed to protect everyone. We didn't realize that there were other models or circumstances. We were able to ignore the reality of women of color and poverty because we rarely ever met them or knew their stories because mainstream entertainment and media ignored their lives.

It bothered me when I noticed that we were all white and middle class when I took my self-defense class. But maybe white, middle-class guilt has a special place in social movements; if the "protected ones" can see and feel injustice that is obvious to other "out" groups, they are in a perfect position to help foster change for everyone. White, middle-class women were primary movers in gaining co-education and the franchise. They have had, and continue to have, a little more access to the tools of the status quo than the completely disenfranchised. They have discretionary funds, more time, more access to formalized power. Maybe, when enough white, middle-class women see the necessity for self-defense, the "out" groups will get more access.

In 1990 these thoughts were only seeds in my brain as Kim and I walked around the classroom, which smelled vaguely of a men's locker room. We were in Van Nuys, California, in the second story of a strip mall. The classroom was large, had an expanse of blue tumbling mats in the center, and Japanese-style screens in one corner. We were there to learn how to defend ourselves. The other thirteen women, all appearing to be middle-class, ranged from early 20's to late 60's. They looked as utterly out-of-place, befuddled, and uncomfortable as we did.

We were to fill out information sheets with questions no one had ever asked me before. Had I been attacked? Why did I want to learn to defend myself? Had I ever been raped? I answered "no" to that, but would end up revising that to a "yes," the more I thought about it. This was only the first 10 minutes of a twenty-hour class and I was already facing things, learning things, questioning things, that hadn't occurred to me before. I noticed how quiet and solemn the women were as we answered our questionnaires. We were terrified. And we were fascinated.

There were people with "Impact Personal Safety" emblazoned on their sweat shirts and t-shirts. I wasn't prepared for the impact that they would have on my life. No wonder they called themselves "Impact."

As soon as our information sheets were collected, we were asked to sit in a big circle. Our instructor, Annette Washington, explained we would open and close every class with a "circle." Since we all needed a safe space, she asked us to keep what we heard in the circle confidential. Our first circle, she explained, would help us get to know each other and why we were there in class. I was tempted to roll my eyes. Another "sharing" circle. "How California," I thought. The circles would become integral to every class and I became the biggest circle fan of all.

We could talk in the circle or pass, but we were to tap our neighbor by holding her hand to pass the "power," to indicate we were passing or done talking. Oh, brother. But pass the power we did, and I heard self-loathing, self-blame, and self-recrimination for violence that had been inflicted on women completely unprepared to defend themselves. I heard giggles about how stupid a woman considered herself for not believing her inner-voice that had warned her about the man who subsequently attacked her. By the fifth woman I had been outraged, touched, and choked up. I couldn't wait to hear every woman's story, including my own. I had never even considered my own unique story as it related to self-protection. Something important was happening. I felt brain explosions and curiosity popping all around me.

Before we got up on the mat, Annette explained more to us, again things I'd never heard about. We weren't going to be learning the martial arts. Aspects of martial arts would be used in what we learned but our method of self-defense had been developed by Matt Thomas, who had studied how women were actually attacked. He'd been dismayed to learn that a female friend of his, a highly trained martial artist, had been unable to prevent a vicious rape from being completed. Why? Why? His discoveries were the basis for a form of self-defense that was being taught by him, and by people who had learned from and since separated from him.

Matt Thomas and his associates realized that women were attacked by men in ways that were unique. Men attacked women in a predatory way, often from behind, whereas when men fought men, there was more often a "squaring" off. Men were territorial with each other but predatory with women. Mr. Thomas had also realized that the martial arts could fail women because they were developed for men's bodies, not women's.

The traditional martial arts had been developed in countries where weapons had been taken away from the lower classes. In order to defend themselves, or to rebel, people had to develop ways of fighting which incorporated their own bodies or weapons that weren't actual weapons, like farming implements and materials.

Annette explained that our bodies are different from men's bodies, and that women often make the mistake of trying to fight like men. Women can't match men's upper-body strength since our strength is in our hips. She laughed, "When they say get up and fight like a man, tell them to get down and fight like a woman." I didn't have a clue what she was talking about. She explained that since many male-to-female attacks involve a man knocking a woman to the ground as a precursor to rape, we'd learn to fight on the ground. Oh. Another new concept. No wonder we'd been in such mystery about what we would learn. We had nothing to relate to, nothing to draw on, at least in the mainstream.

As the time to get up on the mat neared, we were all getting more anxious. There was more giggling. We went from women to girls before my very eyes. We weren't going to learn fighting right away, at least not with our bodies. We were going to learn how to yell "No." Easy, no?

No, "No" wasn't easy for most of us. I had an easy time because I had been educated in the theater department and could do drama-type exercises pretty easily. For more than half of the women, yelling "No," was extremely difficult and stressful. They screamed, yelped, whispered "No," but it wasn't until we'd practiced "No," a simple yell, that we could do it as a group. Very interesting. "No" is truly the first line of defense for any boundary, as in "No trespassing," "No, don't touch me." "No, no, no."

We were timid, we were tiny, a handful of us were bold but "No" was not as easy as even I thought it would be. Annette talked to us about the difference between screaming and yelling "No," another distinction I'd never made.

But hadn't my scream worked? Yes, it had but I also noticed it was the only thing I knew how to do. Yell? Screaming was automatic and something I'd seen in the movies. Was that why I'd screamed? Yelling required something that screaming didn't. Screaming hurt and wasn't powerful; it was stereotypical. Yelling was centered and required that I breathe and give an order, a demand, set a boundary. Wow, the "No" lesson alone was worth the price of admission.

After "No," we went on to physical techniques; eye-strikes, heel-palms, knee-strikes, and then combinations. We worked on footwork, we worked on keeping a safe distance, we worked on creating a stable stance. We worked on holding our hands up in a protective yet not provocative way. We yelled "NO!" as we practiced these "moves" in the air. Yelling "No" was not just a thing to do, it had a purpose, Annette explained. Yelling "No" was a warning, an alarm. It helped us breathe and it gave us power. That's why so many of the martial arts had yells in them.

And then "he" came out. "He" was the reason that Model Mugging had been given such high reviews in all the articles our computer search had pulled up. The man in the padded suit was why I had been so moved by KIDPOWER. Aha. The man in the padded suit was also the source of the locker room smell that wafted through the room.

Rondell Dodson was the male instructor, half of the two-person instructor team. He had padding from head to foot. We giggled when he came out. He was huge anyway, but with his helmet and suit, he loomed over us like our worst nightmare. He proved to us that we couldn't hurt him and that we should not worry. He let us hit his eyes on his helmet. No way could we get through the mesh. Annette kicked him in his groin as hard as she could to prove to us that his "family jewels" were in safe hands.

We acted like kids because, developmentally, we were. I now believe that most of us had been developmentally arrested in childhood in matters of protecting ourselves from the threat of violent men.

Rondell warned us that when he had his helmet on, he was "Chester," and not to be trusted. Without the helmet, we was the kind instructor, feminist, father of four that he really was.

All of the moves were awkward. But as we practiced they made sense and, as with anything, became more fluid. "Ready stance," Annette would yell. We all took a shoulder's width stance with our hands up, elbows in. "Yell 'No'," she yelled. We did. "Step, eyes," we stepped and we all did eye strikes in the air. "Knee to the groin, knee to the head." Pretty soon, she said, we'd have our first fight on the mat. We would go slowly, our instructors assured us. Was it really true that we had learned all of this in two hours? It seemed like two minutes.

Annette demonstrated a fight for us on the blue mats. One of our assistants played the coach role. Here was the routine: we would wait in the line, next to the mat as the coach, the female instructor or assistant, would come and escort us to the center of the mat. She would ask us if we had any injuries. If we did, we'd point them out and she would let the "mugger" know to be gentle to that area. If there were no injuries, she'd say, "No injuries, Annette is ready," and the mugger would advance on us and we'd fight him. That simple.

Our job in the line was to cheer and support the person who was fighting on the mat. "No talking please," reminded a few of us of twelve-step program policy. We really did need to focus on the person who was fighting because we learned as we watched them. When the fight was over, it would be signaled by the whistle blown by Annette or the assistant.

When we heard the whistle we were to get up, look all around us while we yelled, "Look." That was to break the tunnel vision that occurs when adrenaline is pumping through our veins. We were to practice looking to see if there were any other attackers lurking or if we were in danger from traffic or other circumstances. Then we were to yell "assess" which was to remind us to look at the now prone attacker in order to "assess" if he was in fact knocked out so we could run to safety. And then, finally, we were to run back to the line which symbolized safety, hold the hand of the woman at the end of the line, and yell "911," as a symbolic way to communicate that we'd gone to a safe place. Then the next woman in line would fight, and so on.

Annette demonstrated it all as we watched her power, her skill, her rage turned into action. She was tiny and yet she took on "Chester," the over-sized mock assailant with seeming ease. We cheered and she told us that in no time, we'd be doing the same thing.

My first time on the mat "time stood still," the cliché usually associated with falling in love. As Annette announced, "No injuries, Ellen is ready," I felt frozen. My deepest fear. I wanted to run but then I heard Annette coach me to yell, "No!" I did it. And sure enough, I unfroze and moved into "fight" mode. The simple defenses we'd learned were there, not in my mind's memory but my body's, just as the instructors had said. In no time I had Rondell, rather "Chester," on the ground due to my wrecking-ball — my knee to the head blow that knocked him farther than I could have ever guessed it would.

Was he faking it? The whistle shrieked; I looked, I assessed, and I ran to the line and yelled "911" with my classmates. I had won and I was hooked. Finally, the home team was winning.

Of course I won, I thought; it's set up that way. It would take the entire twenty-hour class for me to be convinced physically, mentally, and emotionally, that my classmates and I would have a fighting chance in a real encounter with a real man.

The second round on the mat, Annette asked me if I had any injuries. No, I didn't, other than the hurt of being a woman in general, I thought. The fights this time would come from the back and we'd be "taken" to the ground. I wanted to throw up.

Annette turned my back to that big old padded assailant, held her thumb up and said, "No injuries, Ellen is ready." Then he attacked me from the back and I had my second fight rehearsal. "No injuries, Ellen is ready." Words that changed my life.

We were so proud of each other. We especially loved seeing the meekest and smallest of us open up and fight. "Use your anger," our instructors and assistants would yell. Put your anger to work. Use the anger to hit harder, slow down, take aim, and BAM! Connect the knee, the elbow, the palm to the tender parts that would make the attacker stop attacking.

The next four Saturdays were just as intense as the first. During our opening and closing circles we would share our hearts out. We shared our doubts, we shared our nightmares, we shared the differences we saw in ourselves as we went about our regular day. Annette had asked us to observe our dreams. She'd had women report back that nightmares that had always ended in defeat were turning around. Women were winning in their own terrifying dreams.

We all experienced wide swings of feeling. A few of us would be excited about coming to the next class, but the majority of us dreaded it, even though we loved it once we were there. It was uncomfortable to confront our fears, to face the mugger on the mat, to let go of our childish hopes that someone would always be there to rescue us. We were learning to rescue ourselves, a lesson that most of us had put off, not because we were abnormally irresponsible, but because we were fulfilling our roles as beauties, as damsels-in-distress.

One week Annette gave us an assignment, yet another concept that had never occurred to me. She told us to walk around as if we were dangerous. What would it feel like if we perceived ourselves as potentially dangerous? Me, dangerous?

I wrote down danger and saw for the first time that danger is "anger" but with a "d" in front of it. My world view was changing with the acquisition of physical skills. I was tapping into an area of anger that could be directed and could be used to make myself and others safe. This was revolutionary. Revolutions are by their very nature disturbing.

We were particularly disturbed by the class session where we practiced rape scenarios. We learned that 50% of rapes happen in a woman's own home. Frequently she is awakened by an intruder who happens to take the "opportunity" to rape someone who "foolishly" left their door or window unlocked. The people who leave their doors and windows open in the heat of summer are the poor; they are old people, young people, people of color in low-income neighborhoods. Air-conditioning offers the luxury of security as well as temperature control. This was the class that made us the sickest.

The rape scenarios were called "reversals" because we learned how to "reverse" what seemed like an impossible circumstance. We fought the hardest during those scenarios because the terror was most palpable. We cheered the hardest because of the obvious cruelty involved with a larger man waking up a sleeping, often smaller, usually defenseless woman to rape her.

We learned and practiced that no man's arm was bigger or stronger than the smallest woman's leg, especially if she was on the ground using her hips for power. She could kick with enough force to break his knee. She could kick away any hand that tried to grasp an unwilling ankle. We learned and saw from experience that it was impossible to hold down every part of a woman and also rape her. We learned to look for "openings," that is, opportunities to fight back. We learned to strategize. We learned to speak through abject fear and we learned the nuclear power of "No!"

Every fight, from the very first to the last, accelerated in difficulty and speed. Soon we were fully fighting a man that grunted when we hit, begged us not to hit anymore, slimed us with real sweat, moved out of the way, dodged our blows, and fought back.

In the rape scenarios, or in scenarios of our own choosing where we were most nervous in real life, Rondell and then an added mugger would use the most foul language possible. The language was used so that it would lose its potentially paralyzing effect on us. Many perpetrators know that all they have to do to dominate a female victim is to talk rough. That's enough to freeze her into submission. We participated in our own desensitization by listening to it and letting the vile language go by while we looked for openings to kick his ass.

The last class was our "graduation." We were encouraged to invite our loved ones to watch as we demonstrated our new-found ability to fight back against violent attack. All of us had people we wanted to have take the class. Some of us had people we wanted to prove something to. Most of us worried that we'd fail in front of an audience. We questioned the wisdom of fighting in public. Wouldn't it make us nervous and we'd fall on our faces?

Annette assured us that adding an audience would empower us. If we were beginning to fight as competently and confidently as we were, an audience would add another level of difficulty. We were no longer tender damsels. We were awakened warriors, ready to joust for the court.

With my typical missionary zeal, I made a list of twenty women in my life I wanted to attend and called them, begging them to come. Twelve said they'd come. Two actually showed. I was getting my second glimmer of how hard it is to sell a class that logically should sell like hot-cakes.

We had about 30 people at our graduation. Lisa Gaeta, the co-founder of Impact Personal Safety in Los Angeles, along with her husband, Al Potash, talked to our friends and family in a guest presentation designed to prepare them for what they were about to see. She warned that they might get emotional. She explained the method, how our bodies were different from men's. She explained that this was not an anti-male group but an antiviolence group. Impact was about men and women working together to end violence. She reviewed what Annette had told us in our opening circle. Was it only five weeks ago?

The enrollment process was not "hard sell" like some of us had worried it might be. Many of us had been to motivational guest seminars where we'd been cornered, cajoled, and pressured, and we didn't want that for our friends. We also figured that our fighting would sell itself. After all, watching us fight like we'd been doing it all our lives would be inspirational enough to have anyone who wanted to feel safe sign up, wouldn't it? They'd known us before; after they'd seen our "after," who could resist? During the presentation, we all "witnessed," all fifteen of us, because someone asked if everyone felt they'd gotten their money's worth. Yes, we all had. This was the first time I'd seen a class deliver 100% or more.

I'd had a lot of sales experience, and I would have bet the farm that at least five women would sign up. Out of twenty potential students, only one woman signed up at our graduation. How odd.

That basics class changed my life forever. I continued and completed every class I could. I became an assistant, an instructor, and an advocate of full-force self-defense.

Had I known that within five years I'd write a book about a woman's moral and natural right to fight, I would have asked all of my classmates for "before and after" interviews. Instead, in the next chapter, I'll introduce you to a cross-section of women I interviewed on the phone from all over the country. They agreed to let me speak to them before they started their basics class and after they graduated. They are all unique, and yet they are everywoman — sleeping beauties who finally realized they were asleep. I see myself in all of them. Perhaps you will too.

3

Sleeping Beauties Awake: Before and After the Self-Defense Class

Do not look back in anger, or forward in fear, but around in awareness.

JAMES THURBER

We came together as strangers, but each of our stories sounded familiar to the rest. The self-defense class was, for most of us, the first place we could come out of denial about our daily fears. Most were closeted "scaredy cats." We were professionals who talked about being scared to death just being home alone. We were women who'd lost promotions because we were scared to work late. A third of us had been encouraged by therapists to get into an Impact Personal Safety class. Some women talked about hearing fathers beating up mothers when they were little and about how afraid that made them of all men. We understood, without actually saying so, how similar our experiences were just by virtue of being women. But more than anything, what we all had in common was that none of us had a conscious clue about self-defense, and all of us had altered our lives significantly due to fear, unfounded or not, of male violence.

Like those women in my first self-defense class, most of the women I subsequently interviewed for this book initially knew nothing about self-protection, whether they were in Los Angeles, San Francisco, Montana, Colorado, Washington, D.C., San Luis Obispo, or New York City. Every person in my series of phone surveys reported that what they got out of their self-defense training was far more than they could ever have imagined. In this chapter you will meet some of the women who shared their "before" and "after" thoughts and feelings with me. Some names and identifying circumstances have been changed to ensure privacy. Hopefully, hearing their stories will help awaken the "warrior" within you. Once you can acknowledge your need — and your birthright — to access your natural fighting instinct as they did, you will be inspired to take the defense of your beauty, your body and your dignity into your own hands.

Before's and After's

Rose: "I Can Now Go Anywhere I Damn Well Please"

Rose, a grandmother, is sure her friends are amused by her "religious fervor" about the Vital Victories class she took in New Zealand. Rose is 46, 5'1", 7 stones, or 110 lbs. By her own description, she is extremely middle class, with a conservative appearance. She put off taking a self-defense class for 15 years because she was too busy raising children and working. She now can't believe that she procrastinated so long. Whereas she once felt cautious whenever she was alone, whether walking or at work, she is now confident that she can fully defend herself if she must. She is a completely changed person.

Like most women I've talked to, Rose was afraid that she'd freeze if faced with the threat of violence. She feared being "wimpy." She was also afraid that she'd be the "worst" in the class, which she discovered was not relevant since everyone was a novice. She loved doing the class with four of her co-workers, and said they became close through the shared experience.

Rose works as a mental health professional in a remote area of New Zealand, two hours away from the closest psychiatric hospital. They must drive severely disturbed people over rough terrain in a van. While that professional task used to be daunting, all of Rose's co-workers who attended Vital Victories now feel confident of their ability to handle any of the patients under any circumstance.

Rose told me that other women she knew who had taken other styles of self-defense classes were so "envious" that the Vital Victories class provided a chance to fight full-out and practice on a moving/talking/bigger person.

While Rose lives in a rural community where people still don't lock doors or take security precautions, violence against women is nonetheless very much alive. Rose's former husband raped her anally twice. One of her friends was raped at a "safe" New Zealand beach when she went there by herself. In her "before" interview, Rose lamented that she couldn't go to a beach alone, "tramp" alone, or walk at night by herself. Rose will be going anywhere she damn well pleases now, thank you very much.

Iris: Re-enacting and Overcoming Childhood Abuse

As an R.N., Iris has seen close-up the results of violence. She is tall, between 5′ 8″ and 9″, 130 lbs., and had been sexually abused by her stepfather and three of her mom's boyfriends as a teenager. Her fighting spirit was intact before she joined Bay Area Model Mugging, (BAMM,) due to the healing work she'd done in groups. She simply lacked skills to fight back.

What did she get out of the class? "A heightened awareness of the strength I have, and that men are vulnerable. It was a deep psychological purging. Most significant to me was the opportunity to request a customized fight scenario where I asked the two male instructors to re-enact two of my mom's male friends in their 50's when I was a teen." Iris directed the scenario and asked the female instructor to play her mother. But this time, rather than laughing at her like she did before, she had the "mom" intervene "only a bit," simply because she wanted to do a full fight on her own. "It was a cellular event. I feel like the molecules in my body changed. I was so surprised at how deep the class went; it was physical, mental, emotional and spiritual."

When I asked Iris if any of her attitudes about other women shifted as a result of the class, she answered, "Absolutely. I used to believe that everyone saw things the way I do. Listening to the other 15 women talking about the same things changed me. I saw some get scared and fight anyway — there were very 'feminine' women who were such tigers. It was nice to see tiny women get so feisty and brave."

Amy: Learning to Avoid Foolhardiness

Amy has a B.A., is 30 years old, 5′4″ and medium weight. She is a fighter and seems to always have been. Her dad was a hitter, which made her quick to defend herself. A woman threw a punch at her once as she was walking in Berkeley. She blocked the punch and then threw the assailant into the gutter. Her concern was that she may have been too confident; after BAMM she gained more confidence, but learned how to avoid foolhardiness. She also learned new physical skills and new ideas about how to avoid conflict.

Amy doesn't pull punches with her opinions. When I asked her what she thought would make the biggest difference in eradicating violence against women she said, "There should be no second chance for rapists and molesters. Women who kill abusive husbands ought to be given their dream home." (Author's note: Wouldn't that be the day? Now, most women who kill their abusive husbands get a new house all right, the big house, even if it's documented that he tortured or attempted to murder her for decades.) Amy feels strongly that every woman should learn how to fight, and that the training should start young.

Katherine: "I'm Tired of Waiting for Justice"

Katherine, 27, mother of 4, divorced once, going on her second divorce, is a woman who has overcome odds that could have overwhelmed her. She can remember three specific times she's been raped. She believes her father may have raped her but can't say so for sure. She does remember that he used to wake her up in the middle of the night, take her to the basement, tie her up and beat her. "My father used to say we were being punished, but we were being tortured, " Katherine recounted. The older kids got it worst, but the father beat all of them as his mother used to beat him. He once beat Katherine so badly she missed school for two weeks because of the damage, and she couldn't even get out of bed for two days.

How did she change her life? Reading, listening to tapes, and attending support groups. She has a dream that she will never repeat what her family has done for generations. She attended a graduation of Worth Defending (a full-force self-defense provider in the midwestern states and Northern California) and knew it was for her because of the fear and excitement she felt when she saw women fighting back so powerfully. "I'm scared of my current husband, whom I'm divorcing," she said. "I have a restraining order, but I want to learn how to defend myself in the moment. I'm tired of waiting for justice."

She went to Worth Defending with great expectations and got more than she even expected. "I have self-safety now. For the first time in my life I know I'm not going to be raped, that I'm safe. I love my life and I've never been able to say that before. Worth Defending brought it out."

Katherine is crystal clear that she's the one who facilitated her own growth. She embodies the spirit of "If I can do it, you can too." Katherine wants to be a public speaker so she can help other women fulfill their potential. I believe she'll do it.

Andrea: A New Compassion for Other Women

Andrea, 5'7," 142 lbs., offered a unique perspective as a German citizen. Andrea works in Washington, D.C. as a foreign correspondent for her German publication. Unlike many of the American women I spoke with, Andrea had grown up playing rough soccer and had also been a fighter as a kid. She engaged in fights, she initiated a lot of them, and she felt humiliated if she lost. She was able to beat a lot of boys, not only at sports but "duking it out."

Andrea signed up for D.C. Impact because of its leader, renowned martial arts expert, Carol Middleton. Andrea was in a karate class when she heard about the concept of full-force fighting with a "mock" padded assailant. The idea fascinated her and she jumped in, more or less out of curiosity. Andrea rated herself highly before she took the D.C. Impact basics class, but said her fighting skills progressed immensely.

She also grew in more peaceful and abstract ways. While she'd always been willing to fight, she said, "I learned how to avoid and de-escalate so a confrontation doesn't get physical."

She noted that what she gained most was a new compassion for other women. Before Impact, she'd been bewildered by other women's assaults. "That couldn't happen to me, I would think. That woman must have done something wrong to get beaten up or raped like that. But listening to other women's stories Andrea was moved, especially as she saw them get stronger and stronger with each week. A complete shift occurred; "I admired them and got over my harsh judgment."

Rhonda: Self-empowerment for a Victim of Rape

When she was 19, a man raped Rhonda in a major downtown area during the day. She had ignored the discomfort she felt about a man she'd seen following her. "It could never happen to me" was a myth that was cruelly shattered for her that day. The rape "changed everything about me, changed my whole personality. It took a piece of me away. I feel paranoid; I'm always looking over my shoulder. Rhonda's rapist has never been found.

Now 24, Rhonda, a social worker, decided to take a complete basics Worth Defending training after she attended a less comprehensive self-defense workshop. She is engaged to be married, doesn't consider herself a feminist, and guesses she's more or less "traditional."

What did Rhonda get from her full-contact self-defense class? "Self-empowerment — it totally changed my sense of safety. After I was attacked that had been taken away from me. I could never relax, even for little things. If I wanted to lie by the pool I couldn't close my eyes. Now, if someone's out to get me, I'll get them back. I'm not paranoid now, but I'm not naive either.

"It was an amazing class, especially for survivors — the most amazing experience I've ever had. It was a gift for me. It changed my life. Every woman should take it if it's available in their area." Rhonda certainly wasn't prone to hyperbole when I first spoke to her. Obviously, something major shifted for her. Rhonda now knows the difference between paranoia and awareness; paranoia is debilitating, awareness, empowering.

Gina: Gaining Mental Strength

Gina, 34, medium height and build, had no idea what to expect when she signed up for Worth Defending in Helena, Montana. Since I hail from South Dakota and Montana myself, I was familiar with Gina's Midwestern common sense and no-nonsense approach to life. She'd never really thought about violence too much, although the possibility of attack would occur to her occasionally. Extremely smart, highly educated, a research scientist, she had no idea of what she would do if she was attacked. She'd never thought about taking a self-defense class and wasn't aware of any. She was taking the class because, as a botanist, she would occasionally have to be out at night by herself studying plants. Her employer paid for the class.

Afterwards Gina told me about a man she supervises who had a problem with what he called "such a violent approach" to defending oneself. He thought a gun was OK, but not physical fighting. Go figure.

Gina not only gained physical confidence, she says she also gained mental strength from the class. She was extremely impressed with the training environment and how realistic, yet safe, the simulated attacks were. Even though she was filled with fear, she snapped into a defense mode that surprised her. And she came away with some interesting insights. "I was really surprised at how weak some women perceived themselves to be, even though they were physically strong. It really bothered me until I saw such improvement." She would strongly recommend it to other women, "especially women who work at night — in hospitals, diners, bars, police, those kinds of professions."

Linda: The Changes Were More Mental, Emotional, and Spiritual

Linda, 51, an advertising and marketing consultant, didn't change physically as much as she expected after her basics class with Impact Personal Safety of Los Angeles. Although she had wanted to feel stronger physically, she told me her experience was more mental, emotional and spiritual. It underlined for her how much she's compromised boundaries, and she thinks women in general would benefit from learning that they "don't have to take shit."

Striking a profound chord, after taking the class Linda found herself behaving in a manner very unlike her usual charming "good student" self. She refrained from the clowning around she'd once engaged in. She was able to recognize and start to dismantle how helpless she considers herself, something she hides very well through her gregarious, funny personality.

Linda related how she cried for hours after her graduation from the class and went to bed at 6 p.m. She had two dreams that evening: one in a corporate setting, another in a social situation. The people in both dreams were treating her very badly. Everyone behaved, including Linda, as if that were normal. She woke up crying, with the realization that it isn't normal to be treated poorly, it's horrible. She saw her dream as the beginning of healing a psyche that had always expected to be hurt, humiliated and punished.

Linda also reported that after taking the classes she felt less defensive in a professional situation where a client gave her unsolicited advice. Before, she believes she would have been offended, but now she could relax and understand that the man was simply trying to get the best possible result from their working relationship.

Linda is courageous and thoroughly committed to her own growth. She said she never realized that women could be as tough as she saw some in her class being, even the tiniest ones. She also was encouraged by the example the male instructors set. "Inch by inch I'm beginning to realize there are some real nice guys out there who want to help women.

Marilyn: "Now I Know I'm Worth Defending"

Marilyn, an administrative assistant is 5'2 and 115 lbs. Her "before" interview was full of doubt about the possibility of being able to learn any skills to defend herself since she is "so small, after all."

Marilyn grew up seeing men beat up women. Her stepfather once tried to seduce her. She was able to fend him off, and yet she protected him by not telling anyone. She used to be afraid of her stepfather. Everyone in her family is still afraid of him, but now she's not. She knows she could handle whatever might come up.

What did she get out of class? "A sense of being. I know what my rights are and I know I'm worth defending. I know if something happened I could defend myself. Defending myself is one thing I won't have to carry in my little basket of worries — that's one thing I can toss." Before taking the class, Marilyn told me that she had no idea how she could defend herself, that women are unable to fight back or, if they do, they have little chance of prevailing.

She remembered during our "after" interview that she'd answered "no" in the first interview when I asked if she'd been attacked. She later recalled "thwarted attacks that I just accepted as part of life or part of being a woman."

What about shifts in attitude toward men? " Yes, I'm less afraid. It's so much easier for me to talk to men, and I feel equal to them because

I'm not afraid. I don't have to hate or think bad things about them. I feel tricked. All these years of fear and they were just people like me."

Deb: "Self-Defense Did More For My Self-Esteem Than Any Diet"

Deb, a vivacious woman in her early 40's, was terribly afraid that her body size would get in the way of learning to defend herself. She's bigger than fashionable standards; "anatomically incorrect" is how she describes herself. Deb was amazed at how easily she took to the class, however, in spite of her size. When she saw another woman even bigger than she taken to the ground by the mock assailant, she knew she'd come to the right place. She had a history of being assaulted, starting with an abusive stepfather, continuing with rape when she was traveling in England, and then a violent Hollywood producer boyfriend who beat her up.

Deb knew a profound shift had taken place when she found herself walking down the street in Berkeley, a community full of colorful looking, previously scary, unpredictable types, thinking, "Just try something and you'll be sorry. You don't know who you're dealing with." This is the same woman who, a month or so previously, was "scared shitless" at the idea of a physical assault.

Deb, like many others, had justified her procrastination about taking self-defense because she felt her body wasn't right. "Now, I can't believe I put off something that would make such a major difference in my life. The class has had a positive impact on where I go and how I feel about my body. I've done many diets and lost many pounds, but this 20-hour class has done more for my self-esteem than any diet I could possibly imagine."

Sophie: "I Finally Felt the Joy of Fighting Back Instead of Freezing"

Sophie, 45 years old, has her MBA, is medium height and medium build. She had experienced "freezing" when a same-sex lover started hitting and kicking her after a pushing match which resulted when she tried to keep her girlfriend from driving drunk. Sophie was plagued with the memory and was furious and fearful that if she was ever attacked again she'd react the same way. Sophie had known about Bay Area Model Mugging (BAMM) for 15 years. She'd never heard one negative thing about it, just positive, glowing reports. She'd taken a self-defense class in college, and while she felt it had been a step in the right direction, it wasn't comprehensive enough. It hadn't taken into account the socialization that women go through.

What did she get out of the class? "It erased my fear of freezing. I feel more safe. I'm still fearful, and yet I feel safe. I got skills, camaraderie, and confidence. It was really helpful to see women smaller than I fight hard. If they can do it, I can do it. The rule 'don't judge a book by its cover' was reinforced. Some women I judged to be airheads turned out to be eloquent fireballs. We had a good span of women, 20's through 40's, with varying degrees of ability, hearing problems, bad backs. I was impressed with the staff and how they were able to work around problems to tailor the program to all types and levels.

I asked Sophie if there was anything she wanted to add at the end of our "after" interview. "Yes," she said. "During one fight I cried. I couldn't finish. It took me awhile to get in touch with my anger. It was very hard for me. The last day I was finally able to feel real rage, and I beat the shit out of our instructor. Rage is so different from fear, and I finally felt the joy of fighting when I'm angry. There was a moment where I had to decide to go for it; I knew it would be easier to lie there and give up, but I didn't. I hesitate to call it life-altering yet, because not enough time has passed; but at this point, I think it was."

Demi: "Self-defense Isn't About Man-Hating, It's About Self-Empowerment"

For 26-year-old graduate student Demi, it was important to be in a self-defense class that wasn't "man-hating. She saw that Model Mugging of San Luis Obispo fit the bill when she attended a friend's graduation. Demi 5'2", 112 lbs., had never taken a self-defense class before because she figured, "Why even bother because it's impossible for someone my size to defend myself." Once she saw full-force self-defense demonstrated, she knew she could do it but had to figure out the financial aspect. Thanks to a non-profit adjunct group of men and women in San Luis Obispo called Safe-S.L.O. that subsidized half her tuition, Demi was able to do the class. She knew she wanted the safe environment, the realistic practice, and she knew the person who recommended it wouldn't steer her in the wrong direction.

Typically, Demi's boyfriend was initially unclear about why she would want to go to such an extreme as taking a full-out fighting class. He was afraid something had happened in Demi's past that she hadn't told him about. He hadn't experienced, and didn't initially understand, that most women are constantly concerned about their physical safety. Demi told him that since she worked alone and in the field, she felt particularly vulnerable. Her boyfriend, nevertheless, didn't "get it" — that is, until he saw Demi's graduation. Now he's very supportive about her new-found self-defense skills.

Before her class, Demi said, "I'm doing it not just for self-defense. This is a way to get out my frustration. I'm taking back myself as an empowerment." Now Demi is not afraid to be by herself at night, as she had been before, and she now feels that men don't have power over her. "I'm not easily intimidated now. I'm as strong as they are." For someone who had a constant fear of the possibility of an attack, Demi came a very long way.

I asked her if there was anything else she wanted to say. "I think it's important for other women to know that it wasn't a man-hating class but people-loving. Almost all the graduates I know would agree with Demi. For me the man-hating stigma always brings up the question, "What does a woman's self-empowerment have to do with hating men, anyway?"

Catherine: Re-enacting and Healing From Childhood Abuse

Taller than a lot of women, athletic and confident, Catherine never thought self-defense was necessary if she even gave it a thought at all. Like Demi, after seeing a graduation, she saw that self-defense was more than physical. She waited three or four years, but finally took the class.

I asked Catherine what changes she's noticed in herself. "This may sound odd, but I see more details. Taking a walk, I notice all my senses are more accessible, more vivid. I procrastinate less and I've been giving myself more permission to do what I want, whether it's needlepoint or reading poetry. I'm much less approval driven."

It's common for women to report that their awareness increases and hyper-vigilance decreases after learning self-defense. One explanation is that knowing how to defend oneself allows one to relax and therefore pay more attention to details. It's as if the coping mechanisms many of us use, whether it's denial or paranoia, also serve to decrease the pleasure we can take in our surroundings. Also, knowledge of self-defense seems to serve as a maturing process for some, whereby they suddenly feel they deserve to spend more time on themselves with less guilt and fewer excuses.

Catherine noticed that she gained more sympathy for other women and gave herself and her classmates more credit for being strong than she used to. She also noticed how uncertain a little girl in her neighborhood already was, how listless, how scared of being wrong. Prior to taking the class, she would not have noticed the little girl's wishy-washiness, and would have just accepted her manner as "natural" young-girl behavior.

Had any of her attitudes toward men shifted? "I'm still muddling through that one. But I do see that they are muddling through too. They're definitely not as scary."

During class, Catherine requested a scenario that duplicated a violent incident with her dad when she was kid. She and her father had been talking while she was washing dishes. Katherine had shaken her hands off and small flecks of water and suds had hit her father. He slapped her hard, then went back to chatting as if nothing happened. He then berated her for stopping her end of the conversation.

When she re-enacted the incident in class the scenario changed. Catherine hit her "father" back and then proceeded to knock him out. She explained that she would not really beat up her father if the same thing happened again. Rather, this was a symbolic scene that transformed the helpless child she had been into a competent woman capable of defending herself. The re-enactment was a very healing experience for her.

Finally, I asked if she would change anything she had stated during our first interview. Catherine said she remembered that she had answered "No" to the question, "Have you ever been attacked?" She wanted to change it to "Yes." She'd never thought of her father's frequent and arbitrary slaps as attacks before.

Heather: "It's Hard to Confront Your Worst Nightmare"

Heather, 5'6", 120 lbs., 31 years old, had nightmares that were frequent enough to have a therapist refer her to Impact Personal Safety in Los Angeles. Her nightmares ended because of the class. She attributes her bad dreams to previous irrational fears, and credits their disappearance to finding that she has the tools to take care of herself. Heather's day-by-day confidence has increased markedly since taking self-defense. She said everyone she knows has remarked that she seems changed, especially her husband.

Heather was amazed and inspired by her own untapped power and by the women who started class and couldn't even say, let alone yell, "No!" They started out so timid and yet grew into physically- and mentally-prepared people. She had put off taking a class in self-defense because she simply wanted to avoid confronting her nightmares.

As a writer and producer in the film business, perhaps Heather will be a leader in the industry who will depict women as strong and fully capable of "rescuing" themselves.

Rachel: "Hmm, That Guy Over There — What Would I Do If Something Happened?"

Rachel, 34, 5', 105 lbs., described herself as "always on guard, always watching, ever-vigilant." Never attacked, although she'd had a necklace grabbed off her neck (most would consider that an attack), she had constricted her life to minimize risk — deciding not to travel as much as she'd like because she "chickened out." Rachel is a thoughtful, introspective person. She decided not to complete the last class which is designed to be in front of an audience of interested people. She decided she wasn't ready to fight in front of people she didn't know.

She was surprised at how visceral the experience of fighting back was. She got nauseous at the idea of hitting someone. She learned skills she'd never considered, like getting to the ground to kick at an assailant. However, she said she couldn't be as enthusiastic as she saw other classmates being because she was processing what turned out for her to be a deep experience, emotionally and spiritually. She also found that men are a lot more vulnerable than she ever thought, and appreciated that she could now assess her situation, as in: "Hmm, that guy over there, what would I do if something were to happen?"

She said she wasn't sure that I'd want to talk to her if she hadn't finished or if she wasn't "rah, rah" about the experience. I told her that her experience was just as valid as anyone else's, and I appreciated her candor. I too had been quite disturbed in my first class. I had found it somewhat revolting, and something that elevated my responsibility to others in a whole new way.

Rachel knew that it was a pitfall to compare her experience to others'. She still felt that the class was more than worth doing. While she found it disturbing, she didn't think it was because anything was amiss. She was simply surprised at how upsetting she found the whole subject of violence, and how her responsibility for protecting herself weighed heavily on her. She said she would heartily recommend Bay Area Model Mugging because she found it empowering.

So many of the women I talked to were aware of their desire to take a full-impact class and yet procrastinated — sometimes for years. A common "after" refrain was "Why did I put this off? Why didn't I do this when I was younger?"

Why *is* it so hard for most of us to take that initial step? Self-defense leaders across the country, interviewed separately, agree that fear, terror, is the real underlying basis for women's procrastination, although lack of time and money are common excuses. We put it off because we're terrified of even the possibility of attack. And, like children, we cling to the belief that others will protect us — that self-protection is not our job.

Although, again like children, we frequently blame ourselves for the violence others perpetrate upon us, the blame lies with dangerous notions we have had passed on to us from previous generations in the place we're told is safe: the bosom of the family.

4

Why Beauty Sleeps: The Spells of Home and Hearth

The most potent weapon in the hands of the oppressor is the mind of the oppressed.

STEVE (STEPHEN BANTU) BIKO, 1946-1977
STATEMENT AS WITNESS (MAY 3, 1976)

What's the use of learning to defend myself? I'd never win anyway. This is the most disheartening, home-grown excuse I hear from women who negate the need for self-defense training. Such an attitude not only reveals resignation, it also denies reality. It's like white corpuscles saying, "I can't fight this germ." Such an unrealistic assessment of our potential indicates a serious problem in our spirit's immune system — HIV of the heart. The bad news is I've heard this excuse far too many times. The good news is it's easy to restore one's fighting spirit. The benefits of a fighting spirit go way beyond the physical realm. A fighting spirit affects one's core, confidence and essential self-image. The purpose of this chapter is to explore the role of family in how we view our right and ability to defend ourselves.

Where Beauty and Beast Learn Their Roles

Fighting spirit is either fanned or famished in the heart of the family. Beasts have families that raise beasts. Beauties have families that raise beauties. Some families raise beauties and beasts; the distinctions generally fall along traditional gender lines. Girls are generally raised to be beauties and boys are raised to be beasts. Some beasts have beautiful hearts that can only be liberated by a beauty. Some beasts are predators and want to kill any beauty, whether it's within themselves or manifested in a living woman. Occasionally beauties are raised to understand that being a beauty doesn't mean one doesn't or can't have a "dark" beast side, a side they can call upon when they need to confront the beast in another.

It is in the context of our families that we develop our beauty or beastliness. We each have both beauty and beast within our psychological make-up in varying degrees. When we interact with one another, however, the Beast dominates because Beauty has not learned in her family how to "bite," how to fight or beat the beast back.

Society has forced women to believe that they can't fight back; there is no use even to try. The myth that Beauty is defenseless has become a reality because every structure has been designed to enforce and reinforce women's weakness: religion, commerce, education, family and individual. We are so thoroughly out of touch with the potential of our own bodies to be effective in defense that we don't even consider the knowledge of physical defense as a missing link in our power, let alone our spiritual and intellectual prowess.

Families also shape how we perceive our right to set boundaries, within our own families and in society at large. Our family experience determines whether we automatically give authority to a person because he happens to be male, or if we automatically give a woman less respect. As children we learn how men and women are supposed to relate based on how our parents or guardians interact. We learn which activities each gender is supposed to engage in. And we grow up assuming that these behaviors are just the way things are, rather than the result of cultural and social engineering. We also learn the relationship that each gender has to power and violence. Myriam Miedzian's book, *Boys Will Be Boys: Breaking the Link Between Masculinity and Violence,* is one of the most thorough works I have encountered on what it takes to indoctrinate human males with the belief in and the need for violence. The family is key, because it introduces and enforces the culture's commitment to male dominance, and enforces codes and manners of proper feminine and masculine identity.

Women literally have been domesticated to the point of pathological notions of femininity. On one end of the spectrum we have truly obnoxious men who are pathologically masculine and on the other end, pathologically feminine women. Most of us are in the middle. We've housebroken women to the point that their femininity is frequently deadly when they are confronted with pathologically masculine men.

Pathologically masculine men have many characteristics but the one most deadly to women is that they firmly believe that a woman belongs to them, no kidding. They truly believe it's their duty to discipline, hit, chain, imprison, do whatever's necessary, to keep their woman in line or under their roof. Murder is not out of the question. In fact, the threat of murder, "realistic" or not, is the underlying ultimate control threat. These are all lessons of some homes.

Did your father constantly pull rank on your mother based solely on his maleness? Did he allow the boys in your family to talk assertively to him or your mother, but drew the line when it came to the girls "talking back"? Our gender-role expectations spring from how we see it done in our own home. It can't be helped.

Experts say that our gender molding begins at birth in the hospital. Baby boys are handled more roughly than baby girls. Because of the pink or blue on their swaddling, they are talked to differently. A baby girl is more apt to be kissed and cuddled, nurtured, even in very subtle ways. Baby boys are from the get-go held in such a way as to "toughen" them. And even if the immediate family is very careful to be as loving and warm to their boys as they are to their girls, Uncle Bobby and Auntie Alice may drop by and give the boy noogies and kiss the girl sweetly. The gender messages are pervasive and persistent.

Boys are given a lot more leeway to set boundaries, with each other, with girls, and with adults. The only people allowed to transgress boys' boundaries are bigger boys or men. There is a pecking order that girls are at the bottom of when it comes to saying "No." Boundaries are only effective if they can be enforced. Enforced is a word that has the word "force" in it. Girls are not given many lessons in force, other than to let "boys be boys" or to give in to their force. When I was growing up, I very rarely saw anyone giving a girl permission to meet force with force, whether it was forceful language or physical action.

As a teacher and assistant in full-force self-defense, I have noticed that women from Jewish and African American families tend to be better at verbally asserting themselves than non-Jewish, European American, or Hispanic American women, with glaring exceptions, of course. I've theorized that perhaps Jewish culture honors the intellectual abilities of all its members and has allowed women as well as men to hone verbal skills — to take a stand and maintain it. A greater percentage of African American women seem to have a realistic sense of their own value and validity of their own opinions, compared to other, non-African American women. Perhaps their relatively positive self-image can be attributed to their not having been raised to expect men to rescue or take care of them. These are important factors in setting and maintaining boundaries — intellectual, emotional or physical.

Why Can't Girls Be More Like Puppies?

In recent years, I have begun to identify the process by which I learned to be a privileged, white, middle-class female as being similar to the overt and covert obedience training for dogs. I have been an incredibly well-behaved, intelligent pet whom my normal and actually incredibly kind and progressive parents raised according to cultural gender norms.

Girls of the white middle class, in my generation at least, were reared to breed with the best stud and to show at various events. Even though I was a so-called "tomboy," I wasn't immersed in the culture that would train me to be as successful as a man could be. I wasn't forging relationships which would one day help me in my chosen profession, nor was I developing self-defense skills that would elicit the automatic assumption that no one had the right to mess with me. Underlying all my relationships and undertakings was the unconscious and unarticulated fear that I couldn't really fight back.

As a girl child, I was never encouraged to be anything but obedient. After enough scolding for being "boyish" by teachers, Sunday school personnel, and all the cultural monitors, I started to anticipate displeasure. My ability to defend myself with words was obliterated by the unspoken threat of force or criticism. For decades I had my tail between my legs, afraid of displeasing anyone and very eager to do tricks. And I don't chew shoes or jump on furniture.

On the other hand, I have always had more courage than a lot of girls and women, although others have had more than I. That indicates to me that my "tomness" served me. My parents' and others' affection for my tomboyness was a blessing.

The obedient dog analogy only goes so far. A dog breeder would be considered insane if they separated puppies by sex, allowing only male puppies to play and learn adult survival techniques as they tumbled around "hunting" a ball. We would consider it absurd to train the females not to growl, roll around, get dirty, or fight back if attacked. Notice how dogs behave when they're playing. Their play is a gentle form of fighting, veritable rehearsal for the real thing should the need ever arise. The female pups do not sit on the sidelines watching or cheering the males; they are just as actively entangled in the pile of "fighting" dogs. A bitch that never used her ability to protect herself wouldn't be good for her litter.

Why do humans, for the most part, continue to raise their females to ignore their innate survival instincts? Or fail to teach our girls to confront boys verbally? Isn't it a bit like sending the lambs to the proverbial slaughter? At the same time, aren't males raised to believe that girls and later, women, are unable to fight back in any effective way?

What if little girls were raised as equally as female puppies? Litters are good examples of how useful brothers and sisters and cousins can be in rehearsing for life as adults. Human brothers and sisters could fill the same necessary role in each other's lives. Let's say a brother and sister are wrestling, and she's doing well. She happens to hit her brother between his legs, and rather than her parents telling her, "Never, ever, ever hit a boy down there," they let her know that this is a method that could serve her well down the line. They might tell her, "Don't hit your brother in the crotch unless you truly need to hurt him. Use that move for someone who is really going to hurt you. If any male, including your father, step-father, grandfather, brother, farm-hand, or clergyman is trying to hurt you, go for the gold!"

If girls aren't allowed to engage in physical play with boys, and if someone always intervenes to protect or help the girl, how is she going to handle a date who gets out of hand when she's a teen? How is she going to handle the errant hand at the office copier? By not allowing her the kind of co-ed playtime that puppies have when they "fight," we strip a girl of skills that are vital to her later on. We also strip her daughters of necessary defensive skills, since they won't have a role model from whom to learn, and so on, and so on, and so on. It's no coincidence that many of the women I meet in class who learn to fight quickly grew up with brothers. They have "litter" experience to one degree or another.

I am not saying that one should encourage violence among siblings. Mother dogs intervene when it gets too rough, as should human parents. The pups themselves withdraw, they yelp, they communicate, "enough is enough." But it is a great disservice to pull a girl out of a "litter battle" and not allow her to experience her own power and her own limits. Human daughters thus miss out on self-protection and domination lessons.

Males do not always dominate in a dog litter, nor would they in human "litters." There is usually a dominant female and a co-dominant male. In the animal kingdom, self-protection and rough-housing is not a male-only activity. Both genders partake in physical play in preparation for protection, hunting, or being hunted, in other words, in preparation for real life.

Because so many girls have had so little experience with physical play, I see women come into self-defense classes with fears of injury that are unrealistic and overblown. Had we been raised in a "litter style," we would have experienced rough and tumble activities at home, on the playing field and in our neighborhoods. That experience is essential. When one gets "hit" in a contact sport, it rarely causes serious injury. An injury sustained during play is an important lesson because one learns that the fear of being hurt is often worse than the actual hurt.

Women are often afraid to fight back in real life settings because they are afraid that if they do, they'll get hurt even worse. Not true. Passivity as a defense is a myth unless you're an opossum. Women who fight back are less apt to be raped and no more apt to be hurt any worse than a woman who believes she only makes the rapist more violent if she fights back. In fact, at least one study shows that women who behave passively, who beg or implore their attacker not to hurt them, are apt to be hurt worse because their behavior fits the assailant's stereotypical view of a woman; she's weak, she's whiny, she's hateful, she's not a man, and therefore she's not a person.

The Psychology of Women Quarterly (March 1993) published "The Efficacy of Women's Resistance Strategies in Rape Situations" by Sarah Ullman and Raymond Knight who conclude:

> Forceful resistance strategies such as fighting, screaming, and fleeing/pushing the offender away appear to be more effective for avoiding rape (or at the very least may not exacerbate sexual abuse) than not resisting, especially in dangerous situations (i.e., indoors, when a weapon is present, etc.). Moreover, there is some evidence, corroborating earlier research (Bart & O'Brien, 1985), that pleading, crying, or reasoning during rape are ineffective in avoiding rape and injury (Ullman & Knight, 1992) and may be harmful in both less dangerous situations and in situations in which the risks for sexual abuse and physical injury are high.

Passivity can be an effective strategy. Again, watch puppies at play. Sometimes a puppy will lie still, feigning disinterest or pretending to be at rest. Then, all of a sudden, that same lump of a pup turns into a ball of energy, and the fight is on. Passivity that is passivity because that's the only "method" that the person in danger knows, is not strategy. Strategy is possible when other options are available. By training human females to be passive as the best and only strategy, we endanger them.

Minimizing Intrusions on a Girl's Space Disempowers Her

One story I recall from a friend who grew up in one of the Midwestern states on a farm concerns her encounter with a hired farm hand. He was always sweet to her, so she began to regard him as part of the family. She had brothers, and therefore learned how to fend for herself rather well. She certainly kept up with them athletically, as well as in doing the many kinds of work required around a farm.

One day, when she was that marvelous age of 11, she was in their barn and the farm hand came up behind her, lifted her up, and threw her on a pile of straw. She was playful in return until she noticed that he had a distinctly unplayful look in his eyes. She got scared and asked him to let her go. He refused. She started to cry and that apparently scared him. He pretended to turn it back into play, and then proceeded to lick her all over her face. She wanted to vomit. She said she can still smell his tobacco-tinged saliva. She also said she lost a large chunk of her fighting spirit that day.

She felt completely violated and put in her place. She didn't know that had she been willing to hurt him she could have gotten him off her. She told her mother, who teased her and minimized it as "no big deal. You let the dogs lick you all the time."

One way to judge if there's been a violation or not is to conceptualize a gender switch. How would a budding young man feel if an older man or woman held him down and licked his face against his will? He'd be outraged, and other people could understand why. Not so with girls most of the time. The most well-meaning people, women and men, disregard the boundaries of their daughters, and inadvertently teach them that those boundaries are completely penetrable.

Ladylike Dress Codes and Gender Play Codes

My parents, bless them, certainly never sent me back to the playground to take a stand against a bully. They said, "Boys will be boys, and besides, you don't want to ruin your dress." I kept my clothes clean at great expense to my safety and dignity.

The clothes we wear influence how we perceive our ability to fight back. Rightly so. Look at a picture of a corseted woman in a huge dress with petticoats and lace-up shoes and compare that with the mobility of a young woman of the 90's. Our 90's girl wears Doc Martens, jeans, and a t-shirt. Her clothes would not constrict her from defending herself. Her attitude might, or her lack of knowledge and skill, but not her clothes when she's in casual mode, at least.

Work clothes present another matter. In every self-defense class I've been involved with, someone brings up the concern about work apparel. What if I'm attacked and I have high heels on? (Kick them off). What if I'm wearing a tight skirt? (Let it rip if it must). Try to imagine a man in a self-defense class asking concerned questions about their clothing when discussing self-protection. It's unlikely.

Although dress codes are more relaxed now, they are still with us. Notice how women's clothing can be dangerous, and at the least, not conducive to play or self-defense. Unlike boys' and mens' clothing, which is essentially designed for comfort (with the exception of neckties), women's traditional clothing forces us to be self-conscious. We must always attend to revealing this or not showing that. Straps fall down or dig into our flesh. Shoes pinch our feet or make us hobble. Most women are familiar with the discomfort one must put up with for beauty. Beauty can be unsafe.

As little girls, we were always told to be lady-like. We were to sit properly, while our brothers and boy cousins could engage in play in any setting, whether it was a backyard gathering for a barbecue or a formal wedding. Sure, Mom might get mad at them for mussing up their wedding clothes, but Dad would intervene and let him "be a boy," since, it was only clothing for God's sakes.

But girls saw what their mothers had to do to get clothes presentable. They could see down the road that they would one day have to worry about mending, cleaning, and ironing. Perhaps if boys were taught to clean and mend their own clothes, they'd be more considerate and less rough on them. I could remember hesitating when I'd consider the kind of play I'd engage in, depending on the clothes I had on. Self-defense, taking it a step further, requires reaction, not hesitancy, unconscious or conscious.

Even girls' casual clothing enforces defenselessness. The shoes, the clothes, the hair, the whole package is contrary to physical freedom because of emphasis on looking "put together." Being put together takes a lot of work, whether the look is sloppy or staid. Obviously, sloppy is less constricting but boys' freedom to basically comb their hair and run out the door is far more conducive to physical freedom. Constricting physical freedom for any reason is stultifying in situations where one needs to protect oneself physically.

Another reason girls were made to feel defenseless when I was growing up was the "boys only" aspect to so many of the games and play routines. Boys built tree houses and forts, (with no concern about their clothing), in order to close girls out, even after they had exploited us for our labor to build them. When the tree house or fort was done, they'd post a "no girls allowed" sign, and many of the grown-ups would think that was cute. I thought it was awful.

What was so charming about children's segregation in the grown-up world? Why was an injustice done to little girls considered cute?

Why didn't anyone step forward to tell us to fight back against the blatant injustice of unfair housing, even if it was "play" housing. Again, childhood provides rehearsals for adult life. Is it any wonder that even women minimize their own experience of discrimination? We also learned that offenses toward us were not worth fighting against, physically or otherwise.

From a boy's perspective, it's a shame that playing house or making mud pies or taking care of teddy bears or dolls is cause for humiliation. I knew boys, who probably grew up to be both straight and gay, who really did like to play house. But eventually the Dad or the Uncle or the homophobic Auntie would humiliate them, and the boy would shun his initial instinct to practice nurturing, or cooking, or interacting with a partner. I still see grown-ups being very paranoid about the kinds of toys that their boys play with. In that regard, girls have a lot more room to explore the type of toys they really like.

If you think we've come a long way in the last twenty years, visit a toy store. The entire store will virtually be divided according to gender. There are no toys designed for girls that have to do with learning how to set boundaries or defend space, either personal or territorial.

Boys have dolls, but they learn early on that it's second-class to be a girl so they don't want their dolls to be called dolls. They must be referred to as "action figures." You'll notice in the action figure aisle of your local toy store that, with the exception of Star Trek action figures, most female action figures are incredibly evil, with a drop-dead (phrase used intentionally) gorgeous body, impossible for a female human to have.

What might this teach boys about relating to girls and women? Certainly not healthy lessons that include a female's full personhood. And we wonder why boys grow into men who have a hard time being friends and partners with women? The female action figures are to be either lusted over or attacked — or both!

If play is a form of life rehearsal, what do boys rehearse with action figures? Fighting. They learn self-defense from their dolls. Girls use their dolls to nurture and play house. That's great. However, girls need to learn about fighting as well. I long for the day when I see a girl set up her Barbie in a side-kick position and kick Ken's missing manhood.

If that image of Barbie defending herself from Ken bothers you, ask yourself if it bothers you more than seeing a boy use his G.I. Joe to attack a culprit. If it does, why do you think that is?

Although I don't advocate the "rescuer" role for males, at least rescue is a form of nurturing that both girls and boys can play and benefit from. But even the traditional roles, "damsel-in-distress" or snoozing Beauties are missing from the cast of characters in the action figure world. If the "good" women were present and available in the action figure inventory, a boy might get a sense of chivalry or protectiveness if he had women of so-called virtue to save. They are missing and our boys reflect it. Although there is mischief to be undone from boys playing savior toward females, it's better than creating villains.

Xena: Warrior Princess, is a potent exception to the action figure rule of "no girls allowed." She is good, she is strong, she is able to save the day, herself, other women, men and children as well as animals. She embodies the Diana spirit that has been missing from the play bill for too long.

I don't know how many boys actually want to buy a Xena action figure, but she exists for those who do. Unfortunately, she is incredibly difficult to find in toy stores because they only pack one Xena action figure to a case of Hercules. Interesting business practice, given that when I covered the Xena and Hercules convention in Burbank, California, in 1997, they sold out of Xena figures in the first hour of a two-day convention. It was a convention packed with girls from all backgrounds by the way.

A daughter of a friend was distraught because it took so long to track down a Princess Lea action figure. She had been swept up with the "Star Wars" renaissance and was eager and willing to be a movie-merchandising consumer. But Princess Lea is hard to find as well. I wonder if Carrie Fisher knows that her character is missing and badly misrepresented in the toy world. My friend's daughter interpreted Princess Lea's unavailability as meaning the princess is not as good as the other characters, all males.

The quintessential "action figures" in children's lives are animals. Children learn many things from animals, not as toys, but as non-human playmates to live with and observe. They learn how to be responsible for the care of another being, and most parents don't realize how they can teach kids self-defense by using the animals as examples. Family pets, domestic and wild animals can be terrific tools for parents to teach kids how to defend themselves. I've pointed out to parents how much racket a nest of baby birds can make when they are threatened. A child can mimic threatened animals and thereby learn basic protection skills.

Ask a child to describe what a puppy or kitten does when it doesn't want to be held. He or she will describe wiggling, squealing, scratching, pushing, yelping, growling, running and hiding.

Everything the kitten or puppy does are things that the child can do if someone tries to pick them up that shouldn't.

Recreation and playtime is rehearsal for life. Look at children's play and ask yourself, "What is she or he rehearsing for right now?" The answer to that question may prompt change in their clothing or toys. Playtime affects how the children in your life live their own lives and relate to themselves and others. Pointing out female animals as role models could make a difference in a girls' life when she feels threatened. Showing a girl how Barbie could defend herself if Ken got out of hand might serve her well when she's in college.

Debunking The Damsel-in-Distress Myth

Fairy tales and children's stories are literary instruction manuals that have traditionally been employed to impart proper gender roles and relations.

The bedtime stories told in countless homes across the nation create unrealistic expectations of rescue and confusing double messages to girls and boys. We have generations of girls, now women, who are paying for the Cinderella complex, the obsession with having someone save her. We have rafts of females who wrongly believe that youth, beauty and niceness is enough to keep her out of harm's way. We have loads of mothers who still propose that Prince Charming is out there somewhere and all her daughter has to do is go after him and all will be well.

I suggest that we, regardless of our age, may have to take the time to mourn the loss of our dream that a prince will rescue us. One way to do that is to become your own prince and physical rescuer. The prince often doesn't know how to save himself.

Physical rescue based on gender is an embedded fairy tale and one of the last romances we cling to. Perhaps the romance is gone and you've awakened, Sleeping Beauty, and it's time to fire the prince for not protecting you. Or perhaps it's time to let our prince off the hook, let him know you'll be all right and ride off together on two horses — not behind him on his lone trusty stallion. The single ones of us might consider that perhaps we're not missing out on anything or at least as much as the fairy tales trained us to believe.

Unlearning the lessons of bedtime, digging up what is missing, is a huge but doable task in the realm of self-protection. Self-defense is natural to any living thing. It takes a lot more energy to make someone believe they are defenseless. Even amoebas will move to protect the membrane from too much light or another intrusive amoeba. So when women learn how to defend themselves, they are quite surprised at how easy, how logical, and how available those skills are. Please, it doesn't take a rocket scientist or an Arnold Schwartzenneger to block a blow. Any woman can do it. And we must teach all girls how to do it.

We don't have to throw the fairy-tale baby out with the bath water. But we can use them as lessons. When we read "Little Red Riding Hood," we can ask, "What else could the little girl have done? Could she have called 911? Could she have kicked the wolf really hard between his legs and hurt his jellies?" Use the stories to teach other approaches, other possibilities.

Education is a key to full participation in life. Women are going to have to reclaim their birthright to use powerful instincts of self and family protection. We must understand the power it has taken to strip us of our innate instinct to fight back. Since mothers in other species are the primary teachers of survival skills, human mothers can do that too. We must do it for our daughters, nieces, granddaughters, students, and grandmothers. Meanwhile, in the next chapter, consider how religion and science have played into most women's mistaken beliefs about their physical defenselessness.

5

The Sleeping Potions of Religion and Science

No woman is required to build the world by destroying herself.

RABBI SOFER, 19TH CENTURY

A number of pubs I've seen in England, Australia, and Corona del Mar, California, have the name "The Quiet Woman." Their quaint, Old English-style signs hang from the fronts of these restaurants and drinking establishments. The pub signs include a painting of a decapitated woman who holds her own head in her hands. If a woman called her pub "The Quiet Man" and showed a decapitated man holding his own bloody head, would we find it charming or humorous?

Have you ever heard of "scold's masks," iron head gear designed to keep a woman's mouth shut and torture her if she spoke? They were once used as punishment for a woman who dared tell a man what to do or not do in public. Although these barbaric devices are now merely museum pieces in England and Europe, they symbolize a code which has kept women voiceless for centuries. Is it any wonder that even though verbal self-defense makes so much sense, many women still cling to the notion that asserting oneself verbally is unladylike and wrong — possibly deadly?

Religion and science have each played a part in silencing women and assuring their defenseless position. Science, the new religion for many, has often served to strengthen misogyny and bigotry. Various biological theories have effectively been used to justify discrimination against both men of color and women of every color.

The biological argument, "women's bodies are not as big and strong as men's" is still used to convince women and men that human females are not able to defend themselves effectively. Is this really so? Is male physical domination of women really inevitable and biologically determined because of size? If that's so, why don't larger women attack smaller men? And if power is the exclusive domain of males in nature, why do larger men avoid smaller female guard dogs? The size and gender argument alone is not convincing enough to provide an explanation for men's physical domination of women. Religion originated the justification of female domination; science has simply been used to continue the tradition.

Religion's Role In Suppressing Women

There is ample evidence to indicate that in pre-historic times, women were not dominated by men. According to many feminist scholars working over the past thirty years, there is sufficient physical proof to reconstruct models of social structures other than patriarchy where women were in fact worshiped as deities — where lay women were respected, listened to and followed as leaders in every human pursuit.

When God Was a Woman, by Merlin Stone, explores the concept of woman as God. I had, like most of us, grown up in a tradition that exclusively referred to God as He, our Father, the Big Bearded White Guy in the sky. The idea that entire ancient civilizations once regarded God as a woman, or both man and woman, was surprisingly and enormously moving to me.

I hadn't realized before how remote a father figure seemed to me. While I liked and loved a lot of men, I had rarely connected them to the experience of unconditional love and astounding wisdom. I had observed, however, the unconditional love of many women toward their loved ones.

On Bobby McFerrin's beautiful album, "Medicine Music," one is presented with an image of God as feminine. When I first heard it — and every time I listen to it — it resonates and creates a longing for the divine that I had never felt before. The last cut on the album is McFerrin's interpretation of the 23rd Psalm: 1. "The Lord is my Shepherd, I have all I need, She makes me lie down in green meadows, Beside the still waters, She will lead." The last stanza: 6. "Glory be to our Mother, and Daughter, And to the Holy of Holies, As it was in the beginning, is now and ever shall be, World, without end Amen." "Dedicated to my Mother" is inscribed at the end. One wonders, McFerrin's earthly mother or the divine, or both?

McFerrin's voice, his lyric, sends shivers up my spine. I have always found the 23rd Psalm to be beautiful, but rephrasing it to emphasize the feminine, the Mother, gives it a whole new meaning and intimacy. It also brings a new self-respect and regard toward other women, to see a Her in the role of the Creator and Shepherd. Would men respect women more if their God was a woman or at least genderless?

"Seen but not heard," a tenet regarding the proper behavior for children, was the philosophy that most Christian denominations, Catholic and Protestant, traditionally adhered to with regard to women. St. Paul was one of the major, but not the only, instigators of religiously-based rules concerning a woman's proper behavior in public and the relationship she ought to have to her husband.

Paul's New Testament admonition to husbands and wives in Ephesians 5:21-33, set the tone to suppress women as potential leaders and full intellectual participants. It basically ensured subordinate positions for women, not only in their congregations but at home, even though women held high positions in many Christian communities at the beginning of the Christian movement. St. Paul has been used by some fundamentalists to justify wife beating and other crimes against women. Women who had an inclination to speak out had to learn to suppress their voices in order to ensure their safety at home and in their communities.

The Adam and Eve story has played a pivotal role in justifying men's domination over women in the Judeo-Christian tradition. Even before I read Elaine Pagels, *Adam, Eve and the Serpent*, or Kim Chernin's *Reinventing Eve*, I didn't buy the Eden story as it is presented by Sunday School teachers and most preachers. Even if I did, I'd have a hard time making Adam the boss. What kind of boss would such an inept, gullible, easily swayed and unaccountable person make, anyway? He didn't refuse the apple, and once he was busted, he blamed Eve. Slacker. Not boss material by my standards.

At any rate, given that painful childbirth was then pronounced to be Eve's punishment — and by extension, all womens' burden — torture, rape, beating, humiliation, and murder of women didn't seem such a difficult leap to make if a woman got out of line. After all, if man was supposed to be the boss, and woman was the mouthpiece of the devil, why not bat her around a little? What's the sin in raping a woman if she's a devil anyway? And how dare she defend herself if her husband — or any man — is beating the devil out of her? Many women were convinced of their own shameful status and felt they deserved to be treated inhumanely. Too bad so few women could rebel in the spirit of Jesus' own brand of feminism. He brought about a revolution in regard for women, or at least he attempted it.

Quakers were a major exception to the rule of compulsory silence for women, and it is not a coincidence that Quaker women have been movers and shakers in progressive social movements. It takes language, speaking and writing, to spread new ideas. Both abolition and the woman's movement were largely created and led by Quaker women and men.

A Century of Struggle: The Women's Rights Movement in the United States, by Eleanor Flexner, is a poignant and thorough book on how much it took to get education, property rights and the vote for women, all without bloodshed. Most mainstream religious leaders opposed the vote for women.

Most people are unaware that Mahatma Gandhi publically acknowledged the influence suffragists had on his belief in civil disobedience and non-violent revolution. Gloria Steinem has talked about meeting feminist activists in India during the sixties who were aware of how influential women's rights activists had been in shaping Gandhi's ideas.

The Quakers were in the vanguard of social revolution long before Gandhi and Martin Luther King Jr., the men usually credited with the idea of non-violent social resistance. Perhaps the Quakers' role has been down-played because of their progressive views on women. Quaker doctrine has always allowed women to speak publically in their own churches and by extension, in public places, thereby arguing and convincing new people to hate slavery and liberate women from their subservient status.

Science Seconds the Motion for Male Dominance

Archeology, like other fields, has been dominated by men. A relatively new science, the first archaeologists who dug up graves, tombs and mounds, found warrior skeletons buried along with weapons and symbols of great wealth and honor from their society, and assumed that they were male. Why wouldn't they make that assumption? Lacking DNA tests, carbon-dating and other advanced technology, they had only their prejudice and life experience to draw on. After all, had they ever known any female warriors in their lifetime?

During the late 19th century there were a number of incidents of pre-historic grave robbing. This was a time when many digs were underway, and archaeologists (almost all of whom were men) conducted digs using haphazard classification systems. Numerous items were simply stored away for later examination. Now that there are women in the field, they are demanding more impartial examination and assessment of those artifacts. As it turns out, many of the warriors whom the last century diggers assumed were men, were women. Imagine if girls and women grew up knowing that women had always been warriors. Fighting back would seem more possible, wouldn't it?

The late Marija Gimbutas, an anthropologist-archeologist from UCLA, author of *The Civilization of the Goddess* and *The Language of the Goddess,* spent a good part of her life rediscovering and reinterpreting goddess figures and symbols that had been chalked up by men as mere "sex" symbols or decorations. Male scientists concluded that such figures were antique "playboy bunny" objects for men. Largely because of Dr. Gimbutas, it can now be argued that goddess figures were as ubiquitous and sacred in pre-history as crucifixes are in some countries today.

There are friezes and frescoes discovered in Minoan digs that show societies where men and women were equal. The artwork reveals women playing all roles that have been traditionally thought of as "males only." Women were judges, priests, healers, chemists, musicians, dancers, artists, traders, counselors, merchants, athletes, explorers, and warriors .

What If God Were a Woman?

The context for equality between the sexes in early societies seemed to spring from men and women worshiping a female deity. If God is a woman, how could you ever believe that a woman is inherently incapable? How could you logically exclude women from full participation in a society? Wouldn't that be like denying God her due? It certainly made sense to pre-historic men and women that God was female because of the inexplicable miracle of birth. What a sacred act, giving and sustaining life. Why wouldn't a woman be the holy embodiment of a female creator?

With regard to the subject of this book, wouldn't a physical attack on a woman be tantamount to sacrilege if our culture accepted the notion of a female deity? And if God is a woman, when an evil person attacks a woman, wouldn't she feel that she had absolutely every right, as well as ability, to fight back?

A capsule view of what happened to destroy the goddess-centered, egalitarian societies is that the iron-making and fire dependent societies of the cold north moved south. They dominated the more gentle societies in the temperate and sub-tropical zones. The southerners didn't know how to fight violence since their societies weren't built on violence and domination. The northerners dominated the southerners, the males soon dominated the females, and in the process, female deities were relinquished in favor of battle-oriented and male-supremacist gods.

Even the stories of women as supreme beings were destroyed so as to completely suppress the idea and reality of women's power. Without stories or history, it's easy to convince groups of their inferiority. Further, if you replace stories of female strength and power with anti-female stories, it's possible to intimidate the dominated into agreeing with their dominators.

Selling the Idea of Women's Inferiority and Evil Inclinations

The "natural" inferiority of women was sold and bought, forced and enforced. Today, feminist scholars argue that many stories of the Hebrews were symbolically veiled accounts of the squashing of the Mother and the take-over by the Father, including the creation story. The Hebrews were either originally northern marauders, or they adopted and refined the patriarchal mode as gung-ho converts. They codified the "boys only, no girls allowed" because "God said so" approach to society in the Old Testament. The Christians picked up the misogyny ball and ran with it, as did Muslims.

There were all sorts of religious practices born out of the view that women were inferior to men — segregation, submission, rules regarding menstruation, childbirth, proper roles and behavior, including silence and limited access to learning. Modern Ultra-Orthodox Jews in Israel even want segregated buses. (Of course, the men are not suggesting that women take the front of the bus, oh, no. Where's the Rosa Parks of Jerusalem?)

Deuteronomy 25:11,12 is a humdinger: Moses said to Israel: "If two men are fighting, and the wife of one man tries to rescue her husband by grabbing the other man's private parts, you must cut off her hand. Don't have any mercy." Imagine a culture being so concerned about a woman's potential power that it counsels its men to punish a woman for helping to defend her own husband. What is a male-dominated culture so afraid of when it counsels its men to cut off the hand of a wife who tries to defend her husband by grabbing another man's private parts?

And what does Deuteronomy 25:11,12 say about self-defense? If a woman's identity is completely tied to her husband, the passage becomes a rule against self-defense. What a choice — hand or husband? The woman is terrified of losing her husband, because he is her only means of survival and status in most cases, or losing her hand, another means of survival in very rough hand-to-mouth times.

These days, very few people know that European women were in great and lethal danger in the middle ages. I'll never forget how shocked, grief-stricken and angry I was when I first read that some scholars estimate that between six and nine million women were executed as witches from the mid-1400's to the late 1600's. I was reading *Beyond Power: On Women, Men, and Morals*, by Marilyn French, when I first learned of the female holocaust in Europe. (The last witch trial in the U.S. was in 1692.) That meant that practically everyone in Europe at that time was related to someone who had been killed for not being a proper woman. This was gender genocide, "gendercide" if you will, that still casts its pall at some level, I'm sure.

Woman-hatred became an enterprise, a ritual in the form of witch burnings prompted by the hatred toward women from clergy and learned laymen. This hatred was whipped up even further by the publication and distribution of the *Malleus Malificarum,* "Hammer of Witches," written by two zealous Dominicans, Henry Kramer and Jacob Sprenger. The whole European continent was consumed in ridding itself of Satan in the form of woman. Be mindful that a man could accuse a female neighbor of being a witch if his milk cow went dry temporarily. Or if his neighbor didn't smile enough. Or if she knew how to make herbal remedies, a tradition that had been passed down from mother to daughter for centuries. Or if he coveted her property.

After the witch burnings it was a matter of survival for a woman to learn to be compliant, sweet, pretty, and ladylike. Eccentricity and strong character traits could get a woman killed. *From the Beast to the Blonde: On Fairy Tales and Their Tellers,* by Marina Warner, discusses how cautionary stories warning daughters to comply with male power were self-defensive. Warner doesn't articulate specifically the hidden warnings that must have come into fairy tales due to the witch burnings, but it's not difficult to extrapolate that many stories that modern women feel promote passivity in girls were most likely designed to warn girls to blend in, to not "rock the boat," in order to survive.

The Black Plague is said to have partially been a result of the woman-hating witch burnings, beheadings, drownings and stranglings. Since the zealous witch hunters were determined to wipe out witches, they reasoned they must also destroy everything associated with the alleged witch, their herbal remedies and "familiars." Familiars, or household pets, most commonly cats, were burned right along with their mistresses. If, as some scholars assert, there were millions of women burned, millions of cats were burned too. The fewer cats, the more rats. The more rats, the more fleas, the more carriers of the Black Death. An ironic karmic outcome, no? Also, consider the knowledge of natural medicines that got torched. As a final irony, maybe even cures for the bubonic plague went up in the flames with the women.

Of course the witch hunters in villages across Europe did not destroy the "witches" homes or possessions. These were confiscated by the local Catholic Church, kept, or sold and added to already swollen treasuries. Is it any wonder that wealthy, independent women and widows were frequently prime targets for execution? The witch burnings were a lucrative activity.

Perhaps women's alleged inferior biology, that is, their smaller average size, has little to do with most women believing they are unable to defend themselves, even to this day. Perhaps a woman's well-founded fear of annihilation, and the self-hatred she learns from the culture, has more to do with her unwillingness to defend herself than her size.

Do you suppose some of the women were executed for knowing self-defense and using it or teaching other women secrets of protecting life and limb? Might there have been self-defense techniques that were passed through matrilineal lines for centuries and then forgotten, suppressed out of fear of reprisal? We'll never know.

Self-Defense: The Ultimate Birth Control Method

The miracle of reproduction is a domain of life that has been entangled both in religion and science; both seek to control birth. The ability to defend oneself from unwanted physical "attention," is truly the ultimate form of birth control. Given the Roman Catholic stance against birth control, imagine the bind that a Catholic woman, trained to be a submissive Madonna, is in when she doesn't want to have intercourse — in the middle ages or now in modern times. Or let's say we have a Catholic woman who is willing to use birth control but is too afraid to ask her macho man to wear a condom, even though the consequence of her inability to say "no" could be unwanted pregnancy or even death from HIV and AIDS. When childbirth had a high mortality rate, defending oneself from unwanted sex was definitely a self-defense issue that could mean life or death.

"No!" verbally, and then if the "no" doesn't stop the man, a good swift kick or hit to the testicles, is a natural method of birth control, more natural and immediate than the rhythm method. A good slam to the testicles is enough to quench any guy's fire. In cases of sexual assault, a defensive counter-attack that results in severe injury to a rapist's genitalia may be a form of weeding out violent men from the gene pool. Who knows? We don't know because society, with the emphatic help of religion and science, has disarmed, dislegged, and "dissed" women to such a severe degree we can only surmise what a woman could do in terms of naturally controlling her own reproductive role through physical self-defense.

Rethinking Natural and Acceptable Gender Roles

Until the last two decades, science dispassionately lent credence to the belief in women's physical and social inferiority. Biologists and zoologists, for example interpreted animal behavior in such a way that it most closely resembled a patriarchal human system. Observing animals in the wild, many male scientists could not suspend their own gender bias. Male chauvinist attitudes can still be found in wildlife documentaries on television. The male voice-over says something like, "The female waits in rapt and submissive anticipation while the male asserts his right to have his way." Meanwhile, off camera, they neglect to show the female breaking the male's leg for trying to mount her when she doesn't want "his way" but her own.

Women's equality has been as effectively impeded by science as it has been by religion. When women lobbied for the right to be educated, men of the cloth and men of the lab coat argued that it was unnatural, that if women learned too much, their ovaries would dry up, thereby risking the future of the entire human race.

Prior to the late 19th century, a woman had few if any civil rights. She could be thrown in a mental institution if she "talked back" to her husband, without her even getting to testify at the commitment hearing. She could have her children taken away without a hearing. Doctors, scientists and clergy could be witnesses verifying what was natural and unnatural for females, according to medicine, science and scripture. Even if a woman knew intellectually she was able to physically defend herself from a husband's beating, would she do it? Or would that be an action that would be apt to get her into more hot water?

OK, so that was then and this is now. How do these archaic attitudes affect what modern women do or don't do with regard to defending themselves from violence? A lot. First, we haven't, as a group, truly questioned why women don't defend themselves more. We have simply soaked up old-fashioned attitudes and haven't replaced them with attitudes based in fact. Also, a good portion of the world's women do not have the status of "modern women." Secondly, self-defense attitudes are not talked about very much in the general population and are conspicuous in their absence. Thirdly, our mothers and grandmothers were even more steeped in old notions of proper female behavior than we are — notions promoted by the authorities of religion and science. What images could we possibly draw on to learn how to defend ourselves if our caregivers didn't believe it was possible for a woman to confront a violent man?

Current Religious Views on Self-Defense

I was curious about the effect religious beliefs have on an American woman's attitude toward self-defense. To begin looking for answers, I spoke with women who are leaders in their religious organizations. All had experienced full-force self-defense training.

I spoke with reform Rabbi Kroll of the Stephen Weiss Temple in Los Angeles who recommends Impact Personal Safety of Los Angeles "all the time." She asserts there are absolutely no teachings in Judaism which would prohibit a woman from defending herself. She took the training because she saw how her daughter handled herself after taking a shortened version of the course. She says that she always thinks of her training with gratitude whenever she's out on the streets; she has more street savvy than her husband. She also feels that there is a moral obligation to train women to defend themselves, that it's wrong to withhold the knowledge of self-protection.

Sister Susan Olson belongs to the order of the International Sisters of Notre Dame. The sisters in her order live on their own and have their own financial obligations. She was trained in full-force self-defense when the homeless shelter she worked with hosted a training for its residents. She was amazed at the changes she saw in the women in the shelter, including herself. The women went from wimpy to empowered in a miraculously short time.

"I gained a much better sense of my body and an ability to create a presence. Women don't ordinarily go around creating a presence," Sister Olson said. She is not aware of any articulated position in the Roman Catholic church against women defending themselves.

Minister Verona Criton was trained in an abbreviated, four-hour workshop conducted by the Impact Foundation in Los Angeles. She is a Pentecostal Minister of the Gospel. Her stance on self-defense is simple: "You got to do what you got to do. Jesus lay down his life so you don't have to." Women's self-defense is completely consistent with her faith, and she recommends it to every woman and girl due to the amount of physical abuse in the world.

Ivelisse Roman left her Pentecostal/Charismatic Protestant church of twenty years because of what she calls "toxic faith." She is now ministering with a Reform Presbyterian congregation. She took the full women's basics class with New York City PrePare Inc., a leading provider of full-force self-defense in the nation. Reverend Roman knows that the men in her former church would have big problems with women's self-defense because of varying sexist attitudes, such as: when a woman is assaulted, sexually or otherwise, her Jezebel nature must have encouraged it, or she hadn't submitted to Paul's rules so she deserved what she got. Such men believe that a woman cannot be saved unless she is saved through her husband. They want wives to walk behind men, to stay quiet and follow Old Testament teachings that forbid women from picking up arms or dressing like men. She says sexual abuse, beating, and incest is common in the Bible Belt. She says they even suggested that her husband was gay because she had autonomy.

She, along with Rabbi Kroll, feels there is a moral obligation to obliterate the myth of female defenselessness. She took the class because of her role as a counselor. She kept hearing stories of rape and incest and came to the conclusion that women had to learn how to take care themselves. Donna Chaiet of PrePare, Inc. came to her college to speak, and hearing that talk challenged Reverend Roman to make the commitment. Her life completely changed personally and professionally as a result.

The Muslim woman I interviewed requested that I not use her name, but said that she could not find anything in the Koran that meant that women shouldn't protect themselves. She acknowledged, however, that there are many interpretations of the Koran. The more fundamentalist the person, the less apt they are to grant women any means of independence. But women's oppression is not inherent in the Koran.

Margaret Keip, an ordained Unitarian Universalist minister, is an enthusiastic supporter and advocate of full-force self-defense. Her son is a full-force leader and instructor with a background in aikido, a relatively new style of Japanese martial art. She was amazed and moved when she attended a graduation of one of the full-force classes he'd co-taught, and decided to take it because of her own poor boundary-setting skills. She also had a desire to have more of a sense of personal power, which she had witnessed in the women she saw graduate. When I asked her if there was any articulated position within the Unitarian Universalist organization with regard to violence against women, she was able to give a resounding, "Yes!"

In 1993, the Unitarian Universalist Association drafted a general resolution during its general assembly that called for an end to violence against women. In a moving document, the Unitarian Universalist Association is on public record recognizing the pervasiveness and persistence of the problem of wholesale violence against women. It's no accident that the Unitarians are "cousins" of the Quakers.

Finally, I interviewed Siri Ram, a graduate of Los Angeles, Impact Personal Safety. She is a devout Sikh, a religious group that originated in India. There is not one ounce of religious resistance to women's self-defense in her religion. The Sikhs, in fact, include women in both physical and mental warrior training,due to their history of military oppression and because the woman is considered sacred. Every Sikh carries a knife, ready to defend their lives. They train with knives and swords. The Sikhs' path is that of a soldier-saint. They are taught always to look and behave in a saintly manner but be ready for battle. Incidentally, their creator has no gender.

The only women with whom I spoke who could anticipate a backlash against women's self-defense within their churches were the two Christians affiliated with fundamentalist churches. They felt that men in their churches would react negatively if too many women learned how to fight back. But, they said, "That's their thing, not Jesus' or God's."

Fundamentalism has been rising all over the world, and largely to the detriment of women. Some assert, as Marilyn French does in *The War Against Women,* that the renaissance of fundamentalism is in reaction to the rise of feminism and women's rights.

The Taliban in Afghanistan has ushered in a repressive and deadly climate that gives citizens and soldiers permission to stone women for not covering their bodies properly. Women are no longer allowed to go to school. Public executions, by stoning, are commonplace for adulterers. How do you think a crowd would react to a Afghanistani woman who tried to fight back?

Muslim fundamentalists, however, are not alone in their oppression of women. In Los Angeles, on April 16, 1997, Superior Court Judge James Albracht ruled that two Korean Christian missionaries were guilty of involuntary manslaughter rather than second degree murder for the death of Kyung-Ja Chung, the wife of one of the defendants. Albracht found that the men "may have been misguided and blinded by their religious zeal, but were focused on "saving her from the demons they believed possessed her."

According to the story in the *Los Angeles Times,* by staff writer Ann W. O'Neill, the testimony revealed, "Sixteen of her (Mrs. Chung's) ribs were broken, the muscles in her thighs were so damaged the tissue had died, internal organs were displaced and crushed, and a vein leading to her heart was torn."

Jae-Whoa Chung, the victim's husband, and Sung Soo Choi, stomped Mrs. Chung to death in a demon-cleansing ritual called *ansukido.* In addition to stomping and pressing the woman, the missionaries prayed, sang, spoke in tongues and called out for Jesus Christ to help drive the demons from her.

They decided Kyung-Ja Chung needed the *ansukido* because she talked back to her husband and had been disobedient and arrogant toward him, which was proof enough for them that she was possessed. Did she house demons, the beast in her soul, or was she an awakening beauty, a warrior of the self, someone asserting her own will and spirit? What is the difference, besides method, between the missionaries in Los Angeles, 1997, and zealous witch burners in Switzerland, 1597?

Perhaps the pub signs displaying "The Quiet Woman," holding her own head, aren't so amusing and archaic after all. Women are still being murdered in the name of God for "talking back."

6

The Rules of the Realm of Men

The divine right of husbands, like the divine right of kings, may, it is hoped, in this enlightened age, be contested without danger.

MARY WOLLSTONECRAFT, (1759-1797)

Learning To Be Outlaws

We usually think of outlaws as the "bad guys," wearing black hats or bandannas over their nose and mouth, robbing banks or chasing down trains on horseback. Sometimes they are depicted as heartless terrorists; sometimes they are idealized, like Bonnie and Clyde or Robin Hood.

But there is another type of outlaw as well, and you have probably met or read about such "lawbreakers." They are the women who challenge those written or unwritten laws which are unjust to women.

One such law is the one that says a woman's body is not hers. Although there are no current U.S. laws that state specifically that a woman shall not have jurisdiction over her own body, nonetheless, this unwritten law is supported by factions all over the world. Most of the world's cultures infringe on a woman's right to have jurisdiction over her body by promoting specific practices. These range from genital mutilation and public dress codes, to prohibition of birth control and abortion.

Society says it has an interest in what a woman does with her body because she is the one who bears children. Therefore, it's argued that the society at large has a stake in what a woman does or doesn't do with her reproductive capacity. That position presumes that individual women are not full citizens or mature enough to determine what is best for themselves, their families, and society. Reproductive laws are being seriously challenged as more and more women are willing to make themselves "outlaws." And as more women are willing to be considered outlaws, the faster the laws change through a shift in consciousness and consensus, eventually making them "in-laws." But it takes courage to change laws, inside or outside the system.

A practical problem with women's rights is that with rights come responsibilities. One cannot claim rights and then disclaim accountability or be denied responsibility by those in power over the application of those rights. Those responsibilities include the stewardship of one's own body as well as its defense. When a woman consciously or unconsciously delegates responsibility for her own physical safety, she essentially goes along with the unwritten law that a woman's body is not her own.

Ask a man, "Who is responsible for your body and personal safety?" and he'll respond, "Why, I am, of course." Ask a woman the same question and her answer may not be as clear. A woman who answers, "My husband, my father, my brother, the police," is not considered by our culture to be immature or odd as a man would be if he so answered. If a man answered, "My wife, my parents, my sister, the police," we'd think him odd. Unfortunately, when it is outside the norm for a woman to protect herself, she will not take responsibility for doing so. If,on the other hand, a woman is an "outlaw," she will have discovered that she must be responsible for her own body, or else.

Women who have been assaulted or raped frequently become "outlaws" because their romantic notion of rescue has been viciously dashed. In some cultures a woman who has been raped is shunned and cast out, becoming an outlaw because she's no longer wanted and literally has no choice. Ironically, the incident that victimized her in the first place is the point when a woman will most likely seek out means to defend herself in the future.

If the woman is so traumatized that she's not able to get angry on her own behalf, she will withdraw and use "passive" self-defense that takes her further away from her rights and responsibilities. In other words, there are women who have been assaulted who never go out at night again, who pull back from participation in life. This was too often the case before people began to talk about the trauma of rape. Many women are ashamed of being raped because another unwritten law (sometimes written depending on local case law) was that if a woman is raped, it is her own damned fault. Note, fault, not responsibility. In fact, rape has been used to enforce overt and covert gender laws and to punish women who don't comply.

Commandments which, when broken, can justify rape are:

*A woman shall not be out at night unaccompanied. If she is, she must be accompanied by a male who has proprietary rights over her. He can then, by right, defend her from other men if need be.

*A woman shall not be uppity and enjoy the same freedoms as men.

*A woman shall not laugh at or humiliate a man, even inadvertently.

*A woman shall not "talk back" to men.

*A woman shall not be angry under any circumstance.

*A woman shall not confront or hold a man accountable for his actions.

*A woman shall be neither too attractive nor not attractive enough.

*A woman shall not decide when and where she will have sex with her husband.

*A woman shall not be her own woman but must be some man's woman.

*A woman shall not defend herself from men or be punished by his uncontrollable wrath; and on, and on.

There are also "commandments" applicable only to men which similarly infringe on a woman's rights, such as: "Men shall have the right to...ogle any woman, touch any woman, hassle any woman, punish "their" woman.

An exceptionally fine movie that did not fare well at the box office, "The Ballad of Little Jo," was a heart-breaking story about a real woman who intentionally broke the law in order to live life to its fullest — actually, in order to survive. Little Jo was a woman in the West who, in self-defense, changed her gender identity after she'd been brutally raped.

She scarred her face, she cut her hair and donned the apparel of men, which was against the law. Why would cross-dressing be against the law? Because the law-makers did not want second-class citizens "passing" for first-class citizens and enjoying the benefits of power and privilege. It was, after all, the "law" of the Old Testament that women can not dress as males and vice versa.

Little Jo became an outlaw intentionally, because the first time she was in public alone wearing a dress — hoops, corsets, the whole deal — she was raped. A raped woman in those days had no hot-lines or support groups, and received little sympathy.

Little Jo was good at her masquerade and became not only a man but a successful one — a landowner, a respected citizen, one whom others listened to and followed. When she died the under-taker discovered her charade. In no time the men who had minutes before grieved their loss of Little Jo, the man, turned "her" into an object of intense hatred and betrayal by displaying her dead body on the back of a horse in the middle of town.

Based on the true story of Jo Monaghan of Ruby City, Idaho, Little Jo was a potent reminder to the women of their town that a gender outlaw would be shown no mercy, even in death.

Countless women through history have "passed" as men in order to survive, and many have succeeded in a man's world. Their stories have been suppressed well into this century in order to avoid giving other women "ideas." That the outlaws, the "passers" accomplished so much challenges the lie that men are naturally superior and more capable.

The Rules of Rape and Self-defense

For a long period of history, women were legally considered chattel. Chattel, livestock, possessions have no civil rights. Period. If chattel protects itself, it is stepping beyond chattel status and asserting selfness, something chattel is not allowed or theoretically even capable of doing. With self-defense, there must be a self to defend. When women were thought of as possessions they had no right to protect themselves. They could be beaten, raped, even murdered with little consequence.

In many parts of the world for centuries rape could be punished, not because of the violation of the woman, but because another man's possession had been "damaged." The husband or brother had a right to "undamaged" goods in order to command the biggest and best bride price to his estate when the woman married. Virgins commanded a high price. "Spoiled" girls were "lucky" if they were able to marry at all.

Some rape laws were based on whether the victim became pregnant or not. If the woman became pregnant from the alleged "rape," it was then considered to be not a rape and the perpetrator was not penalized. Some laws required that the rapist marry the woman he raped. Other laws were based on whether the woman was married or not, and then the forced intercourse could be punishable as adultery. In any case, women had no rights to claim victimization, since chattel could not be victimized. Self-defense would therefore be out of the question and certainly the province of an outlaw. No wonder many men still regard women as less than men — possessions. The philosophy underlying archaic, sexist laws and attitudes is still reflected in our contemporary culture and legal system.

Women who have defended themselves have had to confront the "reasonable person" rule, a standard used in tort law and occasionally in criminal law, to determine if a person acted within civilized, acceptable boundaries. A judge will decide if a reasonable person in like circumstances would have reacted as the respondent or defendant did. In most cases, reasonable person has been based on a reasonable man in like circumstances, which has been used to women's detriment when determining whether a woman acted in self-defense reasonably.

Battered women convicted of murder have recently made progress in having case law written that at least acknowledges that a reasonable man standard cannot be applied wholesale to a reasonable woman. Hypothetical: an average-sized male may not see anything reasonably threatening from a man who is smaller than he is. He knows that he could defend himself, or that he could easily deflect any physical force the smaller man may focus on him. Put a weapon in the smaller man's hands and the reasonable man standard changes. A smaller man with a gun is as threatening to a large man as a larger man with a gun. Assault and defense against assault is determined by the threat of harm and the ability to carry out the threat.

Contrast that situation with this: a taller woman is threatened by a smaller man. She has no knowledge of any defense she may have using her own body. Is it reasonable for her to react to a threat of bodily harm that a man her same size wouldn't be threatened by? If the judge or the jury is sufficiently aware from their own life experience that her reaction using "too much" force was reasonable, she'll be acquitted or exonerated. If the judge or jury denies the different realities of men and women, she'll be held to a standard that men are held to. Too bad for her.

Battered women, imprisoned in their own homes by their "macho" husbands, who defend themselves in a "delayed" manner rather than in the heat of the moment, can be compared to a prisoner-of-war who must assess how to escape the enemy camp. If you think that's too dramatic, think about women who live with men who threaten them with death on a daily basis. These men threaten to kill their wives or girlfriends if they talk back, if they leave, if they complain, if they won't have sex, if they burn the dinner or look unhappy.

The Stockholm Syndrome, a condition used to describe men captured in war and their subsequent sympathies with their captors, applies to women under the thumb of violent, dominating husbands and boyfriends. However, fewer people are sympathetic to women prisoners-of-gender-war than they are toward male prisoners because too many people are blind to the very real and uneven battle of the sexes, the "undeclared" war against women.

Given all of the strands woven into the fabric of gender relations: chattel status, double standards in laws, financial dependence, it is easy to see why women are "defensively delayed."

Recognizing a "Nation" of Women

A nation is an entity, a group of people with shared culture: history, language, experience, rules, laws, rituals and boundaries. One way to dominate another nation is to over-run its boundaries, take over the means of communicating, deny the language, and limit the means of production. People who are dominated, or colonized, are then either eliminated or required to uphold the dominant culture while denying their own.

Imagine that you are "Best Man" the leader of the Beasties in an unstable country, Beautland. What would be on your take-over "To-Do" list? What would be on your keep and enforce power "To-Do" list?

1. Seize and maintain all radio and television stations, and newspapers.
2. Create pro-Beasties programs, make the Beautlanders look stupid. Make the Beautlanders look happy to be dominated. Show Beautlanders being killed or hurt for trying anything to over-throw the Beasties.
3. Praise and showcase Beautlanders that criticize other Beautlanders.
4. Ridicule, reject, torture Beasties who help or sympathize with strong Beautlanders.
5. Convince the Beautlanders that their heritage never existed or is a lie.
6. Ban literature depicting Beautlanders as real people.
7. Suppress Beautland leaders and heroes and heroines from the past.
8. Make speaking Beautlandese illegal.
9. Ban meetings of Beautlanders.
10. Deny the existence of Beautlander deities.
11. Make accumulation of wealth or education impossible for Beautlanders without compliance to Beastie values.
12. Convince the Beautlanders that it is hopeless to physically defend themselves against the superior Beasties.

Number 12 is the item most pertinent to this book. However, you must have the other items in place to have 12 be effectively carried out. You can observe this "To-Do" list being checked off time and again in war-torn countries. In Afghanistan's war against women one of the first things the Taliban did was to outlaw education for women. You can also see how the U.S. Constitution was created to protect men from "To-Do" list items 1 through 12, but not minorities and women.

One way to look at women as a group is to consider women a nation. The parallels are obvious. As a nation women have no major newspapers or broadcasting entities. We have had little or no say in the decision-making bodies of the world. We've been excluded from mainstream history. We've been convinced that we are defenseless simply by virtue of being females.

When a misogynist rapes and murders a woman he is not raping and murdering an individual, he is committing a crime against a woman as she represents all women. He is communicating his power over all of us. The nation of men have been warring against women, for centuries. As the patriarchal customs were more and more embedded and enforced, rebels became more scarce, or more suppressed, until women themselves became enforcers of the male nation's rules, in order to simply survive.

It's a Man's World Even With Margaret Thatcher

"It's a man's world." Few would argue with that simply because it's undeniable that men hold the power in practically every country, state, city, village of the world. Almost every institution, whether it's a bank, school, company, corporation, or laboratory, is headed by a male or body of men. That circumstance, looked at from one point of view, amounts to gender dictatorship, or a "men-opoly." There are other forms of domination. In many countries the lighter-skinned people rule the darker-skinned people. But there are countries where skin color is not the major factor in "one-up-man-ship," tribal or religious affiliation is. But women are dominated by men in every society, regardless of the other factors of domination.

There are women who have broken into ranks of power, for sure. But they are still completely and utterly the exceptions, even in so-called developed and democratic countries. We need a critical mass of women to be in power in order to achieve true democracy.

It's practically inevitable when discussing the vision of more women and more female "energy" in government, that someone pipes up with, "Yeah, big difference Margaret Thatcher made in England!" (Elbow, elbow, wink, snort, chuckle.) Never mind that I'm not a British citizen and that I didn't have a vote. That doesn't matter. I'm a female who advocates gender balance.

They're referring, of course, to Thatcher being indistinguishable from the regular white, conservative, hawk males we're accustomed to having as leaders. The comment is supposed to make the proponent of more women in power positions stop, think, and realize, "Oh, yes, how foolish of me to want to have women represented equally in government. It wouldn't change anything. I'll stop now. Thank you for reminding me that Mrs. Thatcher is representative of all women."

Bringing up Thatcher is a conversation stopper. It's also probably thinly veiled hostility to change. Women of all colors and men of color are frequently called upon to answer for all people in whatever subset they are in. What a drag it must be to be an African-American and be expected to explain all other African-Americans. What a burden it is to cringe when another woman does something that's embarrassing. I know that somehow she represents me simply by virtue of our shared biology.

But I don't know a single white man who would even consider being accountable or answering for any other white man just by virtue of his being pale, male and privileged. "As a white man, would you please explain Richard Nixon?" A man would think me nuts for saying something like that.

I have had the experience of being the only woman in a job situation and knowing that all eyes are on me to see "how the woman is doing." I have had the experience of all heads turning in my direction to get "the woman's point of view." I have seen all eyes on me when an off-color joke is told. So I'm frequently put in the position of being expected to defend Thatcher. I didn't like her, couldn't defend her politics, and resented being asked to just because she's a woman. That didn't mean I didn't watch her and wish her well. I wanted her to open doors for other women.

Supposedly the perfect family has a mommy and a daddy. Why wouldn't a perfect decision-making body on a national or global level be balanced as well? Most studies confirm that a healthy dual-parent family is beneficial for children. It's only reasonable then that the family of human beings should have both men and women at the top. Goodness knows that most women and children aren't doing very well in the world. So let's get the "mommy" types in the halls where decisions are made.

Now that I have declared myself not obliged to answer for Mrs. Thatcher I will offer some defense. But only because I feel like it, not because I have to. Has the world been prepared to have as heads of state women who aren't more or less similar to the males on the scene? Haven't citizens been afraid that women would be too emotional, too "soft" on war and criminals, too hormonal? (As if military might isn't some kind of hormone run amok.)

It's important to have compassion for women, the in-laws, who have had to embody traditional male values in order to make way for the rest of us. It's important to understand paradox when a social revolution is afoot. No, I didn't condone Margaret Thatcher's stint as Prime Minister and yes, I appreciate the knocks she's taken and the room that I hope she's made for women with values that aren't men's views dressed in pantyhose and pumps.

Gender dictatorships create hostile climates for women and balancing gender ratios is one of the best solutions we have to ending gender violence all over the world. Imagine the U.N. Security Council or the General Assembly with at least near equal numbers of men and women. It could happen.

Changing the Rules of the Realm: Affirmative Action, Political Power, and Self-Defense

As a self-defense advocate, I firmly believe that affirmative action must remain a policy of this country and other democracies. Why? And what does affirmative action have to do with self-defense?

In order for women to force our society into taking our experiences into account, in order for us to affect official policies, we must have access to the institutions that have traditionally been dominated by white men in this country, men of all colors in countries all over the world. If academia, the corporate world, and government continue to be primarily shaped and maintained by males, the life experience and wisdom of females will continue to be considered less important.

Our voices will not be heard unless there are enough of them to sway policy. The exceptional women who slip through, may not have enough weight to weigh in and make a difference. With affirmative action, women and people of color have more clout, have more opportunity to gain mainstream credibility and then, have a better shot at getting into decision- and policy-making positions. Unless we have leaders who represent large portions of the population with little power and who have had life experiences that reflect that population, social justice will take even longer to achieve.

A government form of affirmative action that's barely been broached in the United States but is "old hat" in many European countries is the concept of "gender balance." Who would you rather have in the legislature arguing for a rape bill? Someone who thinks that rape is a woman's own fault or someone who has been raped and survived it? Or what if a law-making body is considering outlawing pets in public places? What if you consider your dog to be a way to defend yourself from harm?

If a bill suggesting that Title IX funds be used to create required self-defense classes for elementary kids is introduced, wouldn't you like it to be represented by a legislator who has experienced how empowering self-defense can be for women — who has gotten herself, daughter or girlfriend out of a violent situation? Do you really want to be misrepresented by an almost exclusively white male group that doesn't have a clue about what it's like to be a member of any out-of-power group?

It's no wonder that the Scandinavian countries which have gender balance rules for government have the most liberal policies on child care, parental leave and other matters concerning family life. These gender balanced countries have acknowledged through the polls that a true democracy cannot exist without the equal representation of women, half of the people.

What would it take to achieve gender balance in the U.S. or in other countries that have resisted the full participation of women as citizens? Affirmative action, a freer, less biased press that publishes more women's political opinions, and campaign reform.

Campaign reform is a political form of self-defense. As long as the old boys' network thrives, it will protect its own interests through the power of wealth and influence. As long as campaigns cost millions of dollars, only those with access to those dollars will be able to run for office.

If a woman wants to run on a platform that includes supporting affirmative action, liberalizing self-defense laws for battered women, and making self-defense a normal and regular part of physical education in public schools, she must either water down her issues or lose the funding necessary to get her elected. What a Catch-22.

An alternative to costly national offices are state and local positions in which women can still make a huge difference to other women. We need to encourage each other to run for these offices, to support women who run for these offices, and also to participate on local committees and commissions.

How can women make a difference at the local level on the issue of self-defense? Here's an example: Laws concerning a dog-owner's right to rent an apartment or bring their dog into a commercial establishment. This is an issue of self-defense since dogs are excellent protectors. When criminals were asked what they would use to protect their own homes, they said dogs, not alarms. (McCall's May 1992) While middle-aged white men may not understand the security that comes with having a dog, women and senior citizens would. I would rather have strict gun-control laws any day in place of such rigid municipal dog control laws. It's almost impossible to conceal a dog.

One could argue that laws that prohibit dogs in housing discriminate against people who need them for protection. A sympathetic local official who knows how her dog protects her and gives her a sense of confidence will help pass laws making it possible for people with dogs to have access to more places, as many Europeans do.

There are countless success stories involving dogs who foiled the bad intentions of criminals. I know I feel a lot safer when I have my bitch, Maggie, with me. But if you don't have a canine bitch, how about calling for your inner bitch instead? She is part of your verbal warrior. Read on.

7

Veiled Villainies: Covert Verbal Attacks

Any woman who chooses to behave like a full human being should be warned that the armies of the status quo will treat her as something of a dirty joke; that's their natural and first weapon.

GLORIA STEINEM, "SISTERHOOD," IN *MS.* (SPRING 1972)

Women are assaulted verbally at every level of society simply because they are women. That is a self-defense problem. By not identifying and defending against verbal attacks made on women, we all lose civil rights ground. A culture that disrespects women and expresses that disrespect verbally creates a hostile environment where physical violence becomes commonplace, practically ho-hum.

Women are so accustomed to verbal attacks, many of us have become numb or unconscious to their occurrence. We may know something didn't feel good, or we may mull over what we "coulda, shoulda said" in the moment, but we only felt it happening and didn't respond when it happened. We are literally trained to be peacemakers, which is very good. I want people to learn peace-making, but peacemaking must be balanced with conflict resolution. In order to resolve conflicts one must be able to confront conflict, not run from it. Obviously, if we convince / brainwash / coerce half of the population to avoid conflict, we're going to have half the world frozen in the face of confrontation. It's impossible to be an adult citizen of the world without facing conflict.

In order to learn how to defend oneself verbally one must be able to identify an attack for what it is. There are covert and overt verbal assaults on women that are tricky for some to identify, but once you've seen them for what they are, you can do something about them. This chapter will explore common and relatively covert verbal assaults in a woman's world of words.

The Cowboy vs. the Libber:

Uppity women generate personal attacks all the time. As an uppity freshman in 1971, I remember bounding up the stairs to the student union at Rocky Mountain College in Billings, Montana. A cowboy whistled at me. I was new to feminism and hadn't encountered too much open hostility yet. Having completed Robin Morgan's anthology of feminist writings, *Sisterhood is Powerful,* I was inspired to confront sexism. Her book made so many mysteries clear. I didn't like the guy's whistle. It made me feel threatened. I almost ignored him but decided to go over and confront him. I would change him. After all, ending sexism was a sensible, civilized thing to do. He was surprised that this little filly talked back.

She: Please don't whistle at me. It's rude. I'm not a dog.
He: Women like whistles. They've told me.
She: Maybe some do, I don't. Anyway, it's sexist to whistle at women. Women aren't sex objects. We're people.
He: Oh, God, you're not one of those man-hater women's libbers are you?
She: I'm a feminist and I don't hate men.
He: You're probably a dyke.
She: What's a dyke?
He: A girl who can't get a boyfriend.
She: What?
He: You know, she has to do it with other girls.
She: I don't do it with girls.
He: You're so pretty. You just need a boyfriend.
She: I have a boyfriend. (I lied, I was dating but had no boyfriend.) My looks are none of your business.
He: Oooo-yeeee, you're cute when you're pissed off. Don't get so emotional.
She: I'm not being emotional. I just don't want to be whistled at.
He: Don't be such a bitch, I was just having fun.
She: I didn't think it was fun.
He: God, you're so defensive.

When he said I was being defensive I tried to be nicer and smile more so he wouldn't think I was one of "those" feminists. I felt obliged to be a "good" feminist, a goodwill ambassador so that men could see how nice feminists actually are. Somehow we got into my major and minor. I told him I was going to go to law school but was majoring in theater. Yikes! He didn't like that.

He: Girls can't be lawyers. They aren't logical enough.
She: Yes, they can.
He: No, they can't
She: Yes, they can.
He: No, they can't (Whereupon, he had the gall to reach over and pinch my cheek.)
She: Can so.
He: Can't.
She: Can so. Why not?
He: I just know they can't.
She: What are you talking about? Of course, they can! This is America!
He: I've never seen a lady lawyer. Women are supposed to get married and have kids. Men are supposed to be the providers. Name one woman lawyer.
She: I can't, but they exist.
He: Where? Name one.
She: (silent thinking, racking brain, nothing . . .)
He: See? Women aren't supposed to be lawyers or there'd be some. You'll make a really nice wife if you just lose some weight.
She: Shut up. I don't need to lose weight.
He: What's wrong with you, can't you take a joke?

He won. He won through illogic, ignorance, and arrogance. I lost because I was ignorant, and engaged with him in the first place because I had been raised to be nice and to try to see the best in everyone. I also lost because he wasn't really carrying on a conversation.

What I know now that I didn't know then is that the entire "conversation" was off because I didn't realize that practically everything he said was an attack. He was defensive and went on the offensive. I was being defensive, as he so accurately pointed out, because I was being attacked. My response was congruent and appropriate in the context of what was actually happening. And at the time I thought being defensive was bad, something to avoid.

I have a theory that I doubt I'll ever prove: many women gave up their vocal support of feminism after having an exchange or two like the one I had with the cowboy. I believe unidentified illogical attacks like the one the cowboy launched on me created women who started to say, "I'm not a feminist but . . . ." For the rest of the chapter, I'll break down the cowboy's part of the dialogue and expose the attacks for what they were. Some of the attacks are distinct, some over-lap, and some are variations on a theme.

Fencing with Fools — The Whistle

The cowboy's initial act of whistling was a form of verbal attack. In a culture that makes a woman's beauty her most important attribute, a whistle conveys the communication that: 1) Women's looks are subject to judgment and approval anywhere at anytime by anyone; 2) If you're whistled at you're approved of; if you're not whistled at you're not beautiful. A man who whistles at a woman completely disregards the fact that a whistle scares some women, flatters others, angers and insults others. No matter what the individual's opinion of a whistle, it is an intrusion on what could or should be a straightforward activity — walking down the street. The privilege of being male includes being able to walk down streets without hassle, at least within their own turf. There's nowhere, with the possible exception of convents or all-female events, that is a woman's "turf."

"Women like whistles. They've told me."

There are some women who do feel flattered when whistled at, or at least they say so. They have been raised in the same culture with rules that say "Be beautiful, or else." The problem comes in when the dominant culture tries to make a rule about all women from one. In other words, the cowboy might have heard one woman say, "I don't mind being whistled at. I think it's nice."

It's human to try to make rules about "others." Generally speaking, women know that all men are different and grant them the freedom to be individuals. On the other hand, men have been raised to think that "women are all alike," and to try to make rules about all women, instead of knowing each one is different. There's no such thing as all women, all Germans, all Blacks, all men, all any group liking anything.

"Oh, God, you're not one of those man-hater women's libbers are you?"

Who knows where the cowboy got his information about "man-hater women's libbers," but it's unbelievable how many men think they are experts on the women's liberation movement because they read one article or had one conversation about the subject.

I was at a MENSA meeting as a speaker one time talking about my attendance at the U.N. Conference on Women in Beijing. Afterwards, a well-dressed mid-fifties man, a member of MENSA, wanted to argue with me about women's rights.

I stopped him and said, "Before we get into this, give me an idea of how educated you are about women's rights. What books have you read?" Without any embarrassment, he replied, "My former wife read The Feminist {sic} Mystique in the 60s. She told me it was bullshit."

"So you haven't read anything about women's liberation yourself?" I asked, hiding my amazement.

"That doesn't matter," he said, "I have my own opinions."

"Yes, I'm sure you do," I said, "But let's wait and have a conversation about this when you've educated yourself."

This "genius" had formed a negative opinion about women's rights on hearsay and didn't even get the title of the book he hadn't read straight. Why so many negative opinions based on nothing? Because many men are threatened consciously and unconsciously by the idea of their privilege being taken away. They have been exposed to negative media coverage generated by other threatened, privileged males. Mainstream coverage of the feminist movement has been full of ridicule and disparagement. Women have traditionally had little chance to rebut negative images because we don't control or even have much access to the news-gathering organizations or distribution outlets.

Notice just how few progressive women commentators are published or on the air compared to the number of males or conservative females. All views should be aired. A democratic free press should allow access to even unpopular views. But why are the self-defenders of women's rights missing? The movement for votes for women during the last century and the beginning of this century is a perfect example of the role of press coverage in suppressing women's rights.

The suffrage movement saw a lot of opposition. Mainstream media, newspapers and magazines, ran "anti-votes for women" articles and cartoons, full of harridans and "battle-axes," with stereotypical female weapons of domination: frying pans, rolling pins, hat pins, used to cow their unsexed husband into doing "woman's work." The defenders of the status quo, the no-votes for women group, were the "deep pockets" of the alcohol, insurance, railroad and insurance interests. Meanwhile, the women who worked for decades to get the vote could hardly afford ads and could barely get a column inch in the popular press to get their views out. They had to use one-on-one, door-to-door methods of persuasion. Can you imagine how difficult it was to defend the views of pro-vote women when they were constantly attacked by all the big papers and entertainment?

There were silent movies, music hall and vaudeville skits that made fun of the suffragists and their long-suffering families. Even the word "suffragette" was a media-born diminutive of the word suffrage used to minimize a major and global human rights movement, not dissimilar to calling someone a civil rights "activistette." The "humorous" images were used to make men feel threatened and to humiliate those women who were participating in the movement. Women got the message that they would be rejected and ridiculed by men if they came off as one of those "suffragettes." For a woman with no independent means, it was essential for her to stay in a man's good graces, whether father, brother or husband. Of course, the Catch 22 was that in order to become more independent, women needed the vote and needed to be free enough to lobby for it. And in order to work on getting the vote, they needed to ruffle men's feathers.

The dominant message of the mainstream media was that the woman's vote meant the "unsexing" of men and women into unnatural and opposite gender roles. Code for: less privilege for men, more equity for women. Again, no wonder it took so long for women to win the vote.

Today, feminists and strong women continue to be ridiculed in the mainstream press, while many women defensively state, "I'm not a feminist but . . . ." Denying one's affiliation with a group that has been routinely ridiculed is an unfortunate but understandable reaction. Most Americans have no idea of the diversity of style and opinion within the current feminist movement because of the stereotyping that has been put forth by a male dominated culture.

When women who are *de facto* feminists deny their feminism, many are unaware that they have been verbally attacked. They deny support of feminism because they don't know how to defend themselves and a movement that's been good for them but consistently misrepresented. It's difficult to defend the women's movement against attacks unless one knows women's history and can see the pattern of verbal and written attack, masquerading as humor, which has consistently been generated by threatened men.

Today, writers like Camille Paglia and Kate Roiphe get trotted out center stage when they go on their rampages against other feminists. Yahoo! I could just hear the boys in the news room yelling, "Cat Fight!" and sure enough, the air time and the column inches were there in miles for Paglia and Roiphe, not the people they were attacking, however.

The women who are accused of being man-hating libbers, like their suffrage foremothers, barely get any mainstream press to counter the attacks made upon them by detractors, male or female. If Gloria Steinem, Katha Pollitt, Susan Faludi, bell hooks, Patricia Ireland, Andrea Dworkin and Catherine MacKinnon, and many other serious feminist civil rights activists wanted the kind and quantity of press that anti-feminist women get, they could have it too. All they'd have to do is betray their missions, wage a war of words on each other, and take their attention off sexism, racism and gender inequality. How does one defend feminism if the media outlets are often anti-feminist?

Name-Calling and Lesbian-Baiting: "You're probably a dyke."

No one likes to be called a negative name or be identified with a group that is hated or misrepresented. I really didn't know what a dyke was at the beginning of the 70's. But the disgust on his face let me know that "dyke" wasn't referring to a wall in Holland that holds back the sea.

It's getting better but there are straight, feminist women who can still be intimidated by fear that someone may think that they are a bitch or a lesbian. They do not want to be identified with bitches or lesbians. They will be rejected or banished from the power structure, they believe, if they are thought to be a bitch or a lesbian or, God forbid, a bitchy lesbian. Therefore, to question a woman's heterosexuality is a useful political tool not dissimilar to "nigger lover," a phrase I'm loathe to use other than as a vulgar example of sowing hate through threat of association.

There was a media uproar in the 1980's made by some women who complained that the National Organization for Women had been "taken over" by lesbians. Again, we had "cat fight" coverage, between straight and lesbian women, not coverage of substantive issues. If a woman refuses to join a group for fear of being identified as a lesbian, or even "lesbian lover," they allow straight male supremacy to define the agenda for all women regardless of their sexual orientation. N.O.W. had, and continues to have a diverse membership, including men, by the way. Who one loves and who one doesn't love is irrelevant to the issue of confronting abuse and violence against women and children or the broader topics of racism, sexism, and homophobia.

The defense against lesbian-baiting? First, have the "accuser" state the relevance of the attack. What did my sexuality have to do with my confronting the cowboy about his whistle? Nothing. Second, the best defense would be to have everyone sympathetic to gays and lesbians simply "come out," like all the students did in support of their beloved gay teacher in Kevin Kline's movie, "In and Out."

Name-calling is part of the dark side of childhood. "Queer, faggot, fairy, slut, ho, nympho, dyke," are standard modern playground epithets. Sexualized taunts lay the groundwork for violence. Children don't have the luxury or sophistication to withstand vicious name-calling especially if the names that are being used are attached to spurned groups. Name-calling is emotional violence. Name-calling is objectifying someone. The time to stop name-calling is on the playground. We need to help kids arm themselves to fight it. It is vital to self-defense to see what name calling is: vicious.

"You're so pretty."

His statement about my looks, "You're so pretty," implies that pretty women should not have to worry about "civil rights." There's also an implication that women who are not pretty by typical American standards are the only ones who are "libbers." Libbers look all sorts of ways. A woman's looks, her beauty or lack thereof, speaks louder than her actions in current social and political constructs.

Rush Limbaugh and his ilk thrash liberal people for "political correctness" but anatomical or aesthetic correctness is the battle standard they wave all the time. Rush Limbaugh commenting on a woman's looks is like Phyllis Schlafley criticizing women who speak in public. However, it's not just conservatives who harp on the way a woman looks. Even centrists and liberals are obsessed with women's appearance. Thus the media frenzy over Hillary Rodham Clinton's hair changes. Thus the coverage of Simpson prosecutor Marcia Clarke's outfits and hairstyles. Or the writing about feminist philanthropist Peg Yorkin's facial expressions when she gave $10,000,000 to the Fund for the Feminist Majority, the largest gift to a feminist cause in history.

It's politically handy to throw in appearance and grooming habits as a red herring when a woman who speaks her mind criticizes society. I heard Angela Davis speak in 1994. She said her role as a revolutionary, activist, brave human being has been boiled down to her being remembered as the woman with an "Afro." Her looks, not her ideas, were held up and used to deflect her message.

"You just need a boyfriend."

Minimizing, denigrating, patronizing, are words that describe the cowboy's idea that I just needed a boyfriend. Hey, news flash: boyfriends can be great but they are not a panacea for all ills, social or otherwise. "You just need to get laid," is another form of "You just need a boyfriend." As unbelievable as it may sound, at least some women who want their rights aren't horny for men. Perhaps they are horny for justice and equality but let's not mix apples and oranges.

I lied to the cowboy about having a boyfriend when I didn't for two reasons: 1) I didn't want to have to deal with his "hitting on me" so my lie was a form of dating self-defense, and 2) I didn't want him to think that I was "hard up." Women are traditionally respected based on the male affiliation they have. For centuries, it was anathema for a woman to be without a man. It's gotten better but yet there are still women who are mortified that they've never been married.

I wish I'd told the cowboy, "A Woman Without a Man Is Like a Fish Without A Bicycle," and watched his eyes cross but I hadn't heard the saying yet. I could have used that little saying a few times in college.

"You're cute when you're pissed off. Don't get so emotional."

The cowboy's point was . . . ? Commenting on my looks, demeanor, or my emotional state was just more of the same patronizing, demeaning, defensive counter-attack that kept us from talking about his whistle. Meanwhile, he was just as emotional, if not more, than I was.

Beware of anyone who says you are being too emotional, too this, or too that. Usually when someone is commenting on how you're saying something, they are attempting to deflect, and don't want to hear what you're saying. You could say the same thing with less emotion, and they still wouldn't want to hear it.

"Don't be such a bitch."

I wish I'd known at the time that being a bitch is a good thing. (See Chapter Twelve: Bitches, Battle-axes, and Boadiceas.)

" I was just having fun."

"I was just having fun . . ." is an excuse a lot of men make for minimizing and denying their inappropriate intrusion on anothers' space. "I was just having fun . . ." is frequently a precursor to cruelty and violence. White supremacists used to have "fun" with blacks in the South; many a rape has started with wanting to have a little "fun." Bullies like to have fun at others' expense. "Fun" should be fun for both parties.

"God, you're so defensive."

As a matter of fact, he was being defensive during the entire encounter. We both were. But I couldn't see how defensive he was being because he was counter-attacking. As they say, "The best defense is an offense." The cowboy was definitely offensive.

I was sucked into his accusation of my being defensive because I truly was naive in thinking that I could change him. In my first years, as a "baby" feminist, I had no idea just how resistant many people would be to the ideas of women's liberation. I felt that if I was just pleasant enough, reasonable enough, I could sway anyone into my way of thinking about women's rights. Wrong. Now, I generally won't even spend time trying to defend items on the feminist agenda with someone who is closed to the ideas.

There's a saying, "Choose your battles wisely." That is a good self-defense tactic. Save your energy for those who can and want to hear you. Don't reason, argue, or fight with someone you are certain you can't win over; they'll wear you out.

"Girls can't be lawyers. They aren't logical enough."

Ironic that the cowboy had not used one piece of logic, supposedly the province of males, during the entire time we talked. Perhaps it goes without saying, but it's illogical to say that women aren't logical enough to be lawyers.

"Women are supposed to get married and have kids. Men are supposed to be the providers."

"Supposed to" arguments are useless. Avoid arguments with people who have rigid gender rules. The rules are generally born of a religious or ethnic ideology that argument will not change. People only change if they decide that they want to change.

Cheek pinching

Cheek pinching is an assault. It's something that bigger people do to smaller people. The cowboy would never have pinched the cheek of someone he considered a peer or someone bigger. The cowboy used it to tease me, to let me know that he could dominate me. It was supposed to make me feel inferior.

"Women aren't supposed to be lawyers or there'd be some."

Regarding the lady lawyer issue: I was not armed with information to refute him. I'd never had one women's history or issues class in all of my seventeen years of education, nor had the cowboy. He wrongly believed that since he hadn't heard of any women lawyers, there weren't any. I was not sophisticated enough or well-read enough to know why women were missing from history, art, science, all the fields of human endeavor.

It was easy to deduce that women were missing from textbooks because they had never accomplished anything. Not true. They were missing from books because women's achievements had been forgotten, ignored, lost, or rendered invisible by chroniclers who deemed women irrelevant or dangerous to the status quo. Now I know why I couldn't name a female lawyer.

"You'll make a really nice wife if you just lose some weight."

Again he reverted to my looks and my relationship with men, neither of which were relevant to my confronting him about whistling.

Weight and beauty attacks are meant to hurt.

"What's Wrong With You? Can't You Take a Joke?"

Nothing was wrong with me. He wasn't joking anyway. He was jabbing. Men often hide attacks on women in a joke. Many men have also presented themselves as having better senses of humor than women. Stereotypical women, especially women who take themselves and issues seriously, are considered humorless even if they actually have great senses of humor. They simply refuse to laugh at jokes that aren't funny just to make a man feel good.

Now that more women defend their own gender, comment on male behavior, make fun of males, criticize stereotypes, and give some of the "teasing" back, I've noticed some men don't have such great senses of humor. Imagine that. They are suddenly on the defensive as so many women have been for eons.

As I look back at the incident with the cowboy I see how much I've grown. Thanks to so many feminist thinkers and activists, I've been able to analyze my experience as a woman in our culture. We are fortunate, in many ways, to live in the U.S. Some of our fortune lies in the treasury of women's and civil rights writers we have. They are word warriors, intellectuals who practice the adage, "The pen is mightier than the sword." In the next chapter, you can explore how they can help you understand and defend yourself in a sometimes hostile world of words.

8

Awakening the Word Warrior: Defending Our Intellects and Ideas

> *Cautious, careful people, always casting about to preserve their reputation and social standing, never can bring about a reform. Those who are really in earnest must be willing to be anything or nothing in the world's estimation.*
>
> SUSAN B. ANTHONY (1820-1906)

Defending Our Heritage

Knowing history, whether it is the history of women or any other out-of-power group, is an essential weapon of intellectual self-defense. Intellectual self-defense lays the foundation for a group being able to defend itself at all levels, whether it's in the courts or in the streets. When you are the "other," it's a matter of survival to know when you're a target and how and when to defend against an attack whether it's open, covert, or simply ignorant. When you know women's history, you know the patterns. You can see that the ridicule heaped on today's feminists is no different than the ridicule used to keep women from voting for decades.

Sadly, many women are unaware of women's history. Cultural literacy for women is missing for a lot of us. As such, many have been "unarmed" or "disarmed," unable to defend themselves in conversations regarding women's potential abilities and achievements.

Have you heard of Olympe de Gouges? She was prolific in her pamphleteering, educating, playwriting, and devotion to bringing women's status up in the world. Feminists since the 1800's have worked to catch up with the ideas she expressed during the French Revolution. But women sparked by the radical ideas of the French Revolution soon found out that what was good for the gander was out of reach for the goose. Olympe de Gouges was beheaded by

Robespierre because she dared in 1791 to create a Declaration of the Rights of Women which mimicked the Declaration of the Rights of Man. She lost her head over feminist ideals. She implored the women in the crowd to consider, before the guillotine silenced her forever, "What are the advantages you have derived from the Revolution? Slights and contempt more plainly displayed."

Self-defense includes the defense of ideas, of vision, of justice. Ideas are dangerous. Ideas, well, give people ideas. Ideas can get you killed. Ideas grow. They spark passion. Ideas enhance well-being and self-determination. They spark thinking and they create change. Why do you think women were systematically excluded from education for centuries? Why do you think it was illegal to teach slaves to read? Reading gives people ideas and makes them hard to handle, uppity, big-headed, impossible to ignore. They begin to want to have the same rights that they read about. They become visible.

Women and their ideas have been made invisible for centuries, much to our detriment. I believe that invisibility fosters violence.

Defending Against Being Made Invisible

I believe that the ignorant, minimizing, negative attitudes displayed toward feminists and feminist ideas are the same attitudes that generate a tolerance for violence against women. What else could explain our statistics of rape? We have more rapes than any other industrialized nation in the world. We also have a very limited intellectual climate that excludes radical ideas that many European countries simply include as part of their intellectual world.

In order to defend ourselves against being invisible, we must defend our right to be heard and seen, in all our forms, not just beauty queens but eggheads and bookworms, too. Americans don't think much of intellectuals, unlike some citizens of other countries, who have high regard for intellectuals. Female intellectuals in this country are especially subject to being rendered invisible or insignificant. Many American women are unaware of the body of work that women have created, specifically about the subject of women's rights. They have been bamboozled into believing that to be a feminist is to be unattractive.

For a group of women who have been raised to believe that their greatest purpose in life is to be attractive and desirable to men, it's dangerous to court being considered unattractive. It's tantamount to social suicide. It really is. There's almost nothing more powerful than being ostracized. People are pack animals. They need society, love, protection and a purpose for living. Women need to eat. For centuries, with no other jobs than prostitution open — or housewifery and motherhood — the call to an intellectual life was a hard one. And an intellectual life for a woman continues to be hard although we have won major battles to become financially independent, and we have more careers open to us than at any other time in history.

However, many American women continue to be cowed by the specter of feminism. We've got a crowd of women in this country who are prepared to run at the first hint of controversy or association with "them," the libbers. That's not an accident or a character flaw. We are not prepared to defend what we think, defend what we believe in, or fight for what is our due because fighting is not attractive. Therefore most women are not prepared to fight, physically or intellectually. The result of so little "fight" in women is that we risk repeating history. History makes women disappear because we can't or don't fight to be heard, and in turn, fight for each other to be heard in our own defense.

My friend Dr. Betty Brooks, one of the first self-defense advocates in L.A. County, wanted to make sure I knew about Matilda Joslyn Gage, a suffragist, women's right activist, and writing contemporary of Susan B. Anthony and Elizabeth Cady Stanton. I'd never heard of Gage, who also believed women had to be physically independent. Dr. Brooks showed me a well-loved, dog-eared copy of the book wherein she had first become familiar with Matilda Joslyn Gage: *Women of Ideas: And What Men Have Done to Them*, by Australian writer, Dale Spender. (It's brutally ironic that *Women of Ideas* is out of print.) Appropriately, the theme of Spender's book is the "disappearance" of intellectual women's ideas, whether they were in the form of activism, speeches, plays, pamphlets or books. Women have been unable to defend or protect our collective body of learning.

I borrowed Dr. Brooks' copy of *Women of Ideas*. I read the Matilda Joslyn Gage section and was shocked at how "modern," how radical, her ideas were. Her contemporaries, Susan B. Anthony and Elizabeth Cady Stanton, were afraid they'd lose the fight for the vote if conservative women got wind of Gage's ideas. They helped the establishment "disappear" Gage's work. Who knows, maybe they were right, maybe they were wrong. Their decision to disen-Gage was political. They were afraid to alienate everyone because of the ideas of one woman. Men are never afraid that because of one man, their policies or ideas will be at risk.

Defending the Mind, Defends the Body, Defends the Spirit

Learning to defend all three areas, mind, body, spirit, is essential to bringing women into full adult citizenship. The world can no longer afford — men can no longer afford — to pretend that they can handle the management of life on the planet without the full participation of women. Female stewardship is not going to happen without a fight whether the fight is as local as one's own family, fighting for official recognition of women studies at a university, or as global as a U.N. Conference. Even though men have everything to gain from sharing power, many men currently in power do not see it that way. They think that they'll lose everything if they share power. I say they'll lose everything if they don't. Not because women will annihilate them in a "turn about is fair play" way but because we are headed down a road that is going to destroy us without the input of the life experience and intellect of women. Including women everywhere in all major solutions is the ultimate self-defense, the preservation of the planet. Women must wake up — wake up now and begin to learn about power, by themselves and with each other, or be prepared to face heavy consequences. Men are not going to turn over power; they never have, they never will. We must take power.

It's naive and dangerous to think that ideas aren't going to be resisted. Since women are trained to be naive, to be "Pollyanna," (a courageous character, by the way) to see the best, to ignore injustice done to us, it's particularly important that women learn to expect negative reaction for political ideas or for setting boundaries when it comes to women and children. People, regardless of gender, are uncomfortable with change. They are extremely hostile if that change is going to cost them in status, entitlements or money. They will fight it with all their might. Do not underestimate that might. They will hit you where it hurts. They'll lie, they'll misinterpret, they'll question your motives, your sexuality, they'll lump you in with everyone else they despise, and most damaging of all for a movement, they'll "disappear" you, ignore you, make you into nothing; especially if you're a woman. Whoever is dominant has the power to ignore. It is a very powerful and deadly tool, ignoring or ignorance.

Ignoring the Woman's Movement

How do you ignore the woman's movement, a movement that affects everyone? Simple. You don't publish the books, or if they are published, you don't reprint them. If you're the librarian in charge of acquisitions, you determine that this "feminist title is of little general interest," so that people who can't afford to buy books never see it. If you're in charge of charitable grants, you don't make a grant for a "woman's" project you don't understand or care about. You continue to argue that gender studies is not a real area of study. If you manage a broadcasting entity, you don't hire enough female or feminist commentators on a regular basis so people can learn the differences in women. Or if you're an editor you decide a story about women or by women is not interesting. Or you feel, as an editor, that what's being said hits too close to home. Or you give a platform to those who oppose feminism without having aired the original feminist's view, even if she's the one who's being attacked. You present feminism as a joke, you ridicule it, you make sure that it's not attractive to those women who ordinarily would be fully engaged with movements for justice. It's very easy, and it's not even a conspiracy. There's no committee of elite men plotting and planning. It's simply the way it is. Will we ever be able to say that, "It's simply the way it used to be?" It's a miracle that there are as many word warriors, "unquiet women," as there are.

Defending Our Heretics

It's harder to defend oneself, intellectually or physically, when you are alone. Women who have challenged the male power structure have been unofficially declared heretics. We don't burn people at the stake anymore, we just make sure that they are made to seem ridiculous or too radical. Their work is buried or, at best, hard to find. *The American Heritage Dictionary of the English Language* defines "heresy" as: "1. a. An opinion or doctrine at variance with established religious beliefs; especially, dissention from or denial of Roman Catholic dogma by a professed believer or baptized church member. b. adherence to such dissenting opinion or belief. 2. *a. A controversial or unorthodox opinion or doctrine in politics, philosophy, science, or other fields. b. Adherence to such unorthodox opinion."* (My emphasis.) Given that male power is the orthodox structure of today's society, anyone who opposes it, tries to change it, or challenges it is, by definition, a heretic. Roman Catholicism is not the only social or religious organization to embody the "men only" rules.

Read the Works by Role-Model Word Warriors

I arm myself by reading as much as I can. I credit Marilyn French's *Beyond Power: Men, Women and Morals*; Gloria Steinem's *Outrageous Acts and Everyday Rebellions*; Andrea Dworkin's *Woman- Hating*; and Susan Faludi's *Backlash: The Undeclared War Against American Women* for re-awakening my word warrior. I experienced a rebirth of my outrage over sexism as I read their work. After years of knocking my head against walls, I became a born-again feminist.

Gloria Steinem holds a rare position in feminist politics. She's virtually the only household name we have in the movement. She has held the standard for us all, for years. She's witty, wise, and knows a great deal about self-defense, the defense of her ideas. She's also brilliant at using humor to make a point. If you've never read her essay, "If Men Could Menstruate," make it a point to do so. She uses gender swapping to great effect. Far from considering his period a "curse," she has men bragging about the size of the sanitary napkins they use, the size of their flow; customs that women accept as normal suddenly look absurd when Steinem puts men and typical male attitudes in our roles.

Steinem's *Revolution from Within: A Book of Self Esteem,* prompted attacks from within the feminist culture and particularly from some East Coast feminist thinkers. The criticism Ms. Steinem's book received drew more attention than I'd seen about a feminist book in years. (Can you hear the "Hurrah, cat fight!" in the distance?) Since *Revolution from Within* was an autobiographical exploration, what's there to criticize? An academic book is one thing but a memoir, is someone's experience. How can someone criticize experience?

It was as if Steinem's inner exploration described in *Revolution from Within* was too unscholarly, too feminine, too "West Coastish," that some women in the academic establishment cringed in print when they reviewed the book. Some criticized it for fueling people's stereotypical ideas of women. I can't imagine a man criticizing a book because it might give others the wrong idea about other men, can you? Beware of being sucked into the cat fight syndrome or the cringe. You do not represent all women and we do have differences.

Andrea Dworkin, a feminist icon, radical intellectual and public scapegoat, has gotten more flak than almost any other single American feminist. Ms. Dworkin is so devoted to her intellectual life and activism that she decided early on that she had to be prepared to die for the things she believes in and publishes. See how physical life is intimately tied to intellectual life? That willingness to put herself on the line has made her one of the bravest spokeswomen we have for women. Her ideas are always cutting edge. She's not "moderate" and she doesn't intend to be. Her gift is not moderation, it is the willingness to formulate words and ideas that go to the heart of gender politics, economics and survival. Her works on pornography and her theories about the human rights violations the sex industry commits every day should be widely read.

However, true to form, Dworkin's work got more attention because of "in-fighting" between the so-called First Amendment feminists who didn't agree with Dworkin's ideas, and the anti-pornography feminists, Dworkin and Catherine MacKinnon. Dworkin and MacKinnon are the so-called "femi-nazis," that charming epithet coined by Rush

Limbaugh. (What single feminist has the kind of media coverage he has? Is there a political woman who can counter him?) The subject of pornography is a highly charged one; there are real lives at stake, real violence, and huge money interests. But our differences got the press, not the substance of the ideas. The Dworkin vs. other feminists "fight" educated very few people to the real issues behind the differences.

Pornography: Men Possessing Women is the book that put Andrea Dworkin in the eye of the storm as a feminist. It was her fourth book but her first book to be reviewed by the arbiter of what should be taken seriously and what should be ignored, the *New York Times*, "All the News That's Fit to Print." The book editor assigned a woman reviewer who gave *Pornography* a scathing review, accusing her of being aligned with the right. Right. (Note that setting woman upon woman is a favorite tactic of men in control.) Naively, I asked, "But didn't that create controversey which, in turn, made sales go up?" Dworkin told me that it had not. While even negative publicity is usually good for a project, Dworkin feels that doesn't apply to women as much as men.

Dale Spender makes a point throughout *Women of Ideas,* that women are reviewed in such a way that there's nothing attractive about the underlying work. Time and again through her research of women intellectuals, she found reviews that were off-the-mark and so biased, misleading and repulsing, that it would be a miracle for someone to respond to the review with, "Gee, I'd really like to read that." Spender then read the work reviewed and found it to be fascinating, informative, usually well-written. These things had been buried not because they deserved to die but because their existence was too threatening.

Defending Your Radicals: They're Good For You Even If You Don't Agree

Politicos need to be mindful of constituents; writers, activists, and philosophers aren't running for office. They are running their ideas, some for thinking only, some for social change. The ideas behind the Declaration of Independence were once considered too radical. We need people like Steinem, Dworkin, Patricia Ireland, president of the National Organization for Women, pushing buttons, pushing minds, pushing a radical yet common-sense agenda, for change to occur.

I offer these women as examples of women who are on the front lines defending all of us, publically, all the time. We need to turn around and nurture and defend them. It's almost irrelevant whether we agree with their ideas or not. We need to read between lines of reviews.

We, as citizens, need to defend their right to build and expand the literature — the agenda of gender and social justice for women — without fear, and know that women appreciate the difference of opinion that is alive and well in the feminist community.

If we don't defend them, if we stay quiet as they take attack after attack, we create a climate where fewer and fewer ideas see the light of day. Their ideas may be radical today but normal and "of course" in twenty years. We cannot afford to have more of an intellectual chill than we already have. Intellectual chills create violence toward women.

Defending and Differing At the Same Time

It's an old, old trick. Divide and conquer. Men attack each other, and each other's ideas, all the time but no one says, "See how catty men are? See how men can't get along?" The result of intellectual divide and conquer is that women then get sucked into being concerned about how other women are representing them or appearing to the public. I admit I've been overly concerned when a feminist comes off badly because I will be asked to answer for her. Unfair, but true. Women do not yet have the freedom to just be people and have their own ideas.

Differences are used against us as some kind of proof about our inability to lead, to add to the intellectual discourse, to be citizens. Supposedly, East Coast feminists look down on West Coast feminists, academic feminists look down on street feminists, empowered feminists allegedly disdain "victim" feminists. Who knows if any of this conflict is real or manufactured, or both? All I know, is that intra-feminist conflict gets more print than a free exchange of ideas and comparisons of difference.

Defending Our Right to Know: The Press and the Airwaves

Ideally, the press in a democratic society should cover more than just the dominant group's concerns. Yet our press, claiming to be "objective," is frequently biased. It tends to tailor its coverage to appeal to an upper- or middle-class male audience, ignoring major portions of the population or concerns of women and minorities.

There's no free speech right that's been specifically articulated to guarantee that every side of a controversial issue gets a fair hearing in the public press, even though the air waves and press are the "people's." So far, it's extremely difficult to fight for the news and views that are missing. How does one know if something is missing if it's missing?

One needs access to the news outlets to report the news that's missing, at least to the "masses." For instance, feminism is alive and very well, thank you very much, but one wouldn't know that from most mainstream press, given the number of "Feminism is Dead" headlines we've seen over the past twenty years. The press is free all right, free to forward a general opinion of disregard or ridicule for the women's movement without appearing to be biased.

Begin asking, where are the women? Where are the women writers, plural? (I was once turned down by an editor because he said, "We already publish an 'Ellen' pretty regularly.") Where are the female experts that could have been quoted for this article? Where are the reports on the women's conference that you knew was happening but didn't get any press? Where are the women? Why are they missing? We must clamor, be insistent, risk seeming "too" pushy, if we're going to defend our right to know what's happening in our world. Don't get off-track with *ad hominem* attacks, "What's a pretty little thing like you doing with a feminist agenda?" or "Let me play devil's advocate." Beware the devil in any form, advocate or otherwise.

Part of intellectual self-defense is using resources wisely. You know when a person is earnest in conversation. The authentic person who wants to discuss issues might play "devil's advocate" in order to clarify the issue. Choose your battles wisely. It's also apparent when someone is just toying with you, wanting to play devil's advocate — another snare to be aware of and know how to defend against.

Defending Against Intellectual Hijacking

The following story exemplifies how easy it is to verbally disarm someone by being absolutely forthright in your conversation with them. This particular instance involved a man who tried to use the "Let me play devil's advocate" stance to dominate a group of women who were engaged in a serious discussion of women's issues.

My husband and I had a Fourth of July party a few years ago to which we invited mostly close friends except for one couple we thought we "owed." The man had been incredibly persistent in his pursuit of my husband as a business contact. (Such "hounding" in a woman would not be tolerated by most people.) He also happened to be one of the most clueless, arrogant, stupid windbags either of us had ever met. (Otherwise, what a great guy!) He literally trailed my husband, herded him into corners, stuck to him, dominated his time and energy.

Meanwhile, my friend, Kimberlee Ward, two others and I were engaged in a rigorous conversation about women. We were discussing reproductive rights, from birth control to abortion. We knew the chronology of case law in the U.S. and were talking about some of the fundamentalists who were covert proponents of outlawing all birth control, including pills. We talked about pornography and the constitutional issues surrounding it. Kimberlee had just graduated from UCLA with honors. I was no slouch either. We both had read and knew a lot about women's issues. My husband finally made the break from Mr. Windbag and joined our table. He liked to listen to women talking.

Mr. Windbag shadowed my husband, plopped himself down and proceeded to attempt to dominate the conversation. He didn't listen long enough to know what we were talking about but, hey, that didn't stop him. He was taken aback when we didn't stop and defer to him. Horrors, we barely acknowledged his presence. We ignored him much like women get ignored when they join a group of men. He hated it. He grew agitated and spoke louder and louder. Finally, he announced that he would "play devil's advocate."

Before he could hold forth, I took a deep breath and said, "Who do you think you are? Do you have any idea of the years of study, the number of pages of reading, the sheer commitment of purpose that is sitting around this table? We don't need you to play devil's advocate. You seem to think that you can help us, as if we are ignorant school girls who haven't given these issues a lot of thought. You're going to help us be objective, to be thoughtful, to take things that we haven't considered into account? What are your credentials for being able to do this?" Using my words, I verbally knocked him over. He was so astounded by my "unladylike" behavior, he became instantly silent.

Kimberlee jumped in. "Have you read Shulamith Firestone, Audre Lorde, Andrea Dworkin, Catherine MacKinnon, anyone?"

He said, "No, but I know what I think."

I said, "You'd be better off if you just listened."

Oh, did that feel good. I believe it was one of the first times that I experienced saying precisely what was on my mind in the moment, to a man I wasn't related to. I suspect some of my courage came from the assessment that this man could not punish me. Many women are rightly afraid of recriminations — from fathers, bosses, husbands — for speaking their minds.

Imagine if I'd been a woman who had crashed a sports discussion and tried to pontificate on sports but had never watched a game, let alone read a book about it. I plop down and announce, "I'll play devil's advocate." Would the men have sat there and nodded, coddled me, made sure they listened carefully and thanked me for the detour I'd routed them down? I don't think so.

Are you cringing? Did I alienate my husband's business acquaintance and condemn him to a life of feminist-baiting and woman-bashing? Was I a bad example? Did I ruin it for other, more diplomatic feminists? Did I provide one more reason for some women to feel they must say, "I'm not a feminist but . . .?"

Or have you always wanted to speak out in such a forthright manner but feared the consequences? Feared hurting the man or alienating him? I surmise that if the man at our party was someone who had heart and could stomach introspection, he probably thought about what happened and possibly learned from the incident. If he was paranoid and hostile to women to begin with, he probably grew more so. Oh, well. Trying to change people who don't want to change is not my responsibility.

Our party guest faded away in the dusk that evening. We've never heard from him again. I truly am capable of being more diplomatic and polite, especially when I'm hosting. However, I was hungry to talk to my friends, to have a conversation that was among equally educated, interested parties. I was sick to death of men butting in, sick of male arrogance that allows them to believe they always know more than women do, even about being women.

That night, Kimberlee and I defended our right to be experts. We defended our right to have a conversation shaped by our own interests, our own passions. Very few men are used to knowing less than women. They usually experience no consequence to their windbag behavior, so they get away with it; this strengthens their sense of entitlement to blow hot air. Until women are willing to risk delivering consequences to people who disrespect their boundaries, we will continue to put up with those who consistently learn that it's of no consequence to treat women with little or no regard. Or violently.

A person's self is an inseparable weaving of mind, body, spirit. A large component of spirit has to do with being connected to those who have gone before us, and of voicing our collective, analyzed experience. In order to use verbal self-defense effectively, one must learn from others who have been successful. In the next chapter, we'll hear from women who have "talked back" and made verbal defense an integral part of their warrior readiness.

9

The Queen is Not Amused — Commanding Respect With Verbal Self-Defense

I have a right to my anger, and I don't want anybody telling me I shouldn't be, that it's not nice to be, and that something's wrong with me because I get angry.

CONGRESS-WOMAN MAXINE WATERS,
U.S. HOUSE OF REPRESENTATIVES, CALIFORNIA

What is verbal self-defense? It can be listening, it can be sign or body language, a facial expression. It can be silence. Verbal self-defense takes many forms. We usually think of verbal self-defense as a way to persuade someone not to attack us. Verbal self-defense can also be used to verbally hit back, parry, deflect, reflect, charm, distract, absorb, humor, flatter, engage, dissuade, convince, argue, and in this way, protect oneself from verbal or physical abuse.

Those of us who believe we have no authority to stop others from abusing us let things go on that an authority wouldn't. We give ourselves authority to stop abusers from harming our children, or even pets — why not ourselves? Some "put up" with verbal abuse anywhere, whether it's in the home, at work, or on the street. We strip ourselves of authority to draw boundaries.

Many of us grew up on fairy tales and dreamed of being a Princess — royalty who, after all, should have some authority. Perhaps we must graduate from Princess to Queen because the imagery of Queen is more authoritative. A Queen would not allow any of her subjects to cat-call or paw her. There would be consequences.

But since a Queen usually has a government behind her and wise counselors beside her, what do we "commoners" do for counsel when we are disrespected? "Off with their heads" is not an option for those of us who live in the 20th century. We counsel with each other, that's what we do. We share our stories of successful verbal defenses and pass them on to the other Princesses and Queens.

Queens' Chambers — Swapping Strategies

Talking circles or sharing circles are excellent forums for the swapping of verbal self-defense ideas. One reason the full-force self-defense classes are so effective is that they provide an opportunity for women to share their experiences of personal violence. The women feel a sense of sisterhood, an awareness that "I'm not the only one," and an empathy for other women who have also been the victims of violence — verbal, emotional and physical.

But not everyone can be in a formal circle. We just need to talk to each other about experiences of violence, and learn from each other however and wherever we can. We need to swap battle stories, since most of us are veterans of at least a few skirmishes in the so-called "Battle of the Sexes."

Most women are fascinated by each other's stories of violence and how we handled it. We are starved for stories of women, from queens to executives to cleaning women. We don't get stories about ourselves as much as we do about men and boys, or even animals, from all sources of mass media and entertainment. An important part of learning to defend ourselves is to be aware of how others have responded to humiliating or threatening situations. We can learn what to avoid and what to attempt by listening to the experiences of others.

Hearing about other women's encounters and success stories also helps us acknowledge that the attacks made upon us are not caused by some character flaw in ourselves. Women are too apt to blame themselves for anything untoward that happens to them. Talking with other women about violence helps debunk the notion that if you're scared, or attacked, something must be personally wrong with you. Many women begin to see that their "personal" problems are perhaps the result of sex discrimination and our culture's poor treatment of women.

Comparing Come-Uppance Encounters

That stories of come-uppance spread like wildfire, reflects our need to hear them. The first time I heard the story of the woman on the subway who, upon feeling an errant hand on her bottom, grabbed the offender's hand, held it in the air, and said loudly, "I just found a hand on my ass! Does this belong to anyone?" was when I read it in *Her Wits About Her: Self-Defense Success Stories by Women*, edited by Denise Caignon and Gail Groves. Subsequently, I heard that story passed on by several women in various settings. I too have passed it on.

Prior to the U.N. Conference on Women in Beijing, our United Nations Association delegation from the Pasadena-San Gabriel Foothills Chapter toured some of the People's Republic of China. I was constantly amazed at how hundreds of women from all over the world responded when I told them that I was an advocate for universal self-defense for women. Not one person thought it an odd calling; they wanted me to teach them what I knew right there and then. I was consistently called upon to show people simple techniques, no matter where we were, whether in a square, a plane or a train.

During the train ride from Hong Kong to Guanzhou, the city formerly known as Canton, two young women in their twenties from Hong Kong talked about the subways and buses in their city. Public transportation in Hong Kong is a horrific experience for most women. They are veritable pits of groping, poking, pinching and fondling male hands. The young women said that they could not ride anywhere without having their bodies felt up, nor could any other woman. (I have since found that this is a universal problem in big cities with mass transit systems, whether it's Manhattan, Hong Kong, Mexico City or Tokyo.) They felt resigned about it. Women's complaints were routinely laughed at and ignored by officials.

One time, one of the young women told us, a man grabbed her hand and squeezed it as she was waiting for a bus. She felt something warm and sticky. The middle-aged man had ejaculated on his hand and his penis was still hanging from his pants, exposed. Even months later, she had to fight the urge to gag when she related the experience. She desperately wanted to learn self-defense. "How about now?" I asked her. Yes! They wanted anything I could teach them. In no time all of the women in our train car were practicing yelling, "No," and I was teaching eye-strikes and heel palms.

I told the young woman from Hong Kong that the next time she found a hand on her body to yell, "I just found a hand on my ass (or wherever the hand is). Does this belong to anyone?" and watch the men around her clear away immediately. They were delighted with the idea, and had never heard of anyone having a solution to "lost" hands. Our train mates laughed and vowed to try it.

The opportunity to hear stories of come-uppance is invaluable. To realize that you too can respond to rude, obscene, or threatening words by pulling out a sharp verbal sword rather than pleading or whimpering is very empowering. And whether you have a formal "circle" in a class or workshop, or are on a train or plane, you can share what worked and what didn't in encounters with intrusive men. Queens can hold counsel anywhere at any time.

It's Not Nice to Fool With Mother Nature

"Babe, hey, Babe! Bitch! Too stuck up to talk to me, huh, Bitch? Come over here and suck me off!" Imagine the mind that comes up with such a clever come-on. Surely Mother Nature has better mating calls.

Every woman knows exactly how to handle a verbal street assault like that, because we've heard and seen so many examples of what to do, right? Wrong. Most of us stay silent, fume afterwards, and possibly rehearse what we should have, could have said in the moment. Where was our rapier-like wit when we needed it? Why were we unable to come up with a simple statement that made it clear that what the verbal attackers were doing was not okay? Because most of us are afraid of men who verbally assault us. If we feel physically defenseless, it's terrifying to confront someone who is bigger, especially if we wrongly believe that there's nothing a woman can do about a violent man.

Many of us know what it's like to walk down the street and be the target of unwanted and unsolicited male attention which often takes absurd, bizarre forms. "Cat-calls," the lip-smacking, the kissy-sounds, the whistles, the obscenities, the comments on our bodies; it all boils down to a constant reminder of our gender, our body parts and second-class status we have in the view of these guys. It's a way that some men use to put us in our place, to remind us that they can "have their way" with us if they choose; to remind us that nothing will happen to them if they publicly disrespect, taunt and humiliate us, attack us with their words and voices. They are generally right, since few of us ever do anything to defend ourselves against such attacks. If we object or are offended, we are said to have no sense of humor, to be bitches, to be unattractive. You know the litany.

A woman at the last turn-of-the-century might have stuck an offending man with a hat pin. A woman of this turn-of-the- century has many options, depending on the type of assault the bully confronts her with. Our options are much broader than what we were taught as girls.

Advice I have received from adults for handling harassing, bullying, obnoxious boys includes:

1. Pretend he's not there.
2. Walk by quickly and don't say anything.
3. Look away and don't listen.

In other words:

1. Ignore him;
2. Ignore him;
3. Ignore him some more.

Ignore him is literally ignorant advice, born from not knowing what to do or say to intrusive behavior. Ignoring is not a great strategy for bullies. Ignoring usually encourages them to escalate the obnoxious behavior. Great mischief is done when we don't allow girls to try different strategies for handling harassment. While it's quite true that there's no rehearsal for life, all living is the real thing. The closest thing we have to a rehearsal for life is childhood. It's in childhood where we can experiment.

When we let harassers get away with bad behavior, we not only pay but we then inadvertently pass him on to inflict his bullying ways on others.

"Don't you ever do that to me or any other woman again"

Dusty King, a woman who is clear about her boundaries, came out of a theater where she had just seen, "Braveheart." She remembers feeling in touch with both her Scottish heritage and the triumph of the underdog that finally prevails. She decided to get money from the ATM before going to her car.

As Dusty walked over to her bank, she noticed a man sitting on a bench and had an inkling that he was going to hassle her. "Walk, walk, walk. Breathe," she told herself. The man did nothing, at least not on the first pass-by. She withdrew her money, prepared to walk past the man once again as she returned to her car. She lingered at the ATM long enough to put her keys in between her fingers in case she needed to defend herself. True to the Girl and Boy Scout motto, Dusty was prepared.

Sure enough, she had assessed the man correctly. Just as she was parallel to the man, he made his weird noises. She walked over to him, put her key-spiked fist close to his face and said from the depths of her Scottish/Native-American solar plexus, so that anyone within a two-block area could hear, "Don't you ever do that to me or any other woman again!" and walked away.

It outrages me that in our allegedly modern and liberated culture so many women must constantly anticipate danger and their response to it, must constantly calculate whether a man is going to attack her, verbally or physically, while she's going about her daily life. It's even more oppressive and terrorizing for women in developing countries. Women in Afghanistan, for example, risk physical attacks if their ankles show, or if they go out unveiled, or if they look too long at a man. They don't dare verbally defend themselves; their lives are literally at stake.

We can defend ourselves in this country, however. We just need ideas and practice. We need to share stories with each other about what we did that worked. We need to arm each other with word swords.

Was Dusty foolhardy? I don't think so. She talked about how careful she had been. Before she went over to the man she had sized him up and decided that he wasn't armed or dangerous. Her calculations were accurate. Of course, she could have been wrong. But instincts are uncannily accurate. She was empowered because she was fed up. She was offended, not only by this particular incident, but by the countless incidents she'd experienced over the years — men ogling and googling with impunity.

Some of us might have hesitated to do what Dusty did, fearing that it might "start something," — forgetting, of course, that the man on the bench had been the one who "started something." I applaud Dusty's reaction to the verbal assault she faced. I'll bet Mr. Bench will think twice about smacking his lips at another woman. Not every woman can pull a "Dusty," nor is it everyone's style. If Dusty's approach is not your style, what is your style? What would you have done?

The most important lesson in Dusty's story is that she walked away with her selfhood intact and enlivened. She didn't hurt the man; in fact, he may improve as a result of her reaction to his sexist way of relating to women strangers. She did not offer up a passive "thing" to be talked to or hassled with no consequence. Few women know what to do even if they want to when faced with rude "construction worker syndrome"(CWS).

Dusty drew her physical sword in the form of keys between her fingers, and her verbal "sword" in anticipation of the man's challenge. She was prepared because she had given thought the last time she'd been the victim of a walk-by verbal attack to what she would do the next time.

Lying as Self-Defense

It's your right to lie when your safety is at stake: Hey lady, do you live here? No, why do you ask? Is this your car? No. What's your name? Linda. (It's really Trudy.) You are not obligated to answer, or answer with the truth, unless you decide to do it. You have a right to be rude. You have a right to protect yourself and information that could be used against you. One reason it's important for women to know this is because many of us have a niceness compulsion, and nice people don't lie. As parents, we should teach kids that they don't owe someone the truth just because they're older or taller, or even in a uniform. Predators lie all the time. (Rapists of women and children are known to don uniforms because of the automatic credibility their "costume" gives them.) Families can work out a policy in which kids tell their trusted adults the truth, but not just any older person, regardless of who they are.

Flattery May Get You Safety

I've decided that the next time I hear a rude comment from a male stranger on the street, I'll approach him, take out a note pad and lie. I'll tell him I'm writing a story about men who make rude comments. I may even ask for his phone number, so I can send him a copy. It'll be interesting to see what kind of interviews I get. In truth, I *am* interested in what they think about their own behavior, so I may actually write that piece. I anticipate that the "interviewees" will transform once I ask them to tell me about themselves. People are extremely vulnerable, and often sweet, when they think someone wants to know more about them and have their home phone number.

When I was directing a field piece for a television show, my production day was being ruined by an obnoxious teenaged boy who wanted to be on camera. He was hanging around, trying to get into my "shots." Every time we rolled tape, he'd jump around behind the person on camera. The production assistants could not get him to go away. Finally, in a form of professional self-defense, I approached him.

I said, "Young man, you have a very unique look. Do you happen to have a picture and resume for my file?"

He replied, "No." He all of a sudden got very shy.

I said, "That's too bad because you have just the kind of face that we could use in some segments we'll be shooting next week."

He muttered, "No," and left.

By lying about wanting his picture, I made him relate to me and himself as a person, rather than a pest. Humanizing yourself and others is often a good self-defense technique.

"Don't I Know You?"

A woman shared in an opening circle about being called a crude name by a construction worker. Instead of her usual tactic of lowering her eyes, walking faster and ignoring him, she walked up to him and said, "Don't I know you? Don't you have a sister?" Sheepishly, since she was now a human being to him, he said, "Yeah." She said, "I thought so. I know your sister. I bet you'd hate it if my brother did to her what you just did to me." He blushed and shrugged. She delivered consequences to someone who, perhaps for the first time, was held accountable for his verbal abuse.

Actually, this woman lied to the construction worker. She didn't know his sister — she didn't even know if he had a sister. She'd, however, practiced what she'd do the next time she heard disparaging sounds or words due to CWS. Had he not had a sister, she would have covered up her "error" and moved onto other relatives or small talk. It took guts for this woman to confront the construction worker, even though it was a gentle confrontation. She found it somewhat difficult but she'd do it again because of the boost it gave her in self-respect. She also celebrated the fact that she doesn't owe the truth to someone who disrespects her.

Conning a Rapist

Another success story shared in an opening circle dealt with a much more threatening situation than mere street rudeness, one that I'll never forget. A woman awoke to find a naked man by her bed. She froze. He climbed on top of her. She broke her freeze and told him to turn on the light, that she wanted to have more "fun," and while he was at it, "Why don't you go downstairs and get us some beers and we can make a night out of it." He did! She climbed out of the window and called 911 at a neighbor's house.

Her calculated and well-aimed lie, her verbal bullet, found its mark. Language saved her and caught him in his sick belief that women really want to be raped. The women who hear this story will have another idea to draw on when they consider how to defend themselves. They will acquire an additional weapon to add to their arsenal of self-protection tactics.

Lying to Defend Self-Esteem

Lying can be an excellent preemptive type of verbal self-defense. If you feel that you're being disrespected, let the person who has offended you know that you're an attorney or any other position that automatically confers status even if you're not. Just try it as an experiment. If you can't muster that lie, even in self-defense, then find someone in your family who will give you a formal "power of attorney."

I actually am a lawyer, non-practicing, and an inactive member of the California Bar. I've had a smorgasbord of a life with many jobs, some careers. I have had the experience of being at a power party, unknown to most, and have observed the difference in how I'm treated depending on what I decide to say I do.

If I say I'm an actor, which I've been, people practically go cross-eyed and can't wait to move on if the conversation is in New York City or Los Angeles. If I say I'm a homemaker, which I have been, I'm not addressed again and men very rarely look at me or ask me a question for the rest of the event. However, if I let them know that I'm an attorney — wow, what a difference in respect. Suddenly, I'm interesting. I am powerful. I am potentially dangerous because I can deliver consequences. Of course, I continue to be the same person regardless of role but, nonetheless, people give enormous unearned respect to others based on what they do — their perceived status.

Let me give you an example of how differently people can treat you depending on your career status. I was in a doctor's office, and he was responding to me in a very rude manner. He gave my questions about my own treatment begrudging, patronizing answers. He treated me like a child. In his universe he'd decided that I was "just" a homemaker, of no consequence. I decided to tell him that I am a lawyer. He snapped to. Suddenly he became respectful, and the rest of the exam went well. Now whenever I sense someone is being a creep, I use the "I'm a lawyer" verbal defense.

It's harmful to the self to be treated as if you don't matter. It eats away at self-esteem. It creates people who don't want to express themselves because they aren't "important" enough. I am anxious to hear from people who try the "I'm an attorney" phrase. Practice it and have some answers for likely questions like, "Oh, where'd you go to school?" Find a school you would have liked to have gone to, or one attached to a school that you have attended.

What firm are you with? I practice alone. What's your area of practice? Medical malpractice for a real thrill. Sex discrimination law. Whatever tickles you. Don't, however, use the attorney ruse to defraud someone substantively, in legal terms.

The important thing to remember is that you have a right to have others respect you, even if you have to fool them a bit. And be proud of whatever it is you do, regardless of its perceived importance. All jobs in life are important. You can see from my illustration that so-called "social status" is a game. I had fun fooling around with people's lack of respect, and then sudden admiration, and you can fool around with disrespectful people's perception of you too. But you can't fool yourself. You must feel self-respect before you can project the confidence that inspires respect. Self-respect is a major aspect of self-defense. One must respect the self in order to defend it.

Rehearsing "Next Time, I'm Going to Say . . ."

Do you work in an industry that has a "stock" problem customer? Practice what you might say with a co-worker or friend. Come up with at least three ideas and role play the ideas in the mirror or with a buddy. You'll be amazed at how accessible the response will be when you need it if you've practiced it.

Here's an un-credited story that was e-mailed to me about an airline employee's verbal self-defense. This story embodies humor, revenge, and boundary-setting. I like to imagine that this woman came home one night after a long day of dealing with obnoxious passengers, had a glass of wine with a few buddies, and brain-stormed about retorts they could use for the most common situations.

Picture this: A busy airport at Christmas time, harried passengers at every airline but especially United. Cast: Ms. Eunice United and Mr. Matters of Great Importance, thousands of extras. Add: severe blizzard conditions.

Thousands of people are stranded at the airport. Mr. Matters of Great Importance breaks loose from the line where he'd been standing impatiently. He bolts to the head of the line where he confronts Ms. Eunice United with, "I've got to get out of here. I want to be put on a flight to Dallas, immediately!"

Ms. United looks at him and very politely replies, "I'm sorry, Sir, I can't do that. The weather has grounded all flights going anywhere."

He turns beet red and says, "You don't seem to understand. I have a very important matter to deal with in Texas."

Again, she calmly answers, "Sir, all of the flights have been cancelled. There's nothing I can do. You'll just have to wait for the weather to clear up like everyone else."

Ready to explode, Mr. Importance shakes and yells, "Don't speak to me like that. (pause) DO YOU KNOW WHO I AM?"

Without missing a beat, Ms. United clicks on her hand-held public address system and announces, "I have a gentleman here who has asked me if I know who he is. I don't. If there is anyone in line who knows who he is, could you please step up to the counter and let him know? Thank you." Click. Aaaah, Gracie Allen would have loved it.

The entire line burst into laughter and applause, having witnessed the entire tantrum. I'm sure there were many that day who were grateful that Mr. Matters of Great Importance wasn't armed with a semiautomatic weapon.

Japanese School Girl Sees and Does

Self-respect is contagious. I was in Osaka, Japan, with Peggy Renner, my roommate for the U.N. Women's Conference in Beijing. We were waiting for the train that would take us back to the airport. Our line happened to have all women. Four young school girls with suitcases were in front of us, four middle aged women were behind us.

An old yet physically-fit man came up to Peggy. She turned away. Reluctant to be perceived as an "ugly American," I tried to see what he wanted. He spoke no English, I spoke no Japanese. Peggy whispered, "He's drunk." She was right, but by then, he was in my face. My mistake. I put my hands up and said, "Stop. Don't get any closer, back up."

He stopped and his face grew livid with anger. How dare I tell him what to do, I imagined he was saying. He started berating me. I stayed calm with my hands up, telling him quietly, yet forcefully, to back up. He did, without understanding the words, insulting me the whole time.

He then lunged toward the young girls. All four of them looked at the ground and giggled. He started touching them, playing with hair, pawing. They giggled.

I finally said, "Leave them alone."

Back he came to me. I continued with my "ready stance," hands up, knees flexible, ready to defend myself or the others if I had to. He backed off, and back he went to the girls.

This time, the girl he approached mimicked me and held her hands up, signaling him to back up. The man stopped, shook his head in a classic "double take," and backed away. The middle-aged women behind us nodded in approval.

Actions are louder than words. The school girl's action that day may have changed her in ways I'll never know. The desire to be left in peace is genderless and international. At least that day, at that time, the school girl saw a solution, used it, and it worked. It's an injustice that any man can intrude on any woman if he simply feels like it, or he's too drunk to control his impulses. The world often seems unjust when we have an expectation that others will treat us with dignity but ignore our desires instead. Justice is impossible unless we find our voices and enforce our own boundaries.

Strategies, Tactics, Self-Respect

It's common in the legal world to strategize, to figure out the adversary, and create offensive or defensive tactics, in order to fight for justice. Women must give themselves permission to employ tools that men have used forever: coaching, calculating, controlling, and figuring out what will work to one's advantage. However, there's a strong cultural bias at play: notice how derogatory it sounds to call a woman calculating, for instance. But the word used to describe a man makes him sound intelligent.

Successful and respected civil rights attorney Peggy Garrity in Los Angeles has her clients take a self-defense class whenever she can. She sees an enormous shift in their self-respect and ability to speak up for themselves in one of the most important forums for self-defense, the legal system. After their class, they are empowered to take more responsibility for the outcome of their case. If they are testifying in a harassment case, for instance, she sees how they are able to relate their story much more powerfully than they could before the class. And even though her clients are usually plaintiffs, frequently plaintiffs in civil rights and tort cases are put a position to have to defend themselves or their actions.

Lawsuits and testimony, (a word based on the concept of a man swearing on his testicles) are powerful means of verbal self-defense. But there are domains in life between the spheres of home and the public courts where women would benefit themselves and all of society by speaking up before the incident even gets into the system. The verbal scenarios in the next chapter demonstrate how women don't have to depend on police, lawyers, husbands, or judges to defend them, enforce rules or prevent damage before the situation gets out of hand in the first place.

10

A Woman's Home is Her Castle, the World Her Playground — When She Defends Them

Courage is the price that life exacts for granting peace.
The soul that knows it not, knows no release
From little things;
Knows not the livid loneliness of fear,
Nor mountain heights where bitter joy can hear
The sound of wings.

AMELIA EARHART

Re-Parenting Ourselves Defensively

"The safety and self-esteem of a child is worth causing anyone embarrassment, inconvenience, or offense — an adult, another child, or the child at risk." When I first read that statement, the basic tenet of KIDPOWER, I was moved. Most of our parents did not raise us with that idea. We were to remain quiet and not make a scene, no matter what, even if our safety was at stake.

It's difficult to feel at home in the world if one feels embarrassed about defending one's space or dependent on others to create safety. As we grow up, many of us become convinced that there's nothing we can do to help ourselves. That is usually not true. It is true that we are often unable to see the solution(s) without help. There's almost always more than one solution to any given problem. However, when we're being harassed or threatened or intimidated, our thinking is frequently clouded because it's a violation that affects us emotionally and spiritually. When someone else is having trouble with something, notice how often you can see solutions that they don't see.

Harassers, rapists, molesters, physical and verbal abusers, and stalkers — bullies all — thrive on inflicting control and suffering. They also are emboldened by the seeming helplessness of their "mark." The victim's fear that "telling" will only make it worse is often true because women are frequently "abused" by the systems they attempt to enlist to help them. The abusers thereby "benefit" from the woman or child, keeping their mouths shut. In fact, they frequently threaten harm or death, if the person tells. "Don't even think about telling someone or you'll be sorry," or "If you report this, no one will believe you," or "Keep this between us, OK? Or you'll regret it," or "You'll lose your job," are threats that keep victims quiet, with reason. However, the sooner one tells, the better in most cases.

Telling — Playground Self-Defense

Because of the Hill-Thomas hearings, we were exposed as a nation to the problem of sexual harassment in the workplace. True to form, Hollywood soon came out with the movie "Disclosure," a film that depicted Michael Douglas as the harassee. Interesting that the film industry would rush into production over female-on-male sexual harassment when, in fact, it's extremely rare. (Where are the movies about a woman being harassed in the corporate world? It must be too realistic to make good fiction.) Nonetheless, sexual harassment does cut both ways. Sabino Gutierrez of Ontario, California, was awarded $1 million in damages by a Los Angeles jury for sexual harassment by a female executive in his company. A Minnesota boy sued his school for failing to protect him from explicit sexual taunting from other boys. As the saying goes, "What's good for the goose is good for the gander."

But sexual harassment isn't good for anyone, regardless of gender — goose or gander. Unless harassers are stopped and pay consequences, they miss out on meaningful and authentic human relating. I know: I've been harassee and harasser.

I grew up in Huron, South Dakota, home of the world's largest pheasant statue and more than its share of darling Scandinavian boys. In second grade I set my sights on Bobby. I adored him. I wanted him, and I was going to have him. The only reason I chased him was because he was running! If he had only stood there and let me hug and kiss him I wouldn't have chased him, I swear. As it was, I was forced to tackle, straddle, and shower him with my affection.

Obsessed, I would literally lie in wait for him behind bushes, in the coat closet, and behind parked cars. It's a very good thing that children's hearts are strong because I could have given him a heart attack.

The boys razzed Bobby for not standing up to me forcefully. Bobby was fundamentally a nice kid, and I'm sure he suffered because his ordinarily sweet behavior was not a good enough defense against my aggressive tactics. He just wanted to be a nice, smart, cute kid, which is why I had a crush on him in the first place.

Finally, Bobby busted me with the authorities. He "told" on me. I was taken aside by Mrs. Schoolteacher, who told me, "Boys don't like girls who chase them. If you want boys to like you, you must be gentle. Let the boys chase you."

Bobby, Bobby, Bobby! I lost Bobby that day and a good chunk of my self-confidence, misbegotten as it was. Not only was he "The Man That Got Away," but I was told in no uncertain terms that the rules were a lot different for boys than for girls. I also learned that sexual harassment cuts both ways and that, frequently, the only way to stop it is to "tattle." Suffering in silence is for the birds, goose and gander.

Fortunately, I stopped being a bully that day. I realized that forcing myself on Bobby was wrong. Suddenly, I understood the Golden Rule. I didn't want a boy I didn't like to be doing to me what I was doing to Bobby. Unfortunately, I was told that a boy forcing himself on me was not only normal, but that such behavior is expected. Young girls are essentially trained to expect harassment, and boys are trained to employ it or at least to tolerate it in other boys if it doesn't happen to be their style.

Sexual harassment starts young because children see how grown-ups relate. It grows because attitudes and behavior that create and condone harassment are winked at on playgrounds. We haven't taught most of our girls to stand up to bullying, sexual or otherwise, when they're young, and we mess with their instincts to protect themselves.

What could be more natural than defending oneself from unwanted attention? Why are we the only species that trains its females not to defend themselves from assault, be it physical or emotional? It's socialization that says, "Boys will be boys" or "Boys chase, girls don't." And boys aren't "naturally" bullies; they must be trained to be so.

It's important that we address violence, gender discrimination, and harassment in our schoolyards. If we don't teach kids respect for one another regardless of race, religion, looks and gender, we're going to have a heck of an expensive time sorting it all out when those kids grow up. As consumers and taxpayers, we pay for the inappropriate behavior of the few bullies who didn't learn their lessons when they were young.

As for the boys or men who are sexually harassed (rare as it is), it's important that men come forward and "tell." Bullying is bullying, whether the bully is a bull or cow, gander or goose. Sabino Gutierrez and the Minnesota lad have guts. The more people who stand up and refuse to take it, the better for all of us. Bobby protected himself, and I'm a better person for it.

Growing Up With Our Children

I have sprinkled stories of girls and boys throughout the success story chapters because in matters of self-defense, we are often like children. Therefore, it's not too late to learn and grow from stories we never heard as kids. We learned to control our world from lessons we learned on the playground. No wonder it's common for people to feel childish, immature, uncomfortable, unfamiliar with notions of verbal and physical self-defense. Although I occasionally hear stories of a daddy who took a daughter aside and counseled, "If a boy tries anything, hit him between the legs," they are the exception, not the rule. Mostly, the only coaching girls ever got was, "Ignore him," when we'd complain about verbal or physical bullies.

As a rule, women are developmentally delayed in physical defenses techniques. Both genders need remedial work with verbal self-defense, or setting boundaries with words. That is why we have parent's night with KIDPOWER, a self-defense workshop for kids and their parents.

I'm a KIDPOWER instructor and have the privilege of teaching children how to flee from dangerous situations. As part of the workshop, we reserve an evening for the parents only. It's important that the parents know exactly what it is that we'll be teaching their children. We work on the internal aspects of fighting and some external things, like what a snap kick is, what a heel palm is. But most revealing is the practice we do on telling someone what we want or don't want.

In teaching the parents in my KIDPOWER classes some simple verbal self-defense skills, I notice how, at first, their inclination is to avoid defending themselves. We practice verbal skills that are boundary-setting exercises. We know that people have to practice because they haven't seen boundaries being set in their own families by *their* parents. How are they supposed to pass on good boundary skills to their own kids, if their parents didn't have any to pass on to them?

We have people pick a partner during the parent portion of the class. We ask one person to place a hand on the knee of the other, and then proceed to practice having that person take the hand off. The parents revert to childish behavior. They have nothing else to draw on. They get silly, they avoid the person's eyes, they avoid saying anything that might hurt the other person's feelings or making them mad. All the behaviors are avoidance related. We all have enough experience with avoidance to be declared absolute experts. Now we must work on assertiveness in order to make the world our home, our homes our castles.

Assertiveness without aggression is a challenge. Unfortunately, few of us have ever practiced telling someone to stop doing something that offends us, scares us, or simply annoys us. Verbal assertiveness and physical self-defense are no harder than avoidance, it's just that we must learn and practice these skills if we've never used them before. It's that simple.

Defending the Community

Mary E. stopped at the grocery store two years after her basic self-defense class and a month after an advanced class she had taken to brush up. As she got out of her car she noticed a man fall drunkenly out of his huge, gas-guzzling vehicle — the kind with really big doors.

The drunken driver stumbled toward a trash can, crunched an empty beer can in his hand and deposited it in the garbage. He shuffled unsteadily back to his car and started it. Mary couldn't stand it. She'd had friends die because of drunk drivers. Her heart started to beat rapidly, but she knew she had to do something. His car window was down. She walked over and said, "If you don't turn the car off, I'm calling the cops. I'm taking your license number and reporting you for driving under the influence."

He stopped the car and started yelling "Bitch" at Mary as she walked off and into the coolness of the supermarket. She felt great that he'd stopped the car, and she kept her eye out for him as she looked for a pay phone. Mary grabbed a shopping cart, something she could use as a shield to defend herself if the man followed her, went into the produce section, and then saw the man, now walking-under-the-influence, coming toward her.

She put her cart between herself and him, put her hands up, palms out in a conciliatory yet boundary setting way, and said, "Stop! Don't come any closer to me," with the fullness of her voice. The other shoppers suddenly stuck their heads into heaps of broccoli, piles of beans, pyramids of cantaloupes. "You've never seen people try to disappear so quickly into apparently fascinating fruit and vegetables," she later told me.

The drunk man stopped. He slurred, "You bitch, who the hell do you think you are? I'm going to show you who's boss. I can drive whenever I want."

Mary held her ground. "You'll kill people if you get on the road. Back up. I don't want any trouble. Just don't drive until you've slept it off."

The drunk guy's eyes crossed, he mumbled obscenities and left the store. Mary's heart was really going now, but she felt good about taking a stand against drunk driving on a very direct level. She finished her shopping, went out into the parking lot and saw that the man had fallen asleep in the passenger seat. She called 911.

Not everyone will want to intervene in a "situation." Intervention is a private decision because it means you are intentionally putting yourself at risk, taking responsibility for a problem that's not personally yours. It's useful to be able to assess the situation realistically based on information rather than automatically not intervening based on blanket fear. Can you imagine what it costs our communities in prevention when most women and many men are too cowed to stop crimes or activities that could result in crime? What about adults neglecting to comment on the bad behavior of unsupervised children, children who grow to expect that adults will not comment? Perhaps one comment could keep a kid from going down a path that results in gang membership.

It's important to assess if someone you are "ordering" around has a weapon. I would recommend that people use the authorities whenever possible to stop people from doing whatever their dangerous activity is. However, that's the ideal and not always possible. Mary was very courageous and quite likely saved lives by her intervention.

Defending Others

My friend (for years a male instructor of full-force self-defense with Impact Personal Safety in L.A.) and I were strolling by the beach in one of the charming beach communities in Southern California. We noticed two teenage girls being hassled and trailed by a drunk man at least 30 years older than they. He was using obscenities, propositioning them and obviously scaring them.

All the teenage girls did was giggle and walk faster. They didn't tell him to stop. As they spoke to each other, we could hear them saying, "Gross." Their giggles were nervous giggles. He was so drunk that they could have done any number of things. They could have run and lost him. They could have crossed the street to get away from him. They could have gone in a store, asked for assistance. But they were behaving like they had no options.

We decided to ask them if they wanted us to get rid of him. They said, "Yes!" in unison. We faced him and told him to leave or we would call the cops. He did and that was that.

As we were turning to leave I asked the girls if they'd ever thought of taking a self-defense class. They both looked at me like I was strange and said, "That's too weird," started to giggle and left.

When the drunk was pursuing the girls they demonstrated a "freeze" response, even though they were moving their legs and giggling. There were two of them, they were physically fit young women who were probably stronger than the drunk who was hassling them, and yet, they were intimidated by someone they didn't need to be intimidated by. They would never see the drunk again and yet were too embarrassed to tell him what they wanted — for him to leave them alone. How would they be in a date situation if boys they like started to intimidate them?

Defending the Self Within the Family

Verbal self-defense can also solve family problems, especially when there's a bully in the family.

Bridget and Chuck, an early 40's white suburban couple living in California, are active in pro-choice activities. Chuck's brother and his wife, David and Sheila, can't be more opposite in their views. They are ardent anti-abortion activists. All four are college-educated, dedicated and passionate about the issue of a woman's right to have an abortion, or not.

David and Sheila have two young daughters and live in a conservative town. On one leg of a summer vacation they stopped by Bridget and Chuck's home for a lunch break before they continued on their way.

Everyone worked really hard, most of the time, to get along — to find the topics that were "safe" and wouldn't kick up harsh feelings and intense emotions. At one point, however, Bridget inadvertently pushed a very sore button with David. His verbal abuse exploded with no warning. As Bridget stood at the sink, washing dishes, he got within six inches of her face and started yelling at her. He was clearly upset and into a verbal battering mode. His wife and kids were cowering in the other room.

Chuck, the younger of the two brothers, apparently relapsed into a childlike, fear-filled reaction. His older brother, he later said, reminds him of their raging, tantrum-throwing father. Bridget kept breathing, wondering when David would stop, and considered what she should do. She told David to calm down, but he didn't. Bridget simply continued to wash and breathe, wash and breathe, mentally preparing herself to strike David if he looked like he was going to get physical. She was grateful for her physical training. She remembers thinking about David's wife and kids, how they must cower in their own house if he was this out-of-control in his brother and sister-in-law's home.

True to a verbally abusive person's pattern, David finally stopped and then cried from remorse, and begged Bridget for forgiveness. Chuck left the room he was so shaken up. Bridget and David stayed in the kitchen. Bridget said, "If you ever, ever, talk to me that way again, I'll fight back, and if you move to hit me, I'll knock you out. Got it?" David's mouth dropped open; he was speechless. Bridget walked away.

David wrote a letter two weeks later, again to apologize. Bridget boycotted the next family Thanksgiving because he would be there.

That was a triumph of dignity for her. She had always "put up" with unpleasantness in her own immediate family and didn't want to have to be around someone she didn't like, just for the sake of appearances.

Bridget told the rest of the family about the fight and why she was staying away. As the family secret of David's abusive temper started coming out, his behavior improved. Chuck and Bridget then found out that David's in-laws had stopped wanting to be around him too but had not said so directly.

What happened to David was that he finally received some consequences for using rotten, vicious words that hurt. Bridget had verbally defended herself and had warned David of physical consequences should his behavior occur again. Behind a verbal abuser's "power" is the threat of force. Bridget addressed the unspoken threat of force with her own spoken promise to meet his with her own. David was also "boycotted" for a period of time.

Bridget says she finally has forgiven him, but is cautious around him. For her, "Forgive does not mean forget." She's concerned about David's wife, Sheila, and the girls but figures people don't change unless they initiate the change. Both Bridget and Chuck have decided that in terms of David's wife and children, the best thing is to let them know that they are available if they need help or healing from verbal abuse.

Scolding and Showing a Thief to the Door

Laura D., 35, came home on a Sunday afternoon not long after she'd completed her basics self-defense class and slowly realized that there had been a break-in. The TV was on when she knew she'd shut it off. There was a gin bottle on the kitchen table and her dog was closed in the bedroom.

"OK, I have to deal with this," she thought and began opening doors to the other rooms. She went to the back of the apartment and saw a man walking away. She opened the door and yelled, "Come back right now with my things!" He turned, came back, and gave her back a waffle iron. She said, "Leave here this instant."

The intruder explained that he was hungry, homeless and had just wanted something to eat. Laura was indignant and told him his behavior was unacceptable. As he walked away, Laura told him to come back and give her back all of her things, and if he did she wouldn't call the police. The man returned her things, including a granola bar, which Laura told him to keep.

When she asked how he had gotten in, the man lied and said through the window. Laura finally let him go and then discovered that the house key she'd hidden was gone. The thief had not gotten in through the window as he'd claimed and was holding onto the key to use another time, most likely. Laura called 911, the police found the man, and she got her key back. Laura's anger at having been lied to was what prompted her to call the police. She thinks the police are not always the best solution and probably wouldn't have called them had the man given back her key.

Laura wonders now if she should have left her apartment the minute she realized someone had broken in. That is always the safest behavior. On the other hand, she may have had to endure more break-ins because the way she handled the thief led to the discovery of her stolen key. She felt good about her reaction to the incident because she was constantly listening to herself, trusting herself and assessing, moment by moment.

Laura exemplifies an attitude that I've seen in many success stories by women who have completed self-defense classes. She talked to the man, person to person, and humanized him enough to take him to task for what he'd been doing. She didn't freeze, she didn't panic. She commanded authority, which will empower her in other less stressful settings.

Defending at the Castle Gate

Nancy, who completed a twenty-hour basics class with L.A.'s Impact Personal Safety, soon had an opportunity to use the skills she'd learned in class. She came home to her nice neighborhood to find a man ranting and raving near her fence. She took a ready stance (knees comfortably stable and slightly bent, hands up, with palms out, neither aggressive nor passive, protecting her face and neck.) She ordered him to "Back off, leave, I don't want trouble." With that, he continued to berate her, yell obscenities at her, and yet he took her "order" seriously and backed up the whole while. She continued like a "broken record," and he continued to back up until he left.

There are important lessons in Nancy's defense of herself. The class she'd taken had included segments where the male instructor intentionally used abusive language after telling the students that he would be doing that in order to desensitize them. Nancy had gotten over the freeze response that used to happen when she'd hear someone threatening her. Because she'd practiced dealing with verbal abuse in class, she knew how to stay present in the moment and break through a freeze. She'd practiced giving a man orders without having to be polite or pleasing. You'd be amazed how difficult this is, even in rehearsal, for a lot of women. But after practicing a few times ordering a man to do as they're told, women can verbally defend themselves extremely well, as if they'd been doing so all their lives. Nancy was willing and able to fight physically if it came to that, but she succeeded in de-escalating a potentially dangerous situation. When she went into the house she called 911, but by the time the police got there the man had disappeared into the neighborhood.

A week later Nancy and her husband saw the ranting man in their neighborhood again. He didn't see them. This time, Nancy was able to get the police to show up in time to pick up the man for questioning. It turned out that he was wanted as a serial rapist.

Trusting Our Feelings and Instincts

Using language to protect ourselves and our loved ones requires a confidence that comes from trusting our instincts and our feelings. Women's ability to feel is an important factor in self-defense, whether the defense is verbal or physical. Unfortunately, women's feelings have been both belittled and denied in most cultures. On the one hand, our intuitive ("feminine") feelings are frequently denigrated, and on the other hand, too many of us feel we don't have the right to feel and express such a "masculine" feeling as anger.

Women have not been given nor have they taken back their right to feel and express anger to the degree that we need to. We have a right to our anger, our outrage. We still worry about what people will think if we express the so-called "negative" emotions. We fear that our emotions are not logical. The beauty of emotions is missed; emotions needn't be logical to make sense or to be accurate.

Gavin de Becker, author of *The Gift of Fear: Survival Signals That Protect Us From Violence,* says that logic is crawling compared to the soaring that nature gives us through feelings. Ironically, it's our negative emotions — those that make people who are attempting to control or dominate us uncomfortable — that are frequently the guardians of our well-being.

There are other so-called negative attributes that we can call on to help protect ourselves and our families. The next chapter explores our right, and possibly even our obligation, to be a bitch.

11

Bitches, Battle Axes and Boadiceas: Awakening Our Fierceness

A whole troop [of Romans] would not be able to withstand a single Gaul if he called his wife to his assistance. Swelling her neck, gnashing her teeth and brandishing her sallow arms of enormous size, she begins to strike blows mingled with kicks as if they were so many missiles sent from the string of a catapult.

AMMIANUS MARCELLINUS CIRCA 1ST CENTURY, A.D.

Honoring Our Bitch

Go ahead, be a bitch. It's a good thing, nothing to be ashamed or scared of. I've wasted way too much of my life attempting to prove that I'm not a bitch. I have been nice when a saint would have lost it. I have been unduly proud when people said that I'm not a bitch but another woman was. I have called other women bitches in a disempowering way. I'm truly sorry for the way I've abused the word. I would like to see the word "bitch" elevated to its proper place in the English language, transformed from sexist epithet to a word of adoration and awe.

Bitch is actually a wonderful word and state of being. Just as a stud is a potent and valuable male, bitch is the ripe female equivalent in the dog kingdom, er, queendom. As we all know, its human use is usually derogatory because it's a word exclusively used in reference to strong women.

Now strength is a relative term. A man called me a bitch once when I very politely declined to let him cut in front of me in a grocery line. I suddenly understood the absurdity of trying to maintain a non-bitch stance in the world. No matter what, someone will think I am one, so, what the hell, I might as well enjoy the perks of being an actual bitch.

"Bitch" is used as a verbal weapon, a way to keep "uppity" women in line or to keep women who are thinking about being uppity from opening their mouths. "You wouldn't want anyone to think that you're a bitch, now would you? Better not say anything," is how some of the logic goes. OOOOOOOOOHHHHHH, how scary to be called a bitch. Isn't it amazing that so many of us have given the word so much power?

I'll never forget the "Rhymes with Rich" headline about Leona Helmsley. That's acceptable journalism? Of course, the word they were asking us to supply was "bitch." I dare say it would not occur to publishers and editors to have Charles Keating, the infamous cheater of the savings and loan debacle, on a cover with a headline saying, "Rhymes with Sick." The mass media reserve gender-related put-downs for women.

To call someone a bitch as a put-down is to presume that there are bitches in the world and there are "non-bitches"; that the proper way to be a female human being is to be a non-bitch.

What is a non-bitch? She is like the unicorn, a myth, a fantasy that men have dreamed up. A non-bitch is a woman who personifies compliant beauty, who never gives a fellah any trouble. She is always nice and understanding, never angry, doesn't argue, doesn't protect herself, her property or her children. She is always complimentary, remembers every detail about everything, never hurts feelings intentionally or unintentionally, always serves others first, always smiles and does what everyone asks of her, all the time, with no complaint. I'm sure I've left something out but since I'm a bitch, I don't pretend that I don't make mistakes.

The old-fashioned, put-down usage of bitch is like a girdle; it holds women back and in, and in a most uncomfortable and unhealthy way. No one really wants to be stuffed or squeezed into anything, whether it's an undergarment or an archaic form of so-called feminine behavior. Everyone despised girdles, but it wasn't until a few courageous women started refusing to wear them that the rest of us could wiggle out of them forever. (It's amazing to me that bra-burning would become the tired symbol of women's liberation; it should have been girdle-burning. It's even more amazing to me that there has been a recent girdle "revival." Now that's a stretch.)

I hereby proudly declare my bitchness and invite others to do the same. Join me. Everyone in the world has bitchness in them, women and men, girls and boys. Why would we collude in the absurd idea of aspiring to not be something that we all are? There are things to complain about, there are things to be angry about, there are problems to take action on that require the bitch in all of us.

The more who proclaim, nay, celebrate their bitchness, the less bitchy we'll all seem and the bitchier we can all become. If you don't like that idea, take a hike because I don't care. I have better things to worry about. Ahh, that felt good — just like taking off a girdle after a long day. Try it.

Old habits die hard. I admit I still flinch if someone calls me a bitch. But I must remember to be proud that I am no longer invisible and, therefore, pleasing to everyone and anyone. And I think of my favorite real-life bitch, my dog and companion. Now there's a role model.

She's faithful, loving, valuable, warm, nurturing, intelligent, affectionate, and capable of ripping someone who attacks me or my loved ones to ribbons. She's a bitch and, except for the way she drools and sheds, I want to be just like her.

Honoring Our Age, Anger and Outrage — A Battle Axe Asserts Her Rights for Herself and Others

Another name for a woman, usually an older women, who refuses to submit to males just because they are male, is "Battle Axe," a throwback term for a female warrior. She makes cutting remarks, she cuts through the bullshit. The woman who questions male authority is attacked for being unfeminine, and thus, becomes "undesirable." She is rejected and ridiculed by those who don't want to change the rules of the dominant culture, both men and women.

A woman who is not automatically submissive to men is called angry, castrating, a dyke, a feminist, humorless, a battle axe. Isn't it interesting that the assertion of one's rights is such a threat to so-called masculinity? The reason for this is that in our culture, like most others, boys are born into automatic authority and girls into roles of submitting to that authority. One's rights don't automatically take away rights of others. However, automatic privilege based on gender is very threatened by the assertion of rights. Men are privileged in every culture, even if they are relatively unprivileged compared to other groups. No matter what class, the male has automatic authority based on gender, and considers himself to have authority over all women regardless of age and class, even if in reality, he doesn't. The penis is quite a handy organ!

A lot of men and women haven't been able to understand that, just as men feel proud of authority, maturity and manhood, there are women who are (or who are working toward being) proud about mature womanhood and would like the respect that comes with age. Thus the objection some women have had to being called a "girl," regardless of their age or level of professional attainment. But many women are unwilling to object to being called a "girl," since there are so many more pressing life-and-death issues on the woman's-issues burner. However, the underlying belief in men's right to call women whatever a man damn well pleases, "girl" included, is not "semantics." It's a matter of control. Many women have maintained power by simply proudly embracing "girl."

Women who assert rights are often accused of being angry. "Angry" becomes an epithet. In reality, anger is genderless, and is nature's gift to let us know that our boundaries, physical or otherwise, are being trampled.

The following essay, by Randy Mamiaro, is one of the best and only tributes I've seen by a man who honors a woman's anger. "Inside the Helmet" exemplifies the spirit of the men who teach full-force self-defense, the men who put their bodies on the line so that women can learn to fight, literally and figuratively.

Inside the Helmet

By Randy Mamiaro

I had the happy opportunity recently to have a good friend as a student in one of Impact's advanced courses. Although she is a graduate of the basics course twice-over, I had not previously worked with her and so had no expectation one way or another of what the coming fights would be like. We began with rear-takedown scenarios. As I braced her body with padded arms and guided the two of us to the mat she tucked into stance and yelled a very loud and energetic, "NO!" Good start, I thought, and the series of solid elbow strikes and heel-palm blows which thudded against my helmet confirmed that my friend had indeed learned her basic techniques well.

She spun about into side-kick position; through the nylon mesh of my eye-holes I could see the tread pattern on the sole of her upraised shoe. I felt my muscles relax automatically as I prepared to absorb the momentum of her kick. Her foot shot out. POW!

What hit my thankfully well-padded noggin wasn't a human foot. It was a nuclear-powered battering ram! Thank God for foam rubber because — no doubt about it — that one kick would easily have knocked an unprotected person unconscious. For training purposes I kept "Boris" (that's the name of my mugger character) moving to receive another couple of side-kicks and a devastating trio of ax-kicks.

Every one of those kicks hit like a bomb blast. Every one, individually, was a certain knock-out blow. All of our graduates have the capability to successfully defend themselves. All of them can render an assailant unconscious. However, not many hit with such power that every kick is a guaranteed knock-out.

Where, I wondered, was this intense energy coming from? My friend's technique is good, but it's not perfect. I'd call it average. Nor is she a buffed-out athlete with a strong and sinewy Linda Hamilton physique. There was more to those kicks of hers than could be explained by physics or physiology alone. No, the fuel for those strikes had to be something nonmaterial. Each kick was invested with an emotional content that, at the time, I could only think of as anger.

Yet, the word anger doesn't describe accurately what I felt in those kicks. I found myself floundering for the proper terminology so, as I'm wont to do in such a predicament, I ran to my thesaurus and my *Webster's.* My dog-eared *Seventh Collegiate Dictionary* has this entry for anger: "1. a strong feeling of displeasure and usually of antagonism." Well, that certainly falls short of describing the vehemence behind those kicks. The second definition isn't quite right either: 2. Rage. Furthermore, rage is described as implying a loss of self-control in my friend's fight. She hit accurately and deliberately. She did not flail in a blind rage. Hmmmmm . . .Wrath. That's closer, since it suggests an intent to revenge or punish, yet it too seems inadequate. Definitely too biblical.

Ah-ha! Finally, here is the word: OUTRAGE. "The anger and resentment aroused by injury or insult" or, I dare say, by an outrage. That was the source of power in my friend's thunderous kicks — outrage! Of course. Knowing this woman, I know that, oh yes, she gets outraged. She is that too rare being known as an activist, someone who sees the wrongs and ills of the world and refuses to be merely appalled, or scared, or saddened by it all. She gets bloody damn well outraged. Then she tries to do something about it, bless her.

Darth Vader says to Luke Skywalker, in synthesized basso profundo, "Let go of your anger. Only your anger can make you strong!" But that is the Dark Side of the Force talking. Want to stay on the side of the angels? Use outrage, become outraged! Any thug, any robber, any rapist can be angry. Anger is amoral. Good people get, or should get, outraged. Outrage is anger born of a sense of justice, of belief in right and wrong.

I don't know for sure what generated outrage in my friend during her fight. I do know that she tapped into that outrage and it made her strong. Very strong. Stronger than simple anger could have made her, stronger than determination or the will to survive. I wouldn't presume to guess the source of her outrage, and I certainly wouldn't presume to tell someone else what they should become outraged over.

I can tell you what makes me outraged. Children being kidnapped outrages me. Alcoholic parents who beat and heap verbal abuse on their children because of their own insecurity outrages me. Parents who commit the ultimate betrayal and commit incest on their children, breeding their own victims, truly outrages me. Fraternity boys who think that because a woman attends a house party she's fair game for gang rape, or the serial rapist who attacks more than a dozen women before being caught outrages me. Women who fear all men because no man in their lives ever treated them with respect or even common courtesy; men and women emotionally crippled because they never had an opportunity to learn that they have a right to their own integrity and self-worth; criminals convicted of rape and assault who serve maybe one or two years of a sentence then are freed to rape again; all this outrages me. Unfortunately, I could go on and on. And *that* outrages me!

Outrage is not unfocused anger, blind and wild rage, or boiling but impotent ire and frustration. It is the unleashed energy of victims who refuse to be victims any longer. It is a focused, unstoppable laser beam of anger directed against those who would violate our rights, generated by those who know they are right. It is your outrage which kicks out the mugger; your arms and legs, kicks and heel-palm strikes are merely the conduits of that power. Take it from someone who has been on the receiving end of that power: technique by itself is nothing, but technique energized by your outrage is unbeatable.

Honoring Our Bravery — The Boadicea In Us All

The woman on the cover of this book lived. Her name was Queen Boadicea. There is a statue of her in London, not far from Parliament, next to a bridge over the Thames. The statue depicts her driving a two-horse chariot with two young women riding on the chariot behind her. She is large, she is fierce, she is determined to avenge the rape of her daughters. She was a Queen on the British Isles who died in 62 A.D. as she led her troops against the Romans.

Boadicea is the embodiment of bodaciousness, a modern slang word, which according to the *American Heritage Dictionary* means: "Intrepidly bold or daring; audacious. (a blend of bold and audacious)" I don't buy their definition. I'll bet the slang was created by kids who looked up at the statue of Boadicea, and were awed by her. Question the authority of a dictionary? How bodacious.

Look at the *American Heritage Dictionary's* description of Boadicea: "Died A.D. 62. British Queen; led an unsuccessful revolt against the Romans." What an appalling definition that takes a less than flattering "spin" on an incredibly important leader. Dictionaries are written by human beings after all. The human being who wrote about Boadicea could just as easily and truthfully have written: "Died A.D. 62. British Queen notable for her courage against great odds. Attacked a legion of Romans with very few troops." Most likely, there were no women on the dictionary staff to take an editorial stand in favor of Boadicea.

If you make room for Boadicea in your heart, there are three aspects she can awaken in you: the determination to avenge the wrongs done our daughters, the vision to pave the way for a better life for them in the future, and the willingness to take action against great odds.

Honoring Our Cowardice Through Courage

We value valor, bravery, courage, risk-taking, and the ability to withstand pain and suffering in our boys. We don't have the same expectations of our girls. We exclude them from the courage ethic to their detriment. We allow them to be cowards without breaking through to the other side of cowardice: courage. You can't have one without the other.

"Oh, Sally, don't climb that tree, you'll fall and hurt yourself." Yes, she might. So what? Not that I would want any child to break bones. Stanley might hurt himself too, but the gain of risk-taking is the building of heart. Bones break, but so do hearts and spirits when you limit people and assume that they can't handle life. People are disempowered when they don't get a chance to take risks or to test their mettle.

Bravery is actually gender neutral. Physical ability to protect oneself from harm is gender neutral. Systematically training boys to be brave and strong and training girls to be passive and weak is a tragedy that affects everyone. Courage is required of boys and girls, women and men for survival, mental and physical health, and the well-being of our world community.

Many women are guilty of falling back on socially-acceptable "helpless female" behavior when it comes down to hard situations, whether it is climbing a tree, making a difficult phone call, asking for what we need, telling someone to back off or checking out a suspicious sound at night. But it's important that all grown-ups — female and male — come to terms with a fact of life: It not only takes courage to risk your life, it also takes courage to live a free and equal life. Women in dangerous occupations teach us that. Female police officers, soldiers, pilots, astronauts are pioneers who dare to take the all-too-real risk of injury or death. Fulbright Scholar Amy Biehl gave her life in South Africa. Her brutal murder at the hands of a "One Settler, One Bullet" mob came about because she believed in doing whatever she could to end apartheid. Amelia Earhart presumably died following her dream, her heart.

We forget that women actually come from a tradition of courage. For millennia women died regularly in childbirth; thus, marriage and pregnancy were acts of great courage. Sleeping with your husband could literally result in death. Countless colonial and pioneer women threw caution to the often-deadly winds, shoulder-to-shoulder with their loved ones. Native American women died defending their families and tribes. Slave women endured unspeakable torture, rape and inhumane conditions; many who escaped slavery came back to liberate others at great risk. Mexican and Central American women continue to risk their lives, crossing a border to make a better life.

The examples of courageous women are as varied and numbered as there are people. Many women must brave deadly neighborhoods every day. We have no shortage of heroic female role models if we only look. We must take inspiration from these women as we commit ourselves to developing our own bravery. It is only by being role models ourselves that our daughters, nieces, and granddaughters can learn first-hand how to become brave women.

If you look at the origin of the word courage, you find that it means "heart" in the romance languages, from the Latin for heart, cor. "Coure" in French, "corazon" in Spanish, "cuore" in Italian. To have heart, to give heart, are phrases that evoke qualities that most people love and admire. No one likes a coward; even cowards hate being cowards. Yet we train our girls to lose heart, to back away from scary or risky things; we literally "dis-courage" them from experiencing their ability to transcend fear.

Many of us say, "She has balls," if the "she" does something courageous. There is no female equivalent to "balls" that automatically references a woman's risk-taking. "Balls" equals "brave." I've started to say, "She has ovaries," or "She has gonads," when I speak of a woman's valor. Since gonads is a scientific term that refers to both testes and ovaries, it's entirely proper to say of a girl or a boy, "What gonads!"

We expect boys to face their fears. Parents literally "en-courage" them to participate fully in games and activities that involve risk, physical as well as tactical. We can develop courage in young girls by allowing them to do the same. Far too many girls are discouraged from getting dirty, getting hurt, wrestling, out-witting boys, experiencing their strengths and limitations. Girls who have limited experience with athletics have a slim hold on what their bodies can or cannot do. Girls who experience physical activities and athletics gain an understanding of how powerful they really are.

Courage and cowardice. We all have both regardless of gender. Courage requires that a person be responsible for the consequences of his or her actions.

Cowardice is a backing off from personal responsibility. Consequences build character, especially when we have noble expectations of the person who is acting or reacting to whatever circumstances have been handed them in life.

It's always been hard to take stands. There were big chunks of time in my life when I used to not even know what I thought about a lot of things or what to say. I can't say that I was abnormal. I observed women, relatives and strangers, who would literally go dumb around men-folk. Courage to think and speak. That is a very big deal for an entire group of people, women, who have largely had to depend on the men in their lives for esteem. That old outside esteem comes and goes. Self-love regenerates forever. And just as fear breeds fear, the good news is, courage breeds courage. Bodaciousness breeds bodaciousness. You could say that courage is spiritually contagious. You could also say that being a bitch, a battle axe or bodacious is being true to the spirit.

12

The Magic Potion of Fighting Spirit

It's not the size of the woman in the fight, it's the size of the fight in the woman.

VARIATION ON AN OLD SAYING ABOUT DOGS.

Dispiriting Initiation

"Mommy, Daddy, Johnny hit me!" "Slug him back!" I didn't hear that, did you? I heard, "He likes you. Ignore him." He likes me so he hits me?

I whine, "But I don't like being hit." He hits me again. I thought boys weren't supposed to hit girls. Finally, I tire of it and I get in a fight with Johnny. But I'm not really willing to hurt him. I am more gentle than I am rough. He straddles my chest. He uses his elbows and comes down as hard as he can on my budding little breasts, one elbow for each breast. Hard. I cried. He laughed.

"You think you're so tough," he gloated. That was the last time I fought a male in real life.

If there had been movies that showed a girl what to do with an assault, I might have gotten him. Or if it were common for girls and women to share stories about self-defense successes, I could have reached into my memory for something to do. If I'd been unwilling to have him hurt me I would have kicked him between the legs. He went for my breasts. Why didn't I go for his balls? It never occurred to me because I knew that would hurt him. I was brainwashed to never hurt anyone by then. Besides, I'd been told that you never, never hit a boy between his legs. You could hurt him permanently you know. What about me?

I wasn't hurt permanently, physically. But my fighting spirit took a big blow during that cold recess on a playground in South Dakota.

Emotionally, psychologically, spiritually, I was "initiated" into the world of men and women physical power politics. Johnny didn't care what I thought of him, he didn't care what I said about him, and he didn't care about consequences because there probably wouldn't be any for what he did. He was right. There weren't any consequences for his striking me, from me or anyone else. Had I administered my own justice, he'd have been crying like I was.

Think back on school yard days. When I was in first, second and third grades, if a boy hit me, there were consequences. But as early as fourth grade, I was desperate to be an attractive girl. Carol Gilligan identified the slump that girls go into around 11 years old in her book *In a Different Voice*. I related so deeply to her analysis of many things in my own life but she didn't hit, pun intended, on the physical aspect of self-protection and what it costs girls to not protect themselves.

By sixth grade there were no consequences for messing with me and the boys knew it. They knew they had a threat factor that intimidated all of us girls. We had become persons of no consequence when it came to boys crossing our boundaries because of our unconscious fear of physical harm and our reluctance to hit back.

Women and girls will not be free until there are consequences for treating them badly that are just as sure and swift as for treating men badly, whether that justice is administered by ourselves in the moment by hand or foot or by the system. Systems are sometimes the appropriate means for bringing someone to justice. However, a dependence on outside authorities to defend our safety or our rights can be frustrating, impossible and unsatisfactory. We are dispirited when justice is delayed or denied on a consistent basis. Whether we choose to act or not, we should at least know how to deliver our own consequences to bullies and bad guys.

Empower Kids for Self-Defense

There are aphorisms that can be damaging, especially when they are used to enforce compliant behavior by children. Take, for instance, "Children should be seen and not heard" and "What you don't know can't hurt you." Given the prevalence of predators, mostly people we know, some strangers, it's important that we replace the message of those tired sayings with rules that can help children protect themselves.

We tend to think that children are helpless when faced with a grown-up who wishes them harm. Of course, in a full-out struggle, the adult has most of the advantage. However, a child who has practiced very simple self-protection techniques has a dramatically increased chance of saving herself or himself from harm. Fortunately, molesters are not out looking for struggles; they look for a child who will freeze, a child who won't give them any trouble, a child who won't make a scene.

There was an 11-year-old girl who fended off a molester in the San Fernando Valley during the winter of 1993 after a spate of reports about a man who was stalking kids. She had listened to the warnings. She didn't freeze; she fought back. She saved herself from further harm by following the instructions she had received from caring adults: "Don't talk to strangers" and "Run away." However, if she'd had more information — and this is not a criticism of anyone, especially her — the incident could have turned out differently. It might even have led to the apprehension of the man, who was a suspect in half-a-dozen of 26 child-molestation cases reported in the San Fernando Valley in a nine-month period.

The girl was walking to school when she realized she had left her drill-team whistle at home. She turned back, and when she got to her house she suspected that a man was following her. At that point, she could have called 911 when she was in the house simply on the basis of her suspicion.

We must teach our children to trust their instincts and to understand that the worst thing that could happen if their instinct turns out to be wrong is that they might be embarrassed. But to some children, embarrassment is excruciating, especially if it's accompanied by teasing and ridicule.

Other specifics that would have been powerful for the girl to know is that she could have started yelling "911" or "I need help" at the top of her lungs when the man drew near or when he grabbed her. She could have also been yelling out an extremely loud description of him to catch the attention of passersby. Predatory molesters are hit-and-run artists. They don't want a scene, they don't want a child who has been trained to break the "seen and not heard" rule.

If only the girls at Polly Klaas' house that night in Petaluma, California, had made lots of noise. There's no guarantee that the man who kidnaped her at knife-point wouldn't have harmed her or her friends, but hollering for help would have alerted the adults nearby. It's important for everyone to know that it's better to fight at the initial point of an assault, before the perpetrator has the victim isolated.

Children, however — as most of us who love them know — are simply gentle, short human beings, and would rather not hurt someone or make a "fool" of themselves, even when they are being threatened. It's not enough simply to tell children (and adults) to be loud and run when accosted. People, kids included, need to become comfortable about being loud, making a racket, making trouble, making a scene. This takes practice. We know that preparedness drills turn out to be very effective in earthquakes or fires. The same is true in assault situations.

When people freeze it's because they have no experience to draw from. Irene van der Zande, the executive director of KIDPOWER, suspected that her own kids were apt to be just as frozen about yelling as she was herself. She was right; they were mortified at the prospect of yelling under stress. So she took them to a remote area and had them practice, "No! I need help! 911!"

The schoolgirl in the San Fernando Valley elbowed the man, which was a thoroughly effective move, and ran away. That's something else we have to teach kids: when they hit soft tissue on a grown-up with a hard place on their own body, small or not, there will be an effect. "Action" movies and television have given us all the idea that men are impervious to pain. Not true in real life. Rapists and molesters, by the same token, are also counting on what they see in movies and television — that children are easy marks. That has to change.

The Fighting Spirit

Any self-defense or martial arts instructor worth a whit will tell you that the will to live and fighting spirit is the most important thing for a person to have when in danger. Skills are important, but will is the fuel for protecting yourself, with or without formal training. Although I am an unabashed advocate of full-force, full-impact self-defense training, I believe any training is better than none, and that training or no training, a woman (or child) is able to fight back and prevail if the birthright of natural fighting spirit is intact. One way to enhance fighting spirit is to share stories of successful defenses. I have included stories of both boys and girls in this section because we can learn from them — "out of the kicks of babes." All the stories are proof that untrained people with spirit have what is vital for self-protection.

Ten-Year-Old Boy Saves Friend From Attempted Kidnapping

This is a headline from an Associated Press story on Sunday, October 23, 1994. Cameron Noel, ten years old, 4'1", 66 lbs. reacted to an older man, Armando Haramboure, 73, by kicking "him where it hurts." Haramboure allegedly drove up to a group of four kids in Chalmette, Louisiana, grabbed a five-year-old boy and tossed him in the back seat. That's when Cameron let him have it. The groin shot made Haramboure double over. Then, as the man bent over, Cameron kicked him in the head. He proceeded to unlock the car door and got his little friend out of the car.

If Cameron Noel can use his "fighting spirit" to protect himself and others, you can too.

Young Girl Administers Groin Kick

Tommy Li (special to the *Los Angeles Times*) reported in a November 23, 1993 story that a 14-year-old girl "fought off a would-be kidnapper as she walked home from school in La Crescenta, California . . . ."

The 14-year-old victim (sic) had told sheriff's officials last week that a man in his mid-20's grabbed her and demanded that she get into his... truck. When she refused, she said, the man punched her in the back, but "she was able to break free of the attacker by administering a swift kick to the groin area, which caused him to fall to the ground . . . "

The girl did not initially report the incident because she didn't want her mom to be mad. I would guess that she was afraid that her new-teen freedoms might be taken away. Many kids don't want to be punished or restricted as a result of communicating a dangerous event, regardless of the outcome. I think it's interesting that the young woman was still referred to as the "victim," even though the man with the bruised testicles was the actual victim in this success story. "He," as so many people are fond of saying of victims, "must have been asking for it." Only in this instance it was true.

If she could do it, so could you or your daughter or your son.

Jill Goes Ballistic

Even before I learned how to fight, I was inspired by the story of an untrained woman who successfully defended herself against an intruder in Northern California. She was on the phone with her mother, who was at work. As they were speaking, Jill didn't happen to mention that she was presently at her mom's house doing laundry. Jill heard a knock at the door, told her mom to hold on, put the receiver down and went to answer the door.

A man burst through and attacked Jill. The guy had picked the wrong victim. Jill went ballistic on him, scratching, clawing, yelling, kicking, punching, and rolling around on the floor with him. Meanwhile, Jill's mother was listening in horror to the violent struggle over the phone. She held on, used another line to call "911," and dispatched the police to Jill's house, assuming she was there. When the police got to Jill's apartment, no one was there. As it turned out, Jill was able to defend herself; the assailant gave up and ran as quickly as he could from the house. Foiled.

Jill had not had any formal training in self-defense. She tapped into the natural response human beings have when they are attacked: self-protection. Her story reminds me to mention where I am when I call someone.

Fight Now or Die Later

Another woman I heard about was followed into her apartment building's "secure" parking structure. Two men in another car slipped in behind Carmen's car before the automated gate slammed down. As Carmen got out of her car, she found herself face-to-face with a man who had a gun pointed at her. She was sandwiched between her car and theirs with no room to escape. The men had the car door open ready to force her inside. In a split second, the phrase "fight now or die later" came to Carmen's mind. Her thinking was right on the mark. In an upward sweeping motion, she grabbed the man's wrist and got the gun "off-line" — in other words not pointed at a vital spot on her body. The man pistol-whipped Carmen across her forehead, the pistol went off and the bullet shattered her car window. The assailant jumped into his car as soon as the gun went off. The car with the two men squealed away, but when they got to the automatic gate, it wouldn't open. They abandoned the car and ran away on foot.

While Carmen sustained a nasty gash requiring 16 stitches, and some hearing loss from the gun going off so close to her head, she was very much alive to tell about it. Again, Carmen was not trained. But she rightly assessed that she was in a lot of danger and saved herself by not arguing with her instinct. She is a prime example of what Gavin de Becker talks about in *The Gift of Fear.* She used her gift wisely.

People use weapons for intimidation, to force someone to do something against their will. If you are ever in a situation where there's a vehicle, a gun, or some type of restraint, the best thing to do is to fight like hell to not be taken away. Even if you are hurt, there will be a better chance of survival than letting yourself be isolated in a remote place selected by the assailants. People who carry guns, ropes, and duct tape have really bad intentions. You don't want to believe them when they say, "Just do what I say and you'll be OK," or "Come with me or I'll kill you." Listen, talk, but don't take them at their word. Do whatever you can to not be alone with them.

In an article by the *New York Times'* Jane E. Brody, Lieutenant Edward Welch of the University of Oklahoma campus police department talked about what to do if an assailant attempts to force you into a vehicle using a weapon. Lt. Welch advises people to say, "No, I'm not going," and then walk or run away. According to Welch, there's a 98 percent chance the assailant won't shoot, but if you go with him, there's a 98 percent chance you won't survive.

If you ever do get in a situation where you've been forced into a vehicle and tied or taped up, do not give up. Always breathe, plan, look for openings. Negotiate, offer things that are tempting, lie, do whatever needs to be done to save yourself from harm or death.

"But what if they kill me if I fight back?" people ask. That's true, fighting back might get you killed. But paralysis and passivity can get you killed, too. Isn't it better to know how to fight so that fighting back is an option? Regardless of which option one chooses, fighting or staying still, listening to your inner voice or your intuition is a major part of self-defense, if not the most important part. The women who succeed in defending themselves without formal training, do not think themselves into paralysis. They act.

Jogger Defends Against Attack

Los Angeles Times staff writer Vivien Lou Chen reported on July 18, 1995, that a jogger successfully fought off an assailant who was lying in wait for her with a cloth soaked in a chemical substance intended to knock her out. As the 18-year-old woman jogged by herself at 11:00 p.m., John Michael Lew, 34, of Los Angeles, allegedly struck the runner in the face. She responded by "kicking and punching, and finally kicked Lew in the stomach, causing him to double over, the police said. She broke away, running to a nearby home, and gave police a description of her attacker . . . ." Mr. Lew, sore stomach and all, was arrested as he was returning to his car.

Woman, 112, Fights Off Burglar

"Feisty senior provides attacker painful lesson" read the sub-heading of a story by L.A. Johnson, for Knight-Ridder Newspapers. Rosia Lee Ellis, fisher, gardener, occasional snuff-user, beloved neighbor, an "amazing person," has an active life in her Detroit neighborhood of 35 years. When a would-be burglar broke in through the front door of her house, she grabbed him. He was 6 feet, Rosia is 5 feet. He threw her on the floor but she just held on to his crotch. "He didn't have time to say nothin'. He just had time to try to get loose." Neighbors responded to the noise Rosia was making and caused the failed burglar to flee when he heard them outside Rosia's house.

Prostitute's Self-Defense Results in Conviction of Serial Rapist/Murderer

The *Los Angeles Times* reported that a prostitute who was apparently the only known survivor of convicted serial rapist/murderer William L. Suff's vicious attacks provided the key testimony in the *People of California v. Suff.* He had taken her to an abandoned house after she agreed to have sex with him for twenty dollars.

He gave her one dollar, and before she could say anything he started strangling her to the point where she almost went unconscious. She grabbed a flashlight, hit him on the head, bit his finger so hard she broke a tooth and escaped. Suff was convicted of the murder of 13 other prostitutes. She was the only person who could give a positive identitication because she fought back and saved herself from certain death. She also saved other women's lives by fighting back. To me, she is a heroine.

This story also reminds me of the "conventional ignorance" about who rapists pick to be their victims. Some people are so callous that they convince themselves that prostitutes take on the risk of being beaten and killed as an occupational hazard — another way of saying, "they deserve what they get." Others assume that only "pretty young things," "girls who dress to attract the attentions of virile men," or "women who are somewhere where they shouldn't be and should have known better" are the victims of rape. These ignorant opinions are not facts.

"Break out, son-of-a-bitch. You broke in, didn't you?"

And last but not least, one of my favorite untrained defense success stories came to the attention of readers all over the U.S. because of the late Mike Royko's syndicated column. He wrote about Curtescine Lloyd, a triumphant, full of piss and vinegar woman, who rousted an intruder from her home. She took "matters" into her own hands, and the "matters" mattered to the intruder a great deal.

In the dark of the night, Ms. Lloyd, a resident of a small town in Mississippi, was awakened by a man who was intent on raping and pillaging. Ms. Lloyd had other ideas. He did the usual threatening: you're a dead woman if you make noise, keep the light off, shut up and don't make a fuss — the typical midnight rapist rap.

He stripped and hopped into Curtescine Lloyd's bed. According to court records, the tide turned.

Lloyd: "I got it. I grabbed it by my right hand. And when I grabbed it, I gave it a yank. And when I yanked it, I twisted all at the same time."

Let us not forget that the "it" she was yanking and twisting was made of flesh and blood.

"He hit me with his right hand a hard blow beside the head, and when he hit me, I grabbed hold to his scrotum with my left hand and I was twisting it the opposite way. He started to yell and we fell to the floor and he hit me a couple of more licks, but they were light licks. He was weakening some then."

Apparently Ms. Lloyd's elderly aunt never heard the struggle. After some mighty twisting and shouting, the struggle moved from the bedroom to the hall.

"He was trying to get out, and I'm hanging onto him; and he was throwing me from one side of the hall wall to the other. I was afraid if I let him go, he was going to kill me.

"So I was determined I was not going to turn him loose. So we were going down the hallway, falling from one side to the other, and we got into the living room and we both fell. He brought me down right in front of the couch and he leaned back against the couch, pleading with me.

"He says, 'You've got me, you've got me, please, you've got me.' I said, 'I know damn well I got you.' He said, 'Please, please, you're killing me, you're killing me . . . I can't do nothing. Call the police.'

"I said, 'Do you think I'm stupid enough to turn you loose and call the police?' He said, 'Well, what am I gonna do?' I said, 'You're gonna get the hell out of my house.' He said, 'How can I get out of your house if you won't let me go? How can I get out? I can't get out.'

"I said, 'Break out, son-of-a-bitch. You broke in, didn't you?' And I was still holding him.

"He said, 'Oh, you've got me suffering, lady, you've got me suffering.' I said, 'Have you thought about how you were going to have me suffering?' He said, 'Well, I can't do nothing now.' I said, 'Well, that's fine.'"

In righteous indignation, Ms. Lloyd had the erstwhile rapist let himself out of her house.

"And when I did that, I gave it a twist, and I turned him loose. And he took a couple of steps and fell off the steps and he jumped up and grabbed his private parts and made a couple of jumps across the back of my aunt's car.

"And I ran into my aunt's room, got her pistol from underneath the nightstand, ran back to the screen door, and I fired two shots down the hill the way I saw him go. And then I ran back in the house and dialed 911."

The man had identification with the clothes that he'd so cockily stripped off that fateful evening. Dwight Coverson soon had a visit from the police. He was in no shape to run from them. He received 25 years in prison for his little attempt to rape Ms. Curtescine Lloyd.

The most common form of stranger rape is the result of someone breaking into a woman's home. Curtescine Lloyd was middle-aged, at home asleep and certainly not "asking for it," whatever that means.

During the O.J. Simpson trial in L.A., Dr. Michael Baden tipped a hand that many men and way too many women hold when it comes to attitudes about rape. While describing forensic evidence-gathering for homicides that may involve rape, Dr. Baden mentioned in tones of surprise that a homicide victim, a woman in her 80's, had been raped. Does that mean that he's surprised that a rapist wouldn't pick someone younger and prettier, revealing an attitude that rape is a "natural" almost courting behavior, reserved for conventionally attractive women only? Yuk.

Rapists rape women of all types, ages, sizes, colors, backgrounds, economic situations, you name "it," they rape "it." Women aren't people to rapists, they are "its." They rape all women when they rape one, they hate us so. Rape is a brutal, ugly, cruel, torturous, punishing, degrading, vicious crime of violence, domination and power that no one ever deserves. Never forget that.

The only rule when fighting back is that there are no rules. Fighting back can include submitting to a rape if your instinct says that a rape will allow you to keep your life. Most women would rather be raped and deal with healing than die, an event that's impossible to heal from. Conversely, there are rape survivors who have vowed to fight to the death before they would allow another rape.

What these success stories reveal is the importance of "fighting spirit," whether the person has been trained in self-defense or not. In the next chapter, we'll continue with more success stories of women and kids who have trained, mostly in full-force self-defense. They used fighting spirit *and* what they learned in class, and they generously pass their stories on for the benefit of all.

13

Beauty's Battle Tales: Self-Defense Success Stories

While it sickens me that women even have to take a course to learn to defend themselves from men, it is encouraging to know my wife can now defend herself. I know that no man will ever be able to victimize her without having to fight for his life.

CARL JASKOLSKI, MILWAUKEE, WISC.,
MODEL MUGGING NEWS, FALL/WINTER 1989

Trained Women Fight Back

"Amazing," I remember thinking when I first started to get into the self-defense "biz" to find an entire collection of verbal and physical self-defense stories called *Her Wits About Her: Self-Defense Success Stories by Women,* edited by Denise Caignon and Gail Groves. It was both inspiring and infuriating to find out that women of all ages, sizes, colors, and backgrounds have successfully fought back with words and bodies, for years and I didn't know about them. Now newsletters and Web sites from Impact Chapters and other Model-Mugging-type service providers collect and publish success stories of their graduates. They never fail to amaze.

Included are a woman who used her calmness in the face of a rampaging man who charged at her in New York City's Central Park; another who fended off a brash young woman who wanted to steal a portable cassette player; a woman who showed up to give a massage only to discover that her client had really wanted a prostitute instead, and therefore "handled" his "disappointment"; and the woman who walked into a back yard at night as two armed, masked men told her to "go in the house." (See Appendix for the Impact Personal Safety Web site to get the full stories of the above referenced experiences). You name a situation and a graduate of full-force self-defense has gotten out of it using the skills she learned in class.

Trained Self-Defense Success Stories

In my study of success stories out of the full-force defense community I noticed several common threads. One is that women tend to only do enough harm to keep the assailant from doing harm to her or another. They don't stay and beat the assailant up to "teach him a lesson" or "punish" him for the "fun" of it. Unlike a lot of movies where males are depicted as having "fun" with violence, these women were solemn about the responsibility of fending off an attack. The second common theme is that the man who has been hit will respond by saying something like, "Hey, you hit me!" or "What did you hit me for?" even when he had struck the first blow or initiated an assault. It was as if he never realized that what he'd done to women was wrong, or that they had feelings like he does. Third, it was very common for the woman to be amazed at how simple it was to get the assailant to stop once she put up any resistance at all. Perhaps most surprising, in the majority of reported success stories verbal defense was enough to send the guy running.

When the incident did evolve into a physical confrontation, women frequently commented that they only had to strike once. One African-American woman who trained with the Impact Foundation in Los Angeles, reported, "Hey, I hit my attacker once and I didn't have to do all that other stuff; he just ran off!" This is an extremely common and heartening account that serves to break the stereotypes of males being invulnerable and women being helpless.

I think of self-defense in two ways: the use of force to defend oneself or one's loved ones, and the use of force to defend or intervene on behalf of another person unrelated or unknown because of generosity and concern.

Children's Physical Self-Defense Success Stories

Irene van der Zande, co-founder of KIDPOWER, has a collection of children's success stories which she was more than happy to share. Many adults are especially interested in children's self-defense stories because they remember helplessness and powerlessness when they were children themselves. They feel that their ability to draw boundaries got stunted as children and therefore they still feel like children when it comes to verbal or physical self-protection. A common refrain every self-defense teacher hears from adults is: "Is that all there is to it? Why didn't I learn this stuff when I was a kid? I could have been spared so much suffering."

Here are some stories about children who will most likely not suffer the fear of being unable to protect themselves. A nine-year-old girl, a KIDPOWER grad, who lives in the inner city told about her experience of fighting back: "A bully on the playground grabbed my hair and pulled me backwards. I stopped him with just one move. The yard-duty teacher complimented me on how I took care of myself without being a bully too. She said she wished she knew how to do that."

Another little girl, a KIDPOWER preschooler, knew to yell "No," and put her hand up in a "stop" sign when an older gentleman leaned down to give her a kiss. It may be sad to think that it's no longer OK to show affection to any child, anywhere, but it's a cause for celebration that there are more kids now who can stop unwanted touch. They are the ones that can say whether the touch is wanted or not, regardless of the motivation of the toucher.

The Impact Foundation had a graduate report that her teen-aged daughter, a graduate of Teenpower, was with a girlfriend whose car broke down. They'd been drinking and it was late. A truck pulled over to help them. They mistakenly thought it was a tow truck. They got out of the car and started to get into the vehicle when the teen who had been trained in self-defense had a strong feeling of fear. She pulled on her girlfriend to get out of the truck, now. The girlfriend ignored her and stayed inside the cab with the driver. She was beaten and raped. The teen who had training had listened to her instinct and didn't care if she embarrassed herself. Her girlfriend later said that she'd stayed in the truck because she hadn't wanted to hurt the man's feelings by acting suspicious.

Thirteen-year-old Girl Delivers Holiday Message to Thug

This story (and headline) comes from the *Daily News* of Los Angeles. "Andrea Cohn provided the giving this week, but the tall, lanky man running down the street in pain was in no shape to say 'thanks.' Pass this one around the Thanksgiving table today and watch the smiles."

Andrea, 13, was on her way to pick up her younger brother from school when in broad daylight, she saw a man leap over a fence and close in on her. "He grabbed me from behind and twisted my arms back so I wouldn't struggle," Andrea reported.

"I back-kicked him in the groin, (he let go, she turned to face him) grabbed him from the ears and kneed him in the face. Then I ran to my brother's school . . . (she looked back once) . . . He was just getting up off the ground. I saw him run in the other direction."

Andrea's parents had made sure that the family took karate lessons. Andy, Andrea's dad was quoted as saying, "Even the police officers smiled and said it was gratifying to see an incident like this where a citizen wins for a change and beats the bad guy."

It's parents like the Cohns who will usher in an age where kids and women won't be "easy marks." As a nice capper, one of the officers signed up for the same self-defense class that the Cohns had been attending.

Felon Caught When Woman in Her 50's Fights Back Against Purse-Snatcher

Susan Wilde, Director of Worth Defending, a full-force organization serving northern California, Colorado Springs, Colorado and Helena, Montana, writes a newsletter called "Amazing Feats" that carries news and success stories of graduates of the program. In the April 1994 issue, there was a story of a petite, quiet woman in her 50's who started her first class not being able to yell. But after she graduated, she was returning to her car in a parking lot in Colorado Springs when a man ambushed her as she was getting into her car. She was able to get into her car before he could attack her. She elbowed him, wasn't sure if it connected with him or with the car door, but made a lot of noise. They struggled over her purse which he was finally able to get away from her. She chased him on foot long enough to get an idea of where he was going and called the police.

While I have decided that I would probably not fight for property, what one will or will not fight for is a highly personal decision. This woman not only conquered years of fear, she was also able to act on her feelings of having been violated. While she didn't stop the robbery, she succeeded in keeping herself in control and didn't allow the incident to traumatize or victimize her as a person. As a result of her indignation, she assisted in the arrest of the robber and his cohort who were wanted on other felony counts.

Some people think that living in the Midwest or mountain states, or residing in suburban or rural areas, means they're less likely to be the victim of attacks, sexual or otherwise. They consider this type of violence more of a big-city or coastal problem. That's not true. While stranger-attacks may still be less likely in smaller communities, the most recent Department of Justice results from "Violence Against Women: Estimates from the Redesigned Survey," released on August 16, 1995, say, "There was little variation in the extent to which women living in urban, suburban, and rural locations experienced violence by intimates.

However, urban women were more likely than either suburban or rural women to experience violence by strangers." The redesigned Bureau of Justice Statistics National Crime Victimization Survey was written by Ronet Bachman, Ph.D. and Linda E. Saltzman, Ph.D., as a special report to correct an old BJS survey that vastly underestimated women's experience of violence.

Stranger or intimate, violence is violence, crime is crime and can be held off using the same skills. Also, if rural and suburban women travel, they'll need so-called stranger awareness and defense skills regardless of where they may reside. In fact, self-defense for travelers is as important as a current passport.

Preventing a Theft By a Stranger On a Train

Another Colorado Springs graduate of Worth Defending was traveling at night by train in Italy. She found an unoccupied compartment and fell asleep. Karla M. continues, "The next thing I knew, I was clasping onto a man's wrist and firmly saying, "No." I have no recollection before that moment. In fact, I woke myself with my own "No." It was 1:15 a.m. and a man was sitting next to me, going through the top pouch of my backpack. I grabbed the papers he was holding and escorted him to the door of the car, where he mumbled something about looking for cigarettes (Right). Though I will continue to travel alone and will likely go by night train, I will secure car doors from the inside to prevent events like this one. I know that the Worth Defending class has greatly affected my confidence level and my ability to take care of myself."

Married Couple Fights Off Two Assailants

Impact Personal Safety in L.A. got the credit for a married couple's ability to fight off two assailants. According to a *Los Angeles Times* story by Chip Johnson on May 23, 1994, both the wife and husband had learned how to fight. One evening, they were leaving a restaurant at night with another couple when a young man held a gun on the husband while the other assailant attempted to steal his wife's purse. She held on to her purse and kneed the man in the groin, whereupon the man holding a gun on the husband, saw the "scuffle" and began pistol-whipping the husband. His training came back, and he stopped the attack even though it had been two years since he'd been in class. The other couple retreated and used a cellular phone to call 911. The assailants gave up and ran away.

Barbara: Bravely Defending a Stranger

Barbara C. was walking to her car in a parking lot in Hollywood, California, when she saw a nightmarish urban scene: a man was beating a woman as two parking lot workers did nothing but watch. Even after entreating them to intervene, they refused. By then the man was holding the woman by the back of her head and smashing her face into the trunk of the car. Finally, Barbara couldn't stand it anymore. She yelled, "Hey, Hey, Hey — enough's enough." She got closer to them and the man started threatening her, hurling every obscenity in the book.

Undaunted by his verbal attacks, Barbara asked the woman if she wanted help, to which she said, "Please." The man turned back to the woman and struck her again. Barbara threatened to have him arrested. Then the man started moving toward her.

Barbara said, "I'm not looking for trouble," as she put her hands up in ready position, "I just want you to leave this woman alone, and I am going to call the police."

The man continued cursing Barbara and telling her what he was going to do to her. "With that he lunged and grabbed my wrist, pulling me forward to the car. I realized he intended to beat me up too. I dug in, dropped to the ground and shouted.

"He didn't know what happened — although he still had my wrist, I had dropped out of sight. He soon found out where I was — I kicked him in the right knee. I twisted my wrist from his hand and counter-grabbed. I shot my foot up between his legs into his groin, which lifted him off the ground somewhat. I let go of his wrist as he grabbed his crotch and fell to his knees. I saw that his eyes had literally rolled back into his head. He was falling toward me, and since his face was headed for my foot anyway I gave him another shot to the face. He fell back, limp. His nose was bleeding and he was completely still. At first I was afraid I had killed him, but I looked at his chest and saw he was still breathing."

Barbara stopped the assault on the woman. She took charge of the scene, told the attendants what to do and had them call the paramedics and police for the woman and her assailant. A hero in my eyes, Barbara got flack from some of her friends who called her foolish for taking such risks. She answered that she simply could not stand by and watch another person get killed.

Barbara was asked how it felt to fight an unprotected assailant. She said, "When the man fell over after I kicked him in the face I remember thinking, 'well, why are you just lying there?' In class, a Model Mugger would have been right back up. It's a different feeling — it's softer, plus I could see his face react with each kick, I could feel his knee crack, and when I kicked him in the groin I could feel everything squish. His face also realized the importance of practice with verbal attack in the classes. Instead of being victimized by it in the real-life situation, I just thought it was sort of silly. I didn't like being talked to like that, but they were just words."

Linda: Triumphing Over a Real-Life Nightmare

Recent Bureau of Justice Statistics verify that most attacks toward women are by people they know, intimates as well as acquaintances. Linda S. agreed to give her old friend a ride back to his docking place in Long Beach, California. He lived on a boat and had a serious history of mental illness including bouts with paranoia and schizophrenia. He had suffered psychotic episodes but had no history of violent incidents — until the day Linda took him home.

The friend started rambling, threatening to stab a mutual friend of theirs. Linda then realized that he had turned his hostile attentions toward her. He pulled a knife and charged her. Linda continued, "With a deep breath, I dropped to the ground. He was out of his mind, breathing hard, eyes wide and staring into nothing. He lunged with the knife, missing my left leg by inches. I delivered a strong kick to his groin. He never felt it connect. I knew then that I was in very deep trouble.

"In his frenzy, he whisked down, picked me up around the waist, and attempted to plunge the knife into my stomach — dead center. I doubled over hard and fast, instinctively putting my hands in the way. The blade hacked into my knuckles, and the first blood was drawn.

"I dropped back to the ground taking him with me, now screaming for help. It was midday, but no one was around the dock. I realized I was a goner if I didn't stop him. I punched hard again, up into his testicles. Still he came with the knife. Five more times, he lunged. Each time I turned, twisted, and moved just fast enough to remain a hair away from serious injury. We wrestled, tossed, and turned on the dock.

"I grabbed for the knife, placing my left hand on the blade. It hurt, but not as badly as I thought. Better my hand than my heart, I thought. With a death-grip on the blade, I used my other hand to come down hard on his wrist. I considered biting his wrist, but should the truth be known, I have a partial dental bridge and knew I'd lose it. Besides, pain was not affecting him. Thank God we had worked with this type of assailant in the Model Mugging class. I had been trained not to give up.

"I kicked again, with no effect. Miraculously, he lost his grip on the knife and it clattered to the dock. I kicked it into the shallow water. He ran to the edge of the dock to retrieve it and I pushed him hard over the side."

Linda lived through real-life elements of a horror film, with a very big difference. Here the woman wasn't maimed or killed by the "crazy," nor did she depend on some man to rescue her. Had Linda waited for someone to intervene and rescue her, she would have died. The police couldn't believe it when they arrived; they had to keep her friend at bay with drawn guns as they pulled him out of the water. Linda sustained minor injuries. The cuts on her hand amounting to little more than a razor cut or two.

An officer asked her, "What the hell did you do, lady?" When she described her actions and the course she'd taken, he replied solemnly, "That course and your instructor saved your life."

Elizabeth: Petite Grandmother Knocks Out Three Assailants

A sixty-year-old Asian executive, Elizabeth, had two young grandchildren visiting her in Minneapolis. She had not yet completed her full basics class when she decided to take the grandkids to see her sister in a rest home. She parked her car and got the youngest child out of the car-seat in back, when three young men approached her. She sensed danger and quickly stuck the six-month-old under the car, and took the toddler into the enclosed yard of the rest home. That done, she took a deep breath and faced her attackers.

The first boy, ostensibly the leader, told her to "suck him off." She attempted to talk him out of his plan. He threatened to kill her, so she kneeled down in front of the car where the boy was and started to unzip his pants as she hammer-fisted him in the groin. He fell down and threw up. The second boy ran in; she had time to get up and heel palm him and kick his head. She knocked him out. The third one, obviously not understanding what he was seeing, started yelling at her, "Bitch, you can't do that!" He charged her, and she heel palmed him and knocked him out with one blow. Not all success stories have that large a cast or are that dramatic, but all of these stories provide models of real people in real situations.

14

Knights We Know: The Good, The Bad, The Clueless

> *Once, in a Cabinet meeting, we had to deal with the fact that there had been an outbreak of assaults on women at night. One minister suggested a curfew; women should stay home after dark. I said, "But it's the men who are attacking the women. If there's to be a curfew, let the men stay home, not the women."*
>
> GOLDA MEIR, PRIME MINISTER OF ISRAEL, 1969-1974 (1898-1978)

The Good

Silly me, I thought that the only men who would have a negative reaction to the idea of women's self-defense would be rapists or woman-beaters. After all, logically they would be the only people to experience the business end of a well-aimed foot or elbow.

Violence prevention and a movement to create more safety in this country will not happen until more men understand the issues and become allies with our efforts to learn self-defense. However, even "good" men seem threatened by women who know how to fight back. I have now come to expect a certain reaction from the good guys when I tell them I teach self-defense. Predictably, they cover up their groin or say something like, "Gee, I'd better be nice to you!"

Well, yeah, that's a good idea. Not that they wouldn't be anyway, since these men are, in my experience, gentle and respectful — "good" people, toward men *and* women. So why do they feel threatened by women learning self-defense?

Many men think that knowing self-defense doesn't fit with "a woman's true nature"; women being prepared to fight back is seen as a radical over-reaction to the world around us. A lot of good men think they know about what women go through and attempt to apply our experiences to their own lives. Men have a tendency to not acknowledge that a woman's experience of physical safety, and the lack thereof, is unique. Because very few men of any race experience persistent and pervasive sexism and fear of male violence, a woman's fear of these twin threats is either minimized or blamed on the victim.

A close friend, Laura, wrote in response to my self-defense survey, "I think about the possibility of an attack daily. Wherever I am, I always look around. I always lock all my car doors, and all the doors in my home. I don't let my children go anywhere alone. I avoid certain events that are in less safe parts of town. I worry. I argue with my husband who thinks I'm paranoid. (So did my first husband, by the way.)" Laura's husbands are squarely in the "good" men category but are not tuned in to the very real fears nearly all women feel.

During a gathering I recently attended, several of us talked about how reluctant women are to hurt another person, even if they are being hurt themselves. I shared about how terrified I was in High School of giving a boy "blue balls." I went farther sexually than I would have otherwise out of guilt; I didn't want to hurt the guy. "Don't give me blue balls" was a form of white male blackmail in my high school.

One of the "good" men at the party scoffed and said he didn't believe boys used blue balls as a manipulation. The women were aghast, amazed, and amused at his view because *every woman present* had experienced the blue balls ploy, whether she was from South Dakota, California, or New York. I asked him, "How many boys did you date in High School?" Straight as an arrow, he laughed and let me have that argument.

Another time I was driving in Hollywood at 7:30 a.m., on my way to work. I looked in the rear-view mirror and saw a good-looking, well-dressed white man in a Mercedes behind me. When he caught my eye he put his tongue between his fingers that were in a "V" and did a lewd cunnilingus simulation. I was shocked and scared because I didn't know how long he'd been following me or if he would continue to follow me. He didn't. I related the story at another party and one of the men declared, "I don't believe you. I've never seen anything like that!" I asked him, "Why would you?" Why would sleazy, possibly dangerous, heterosexual men employ behaviors they use to intimidate women toward other males?

Many "good" men believe that if they don't see rude or threatening behavior toward women it doesn't exist. I remember playing hide 'n seek when I was four and thinking no one could see me if I closed my eyes. I grew out of it. If these guys don't see the behaviors that women complain about, they figure it must not actually happen. Most women know men who argue with them about what women do or don't experience. It's as if men don't want to let women be experts at anything, even the experience of being a female in a male dominated culture.

A male friend was at the last class of basics self-defense, where friends and family can come and view what the women have learned in their twenty hours of class time. Referred to as a graduation or demonstration, it's frequently an emotional time for people, ranging from the joy and celebration of twelve more women being able to experience less fear and more freedom, all the way to grieving for loved ones who have been hurt in real assaults. This man and I had a mutual friend whom we had come to support.

After the women fought, the instructor talked about up-coming classes, dates, times, prices. She mentioned a class called Advanced Basics where the students learn how to fight in the dark, with bed clothes covering them, in realistic "home" attack scenarios. My friend, always charming and social, leaned over to the older fellow sitting next to him and said, man to man, (wink, wink) "Sounds like married life to me," referring to sexual attacks in "home" scenarios. Yuk, yuk. His joke was in terrible taste and insensitive. The older man did not appreciate the quip and looked at him with contempt. (Women hear tasteless jokes about sexual assaults a lot and are considered humorless when they don't laugh.)

When my friend related what he'd said and the subsequent cold shoulder from the man, I said, "Don't you get it? He's probably here because a woman in his life was raped, maybe in her own bed, and this is a part of her healing." He withered.

"Oh," he said meekly.

Still not quite getting it, he proceeded to comment about the fighting women he'd just witnessed, "Well, I like the women in *Little Women*, they're nice and gentle." Exasperated, I turned to him and said, "The women in *Little Women* would have been in this class if they could have been."

Again, my friend is a decent, nice guy — just ignorant and a product of propaganda about how women ought to behave. He is tied into the romantic notion that women should be gentle Beauties, not Beauties prepared to beat back Beasts. He has suffered from the same educational and news blackout we all do. He's not seen the statistics on rape, assault, and homicide as they pertain to gender hate crimes, male-inflicted violence on women. He doesn't consider violence a big problem for women. He would never condone the violent acts against women which result in injury or death. He's just thoughtless when assessing how real the threat of such acts are to most women.

My male friend's thoughtlessness epitomizes the gap that exists between a lot of men and women in attempting to understand one another. The dangerous aspect of this gap is that it is manifested in laws, policies, and cultural products (such as movies) that are created by "good" men who do not understand the jeopardy in which women are placed simply because they are women.

I interviewed John Stoltenberg, one of my favorite feminist authors, and asked him about "good" men's reactions to self-defense for women. I related my experience of "nice" men covering their crotch or saying, "Gosh, I'd better be nice to you," when they find out I teach self-defense. What was his take on such reactions?

Stoltenberg thinks that men's experience of their vulnerability is much more constant than they are willing or able to admit. Men know in their gut that, not only are they physically vulnerable, their own hold on their imperious gender identity is tenuous. They are on guard against threat a lot.

The presumption that physical force and aggression is a male trait and one that women will therefore not use creates a man's sense of entitlement to the tools of violence. Most men can't articulate this because they haven't thought about it. But when they find out that a woman is also capable of holding her own, it's a threat. It's not a threat because they were planning on assaulting her, but because now they may have to be cautious and vulnerable around the "other" half of humanity.

So aren't there any really "good guys" out there — men who specifically defend women's rights, fight sexism and forward a feminist agenda? Yes there are. And, guess what? They struggle with put-downs from men, too. When Stoltenberg and I discussed how feminist men often get criticized for being "turncoats," he talked about how any civil rights activist needs "self-repair," a form of self-defense. He told me, "My own self-repair mantra is contained in a keynote speech I gave to a national anti-sexist men's conference in 1990 called "A Coupla Things I've been Meaning to Say About Really Confronting Male Power":

> [W]hen you really confront male power — when in your lives and in your activism you actually do something or say something that makes trouble for male supremacy — you're gonna catch shit. In fact, that's how you'll know you did something that made trouble for male supremacy: you catch shit. Don't think male power is stupid. It knows, and it lets you know it

knows, even if the folks around you are still somewhat in a daze. As profeminist men take on some of the responsibility for confronting male power, we'll also take some of the heat, some of the retaliatory anger that radical-feminist women have been getting, pretty much all alone for far too long. It's supposed to scare you and make you quit, but it's actually the best way to find out you might have hit a nerve and you might be getting somewhere. This particular revolutionary reality boils down to what I call the First Principle of Really Confronting Male Power. It's worked pretty well for radical-feminist women; it can work pretty well for us profeminist men too:

"If you ain't caught shit, you ain't done shit."

The Bad

This may seem like a perfect section to cite all of the terrible statistics about "bad" men. There are other books for that. This book is about awakening the warrior inside you so that you don't become a statistic of a "bad" man. The odds are high that a woman or child will be prey to a "bad" man. Women often ask me about statistics on violence when weighing a decision to learn self-defense. I used to respond with the statistics I knew. Now, rather than parrot statistics, I ask women, "Are you playing the odds?" I urge women to stop gambling and focus on changing themselves into people who can confront the possibility of violence.

So far, changing violent men seems to be a futile exercise, similar to the attempt to change the properties of water. You can contain water, you can control it to a certain degree, you can probably avoid ever having to be around it. Similarly, you can contain violent men in prisons, control them through drugs and jail terms, and on the extreme end, you could possibly avoid being around men in any meaningful way. But what kind of life would that be? Doesn't it make more sense to change the woman from a non-swimmer to a swimmer? She, after all, has the most to gain, the most freedom to enjoy from the learning. Doesn't it make more sense to teach women what to do in the event of being confronted with a violent man?

People don't change unless they are motivated to change. It's futile to try to change men who are violent unless they themselves desire the change. It isn't futile to provide the opportunity to learn and change for women who have the desire to stop limiting their lives based on the fear of violence.

One thing is clear. The men intent on hurting women or who view violence toward women and children as a "right," aren't going to stop hurting women and children, no matter how nice we are. Their victims' behavior has nothing to do with their behavior. We can't change them, we can only change ourselves. It's the only real power we have. We need to let the experts in human behavior worry about changing violent men's behavior. Meanwhile, we need to concentrate on altering women's romantic notion that they must depend on men for violence prevention.

The Clueless

Whether men are "good" or "bad," the majority of them are clueless regarding what it feels like to be a woman in a male-dominated culture. By "clueless" I mean ignorant. Ignorance is not a fatal flaw; it can be overcome through education. Therefore, as an educational tool, I offer a parallel that will hopefully enlighten our brothers with respect to a woman's experience of male power, intimidation, and violence. Nothing I say in the following section should be construed as indifference or mockery toward rape or any kind of physical assault toward anyone, male or female.

What if men were kicked in the groin at the same rate that women are raped? Laws and attitudes would change. I'll grant that rape and kicks to the groin are not exactly parallel acts. Still, I find the comparison useful because the two acts of violence involve sexual and reproductive organs and can affect the way the victim relates to normal sexual activity and the other sex forever.

If Men Got Thwopped

There is no word in the English language that means "a hit or kick to the groin." For the sake of this conversation, I'll coin a word for it. "Thwop" is good. It sounds like a good solid hit to soft tissue, and it's a terrific opportunity to use onomatopoeia in real life.

Let's play "switcheroo" for awhile, shall we?

What would happen if a young man with a muscular body, skimpy t-shirt and tight jeans scratched his nether parts, muttered, "Nice tits" and a young woman saw and heard him. Let's say her reaction was to walk over to him and thwop him? Could she say, "He was asking for it?"

Or let's say that a sorority had over the years developed a tradition of getting a freshman boy sloppy drunk and taking turns thwopping him in a dark room. Could he prove who thwopped him? Why was he there in the first place? Why was he drinking with a lot of young women around?

Could he in fact prove that he had been thwopped? Perhaps he had fallen on a bicycle as he rode over a speed bump? Why wasn't he wearing a strap or cup? We shouldn't jump to conclusions and ruin young women's careers over the word of a slutty jock. And you know how them males really are, "They all want it, really. Otherwise, why would they act the way they do?" We heard that some freshman boy had yelled, "Thwop!" in high school and gotten the Homecoming Queen unfairly suspended.

Or what would the Senate do if they heard testimony that 78 men are thwopped per hour every day, without fail, in this country? That 84 percent of those thwops go unreported because the victim is too ashamed to tell anyone?

We've been trying to educate men to not be ashamed of thwop and to report it, but it's difficult. Thwop victims feel humiliated and are afraid of being made fun of or of feeling like they could have prevented it.

Thwop prevention has to start in grade school. Little girls have to be taught that it's not OK to hurt little boys even though the boys give ambiguous messages. You know how boys are. They wear tight pants, loose pants, no shirts, loose shorts, bathing trunks, clothes in general, because they want to be attractive. But they don't want to be kicked, even though they act like they'd like to be kicked. Some males actually do fantasize about being thwopped but you've got to be gentle in fantasy thwopping. But if you get too rough, that's OK, because they really want it.

Imagine the headline, "Palm Beach Florida Man Charges Woman With Date Thwop." Date or acquaintance thwopping is on the rise but it's very difficult to prove. Some guys are interested in making out, some get into petting, but when it comes to "going all the way," well, they'd like to stop but once a woman gets too worked up she just can't be held accountable for what happens next. Thwop.

Some states don't recognize marital thwop. Some women feel that if they've married someone they should be able to have sex any time or just force their husband when he's holding back. Thwop.

Gang thwop is probably the most horrible of crimes and is on the rise because of various societal factors. When the economy gets bad, men tend to become scapegoats, and the incidents of sexual violence against them goes up, including multiple thwops. Sloppy, thwoppy seconds are a real turn-on in a female bonding ritual sense.

We must be wary of false accusations of thwop. You know, these guys, they think they can get some attention and get a woman in trouble just because the date went badly. Or just because the sex that night wasn't good, he yells "Thwop." What's a gal going to do with these wily boys? You know, these guys, they really do deserve whatever they get; and, besides, they really do want it.

Don't despair though because there's some good work being done. There are thwop crisis hot-lines where recovering thwop victims can counsel those who've been thwopped. It's important that those who've been thwopped have someone to share with, talk about their concerns of impotence, infertility, attractiveness after thwop. Unfortunately, funding thwop hot-lines is difficult because it's not perceived as being as important as other philanthwopic concerns.

It's truly a shame that most of the men who have been thwopped find it hard to trust women again. Every female becomes a potential thwoppist in his eyes and the thwop survivor unconsciously bends forward and covers his crotch whenever a woman makes an unpredictable move. It's hell going through life mistrusting 50 percent of the population and involuntarily bowing before them even though you don't even like them.

Fortunately, with gentleness and understanding, the women who relate to thwop victims can eventually regain their confidence. Tragically, there's no guarantee that he may not be thwopped again because as we all know, "It's a jungle out there" — one wrong move and you can be thwopped.

Experts recommend many solutions: that men restrict their clothing to modest styles and incorporate thick padding in the crotch; stay indoors at night and make sure they don't send double messages to women; that men should stay attractive, (although that makes some women want to kick them) but not too attractive (which makes other women want to kick them.)

Men should also become highly sensitive to what women are thinking and doing and then be responsible for whatever consequences there are. The latter is the best approach because that way women won't have to change, which makes it easier on everyone. It's also advised that if a man is being thwopped, he not fight back because that just might make the thwoppist angrier. Who knows? She might kick him in the head and kill him. If he's getting thwopped, a man might as well relax and enjoy it. Better thwopped than dead.

OK, OK, I've made my point. I'm not suggesting that women begin thwopping and pillaging. I'm not advocating squads of gonad-kicking bitches from hell or wanton soprano-makers.

I *am* suggesting that we tell the good men to get the clueless men clued in now — and let the "bad" beware. Criminally assaultive behavior will be dealt a hard thwop by trained women who are taking their safety into their own hands — and feet. Maybe if more first-time rapists were greeted with a sound thwop, there would be no second or third or twelfth time.

Hurting the Other Sex "Down There"

If you have never witnessed a "group groin groan," try talking with a group of men about what it feels like for a man to get hit hard between the legs. The emotional and visceral reactions that explode will obliterate the stereotypes about men being unemotional and non-expressive. Men grimace, scream, and double over from the mere idea of getting hit in the testicles. They love their gonads more than their favorite team or automobile. (Women have a lot to learn from men, because we don't seem to love our bodies as much as they love theirs.) Conversely, insensitive men's reaction to hearing about rape frequently borders on hearing the game score of a team they aren't too interested in. Why is there such a discrepancy between a man's fear of being kicked in the groin and his lack of sensitivity regarding a woman's fear of rape?

Girls and women are told to never, ever hit a boy or man "down there," so we don't. What if little boys and men also learned to never, ever assault a girl or woman "down there"? And what if males were told that if they acted violently toward girls or women, they would receive a hit or kick to their testicles?

We're told that incest and rape are taboo. That's not exactly accurate. It has been taboo to speak of incest and rape until recent years, but the actions themselves have not been taboo. The real taboo action in society is to land a good hit or kick between a man's legs. That is the true taboo. So taboo that there's not a word for it in English. Rape and incest happen behind closed doors. I seriously doubt that there are hidden groin-kicking secrets lurking in families all over the world. There is a strong code that says that hitting a man below the belt is absolutely forbidden, for men or for women.

"Hitting below the belt" is a euphemism for being unfair. I propose a shift in consciousness: hitting below the belt is not only fair, but effective in self-defense. Perhaps we should think of testicles as our friends — allies in self-protection.

I Was Date-Duped

When I was a Junior in college at the University of California, Irvine, I was asked out by a dark, tall and handsome upper-classman. He was probably good, bad, and clueless, looking back now. We went to dinner in Newport Beach. We came home to my ocean-front apartment on the Balboa Peninsula. My roommate had returned to central California for the weekend so we were alone. My hunk of a date had too much to drink. We made out for awhile which was fine with me. I did like him and thought that I wanted to see him again. I wasn't, even though I was turned on, interested in getting naked with him. I didn't want to sleep with him. He had other ideas.

I wanted to stop making out. He pinned me to the back of the couch. I thought he was kidding so I continued to kiss for a bit and he let up on the pressure. Then I decided that enough was enough. I told him that I needed to get up to study in the morning. He argued with me that it was Saturday and that I didn't really need to study. I got up — he pulled me down. That's when I started to get scared.

He was 6'2" and weighed around 190. I was 5'4" and weighed 125 pounds. I assessed my situation. He'd paid for dinner. There has been — and it's still present for many young people — an unspoken rule that if a guy pays, he expects to be paid back with sex. So much for gentlemen's codes. I had no idea what to do if he got violent. He hadn't gotten violent and I didn't know for sure that he would. However, I was not willing to take the risk of violence by putting up a fight. What the hell, I wasn't a virgin anyway. I was on birth control. I decided that it would be easier, and *safer,* to sleep with the guy. That was *safe sex* 70's style. Sleep with him and get it over with.

My fear of the unknown, my lack of nerve sprang from ignorance and a lack of confidence in being able to handle a situation that might have gotten out of hand. Looking back, my behavior was totally rational for who I was and what I knew and didn't know at the time. As far as I can tell, so was his behavior. After all, he'd been raised as a boy in this culture which says over and over that girls' "No" really means "Yes," and that his biological urges weren't his responsibility. Whether his urges were or weren't his responsibility, by virtue of the way we were raised his urges became my responsibility and my problem.

I had no confidence and no courage. My lack of courage came from having no point of reference from any source at all that I could take on a possibly violent man who out-sized me. I had no precedent provided by family or society. Plus I didn't want him to think I was a bitch and to spread it around that I was. How sad. How discouraging. How dangerous. I was afraid of rape, ridicule and rejection, so I didn't hand him any consequences for disrespecting my "No." Just like in the movies.

I listen to the debates about date rape these days and I rarely hear any mention of the fact that women are not taught how to fight off a guy. Self-defense is a very big chunk that's missing from the dialogue. I also know that the language is sorely lacking when talking about gender relations.

Was the guy a jerk? Yes. Would he have wanted a loved-one — a sister, niece, a girl he loved — to be out with someone like him? I doubt it. I gambled that having sex with him would be less dangerous than not "agreeing" to having sex with him. There's no way that I could say if I was right or wrong about that. It was my instinct and my judgment call.

There are people who would identify my college date as a date rape. I wouldn't. Was it full and freely given sexual expression? No. I'd rather not have done it. I thought less of myself as a result of the encounter. It was damaging to me as a human being. It assaulted my dignity. But rape? No, there's no way that my date raped me even though I felt raped. There is no language for a "not rape, but not consensual, mutual sex," and that is the area that gives everyone the most trouble. It is also the problem area in office gender politics. The cultural difference between men and women is vast when it comes to subtle and almost invisible intimidation.

This is a difficult area for most people. I do not want anything I'm going to say to be accidentally interpreted as "blaming the victim." I have nothing but compassion for the woman who tells me she had sex because she was afraid, or that her boss feels her butt, or her co-worker drools and makes lewd noises at her. She shouldn't have to deal with her sexual identity in a work context, but unfortunately, deal with it we must. I'm not surprised either when I ask her if she did anything about the unwanted attention and she says, "No." Weren't we taught to ignore the bullies so they'd go away when we were in grade school? Or perhaps she considered alternatives. She, like I did, could have weighed the consequences and decided her best option — perhaps her financial survival depended on keeping that job — would be to stay out of confrontation and to just put up with it.

Laws, lawsuits, policies are important as back-up but those of us on the front-lines can't depend solely on after-the-fact remedies. We've got to start exploring and experimenting and preparing ourselves for incidents as they are happening. To end sexual assaults, verbal through physical, whether they are in the office, in our homes or in public, we've got to have an approach that includes empowering women to stand up, before, during and after.

It's so seductive to put the attention on men. But the harassers and assailants don't want to change. If they wanted to change, they would. It's vital to point out who's doing what to whom. It's vital to identify manipulation, to point out when the guards of the status quo, "don't get it." However, where we will get results as women is to empower ourselves, financially, physically and emotionally.

A lot of feminist detractors are critical of women for being "whiners." I understand that complaint. I don't agree with it but I do understand it. It does smack of "cry baby," all the epithets that are associated with the behavior of children who can't take care of problems themselves and have to run and "tell." I don't think anyone really likes a cry baby or a snitch. However, it's one thing to dislike someone for being a whiner and it's quite another to give her some tools besides her culturally encouraged helplessness. If she's been trained to whine, she'll whine. If she's convinced that her situation is hopeless, she'll behave like a victim. Or if she thinks that the key to changing something is to change someone other than herself, she'll be frustrated.

A large part of Katie Roiphe's book *The Morning After: Sex, Feminism and Fear on Campus* is a put-down of what she considers victim mentality feminists. While I found Roiphe's book useful for understanding some of the campus controversy, she offered nothing to solve the problems we face as women and men trying to get along. Ms. Roiphe got carried away with the strokes she got from the male establishment for being an anti-feminist feminist. I do believe we need to address the way we raise girls to be victims. Are we so surprised that they behave like victims when they're confronted with harassment, crimes against women and sex discrimination?

No, I was not raped in college although there are states where my experience could be interpreted as rape. I defended myself from consequences I was too fearful to confront. Perhaps I was duped, not by John (not his real name) but by a body of tradition that hid my ability to fight back from me. I was date-duped — not a good phrase but you catch my drift.

Had I known how to fight — had I known that there were any number of things I could have done to "turn off" my suitor, I could have avoided being duped. Bodies are very easy to cool down when one person doesn't want to have sex. I could have lightly hit his groin and he probably would have been more interested in getting away from me than getting in my bed. I could have pinched him. I could have hit him in the throat. I could have shoved him away if he persisted. Worse case scenario, had he gotten me down on the ground and attempted a forcible rape, I could have kicked the shit out of him. Any woman can. We have been duped. The good news is that self-defense is a good way to un-dupe ourselves. We must be brave and we can be. There must be consequences for messing with women that we administer ourselves.

So many of us thought that women would gain equality when we insisted on education and literacy, or when we finally took the vote. Most of us know that was an illusion. The vote was an important first step toward solving an iceberg of issues. The next step, or should I say kick, toward equality is equal access to peace without fear of physical harm.

I suspect that many men are unconsciously afraid that if we women got more power, they would be subjected to cruelty just as women, with men in power, have been. I don't believe that women would reverse roles. The fear that women will retaliate in kind may be the product of guilt for the way men have treated the "other," whether the "other" was a different color, religion, or gender. Thankfully, there are a lot of men in the world who are ready to stand shoulder-to-shoulder with women to make gender-hate violence stop. Education is powerful. Sisterhood is powerful. So is real brotherhood. After all, we are all part of the same family.

Unfortunately, as you'll see in the next chapter, most of our sisters and very few of our supportive brothers make history, or get the amount of media attention meted out to our misogynistic or criminal "brothers."

15

The King's Messenger and Village Crier: News and History

Have you ever noticed that our news stories and language hides a rapist's responsibility in rape? The rapist is missing. We say, "She was raped," passive language, rather than a man raped her. We need to stop that. We need to change the way we speak so that we're clear about who's doing what to whom.

PAXTON QUIGLEY, AUTHOR OF *ARMED AND FEMALE*,
AT 1993 IMPACT PERSONAL SAFETY GRADUATION IN LOS ANGELES
DURING A CONVERSATION.

"Woman Disables Rapist" Rarely Makes the News

Myths, the formative stories that are the foundation of society, are made up of news, history, and stories that are selected by the "King," our male-dominated culture, and delivered by the "King's messenger and Village Crier" in order to pass on values, beliefs and warnings.

In a recent example, people were warned via the news about the dangers of pit bulls (Staffordshire Terriers) and now take precautions to stay out of their way. Pit bulls were not newsworthy until a few of them used their super-charged jaws to maul the limbs of a few people. I remember the days when people weren't automatically afraid of pit bulls. In fact, most folks didn't know a pit bull from a weeny dog. It's not that the dogs changed overnight. Pit bulls simply hadn't been in the news yet.

Public awareness changed with news coverage. Pit bulls are now feared as much, if not more, than Dobermans. Concurrently, pit bull breeding and sales sky-rocketed. The news stories on pit bulls served to advertise the pit bulls' ferocity. Those in the market for a vicious dog ran out to buy them. Those afraid of dogs or confronting dogs had seen the "ads," that is, the stories, and knew to be afraid of pit bulls.

A journalistic fundamental is that "Man Bites Dog" is a rare, and thus a better story than "Dog Bites Man." "Woman Disables Rapist," now that's a very rare story. It's not that women never disable rapists. Rape attempts simply don't make the news as much as completed rapes. I wonder how many reported incidents of successful defenses it will take for women to be as feared as pit bulls in situations of contemplated or actual sexual assault?

How many "Beauty Bites Beast" headlines do we need before would-be woman bashers, rapists and sexual assailants at least consider that they may be seriously damaged if they attempt to hurt a woman? How many stories of a woman defending herself successfully do we need for other women to learn that they can be effective, dangerous in fact, to a potential perpetrator of violent crimes against women? Right now the current state of news is a virtual advertisement for how easy it is for a man to rape a woman and how hard it is for a woman to defend herself.

Most people have a healthy respect for strange dogs regardless of their breed or size. Humans don't call the dogs "people haters" either because they growl or distrust a new person. Why is it then, with the statistics of male-inflicted injury on females, that women who complain and attempt to eradicate violence against women are frequently accused of being "man-haters"?

Women need to reserve the right to be wary and to growl until they know that a man they feel threatened by is OK. We also need to undo social conditioning that says anger or physical defense is "unladylike." Violent men need to be aware that more and more of us will "bite" and do everything in our power to protect ourselves and other women. Some statistics say that, on average, rapists rape twelve times before they are caught. More of us need to say, "The fuck stops here," and not inadvertently put a subsequent woman in the position of having to deal with "the man that got away."

Hopefully, if enough of us "bite," and bite hard enough to gain media attention, we'll have less occasion to have to. I never dreamed that I would devote my life to having women treated as respectfully as dogs.

Stories About Women's Self-Defense Might Give Women "The Wrong Idea"

I was appalled during a success story interview with Nancy (Chapter 13) when she recalled what happened when she told a writer friend about her encounter with the verbally abusive man who turned out to be a convicted serial rapist. It was a serious commentary about the power of the "King," who decides what is news and what is not. Nancy was rightly thrilled that she had successfully kept a dangerous man away from her by using what she'd learned in class about verbal self-defense. The friend was inspired and felt it was important to let others know about the successful defense and how simple it was. She wrote it up for her paper, a local weekly "throw away," and turned it in on time for the deadline.

Her managing editor, a white man, rejected it, saying,"I don't want to give women the idea that they can defend themselves." Pardon me? Was he afraid that the story would give us poor little beauties the false hope that we might be able to depend on ourselves instead of a man or the police to protect us? I can't imagine an editor not running a story about someone, female or male, who'd saved themselves from drowning. "What if it gives people the idea they can save themselves from drowning?" This incident is an example of dangerous censorship. It gives rise to other questions. How many other stories are missing? How many have been rejected for lack of interest or fear of "giving us ideas" that we supposedly cannot handle?

Another publishing anecdote, this one related to book publishing, gives us yet another glimpse of what may be "missing" in print and why. It concerns the controversial feminist philosopher, activist, and writer, Andrea Dworkin. She told me about a "gentleman" publishing executive who was anything but gentle. He was the head of the paperback division of the publishing house that published the hardback version of *Our Blood*, a collection of Dworkin's lectures.

After reviewing *Our Blood* for a possible paperback version, Mr. Gentleman Publisher walked into Dworkin's editor's office. He said he wouldn't make it a paperback because, "She left out how gentle men can be!" and threw the manuscript at the editor's head. How fascinating that it's women who have the reputation for making decisions based on emotion.

And how do women's self-defense stories fare in the broadcast media? The person who decides where the resources, reporters, and remote units go that day is actually deciding what's news from his perspective. Yes, this position — whether it's producer, editor, or managing editor is usually a he. Rarely do broadcast media report the news from a female perspective.

In *Backlash: The Undeclared War Against American Women,* Susan Faludi nailed the media when she exposed the overblown, scientifically inaccurate story of the so-called "marriage crunch" that got beaten to death by every news outlet in the country. TV writers of sitcoms and dramas even got into the act. Faludi's angle in *Backlash,* was that any news that discouraged career women was the news that got "aired" and printed. Briefly, the news purveyors warned professional women about how their chances of marriage were extremely low if they waited to establish their career first. I was a reporter at an NBC affiliate at the time and we were inundated with every pundit's take on the "findings." Headlines screamed about the "new" cost of career — spinsterhood!

STUDY FINDS THAT SELF-PROTECTIVE SKILLS INCREASE WOMEN'S CONFIDENCE IN THEIR ABILITY TO CONTROL THE THREAT OF SEXUAL ASSAULT. That was the headline on a press release in 1990 announcing a study published in the March 1990 issue of the *Journal of Personality and Social Psychology.* "Mechanisms Governing Empowerment Effects: A Self-Efficacy Analysis," by Elizabeth M. Ozer and Albert Bandura of Stanford University was good news for women. They could positively and quantitatively impact their psychological lives through the "Model Mugging" form of self-defense training.

The release said: "Ozer & Bandura found that the self-defense program substantially enhanced the women's perceived capability to defend themselves physically if attacked, to exercise precaution in different social situations, to engage in various everyday activities, and to control negative thinking about sexual assault.

"Women judged themselves much less vulnerable to sexual assault and lower in anxiety. They expanded the number of activities that they engaged in and reduced the number of everyday activities that they wanted to do but had previously avoided out of fear of sexual assault. (For example, outdoor exercise during the day or attending evening concerts or movies.)"

Good news, right? Certainly, had the Ozer & Bandura study made the national news, many women would have registered in classes nationwide, and that would have saved lives and reduced injury. Dr. Bandura is such a big name in social psychology, that mental health professionals would have taken it as important, and referred more clients to full-force "Model Mugging" programs.

The Ozer & Bandura study press release is exactly the kind of story that I, as a commentator/reporter, had I seen it, would have fought to cover. Concurrently, it was the kind of release that a number of my former supervising producers — kings in their little kingdoms all — would have declined to cover. They would have won since they had the clout and reporters don't. If it was a "big" news day when the press release came out, a positive study would take a back seat to "hot" news. Women's safety, the prevention of violence and reduction of women's stress is not sexy or "hot." Sadly, so many news decision-makers are completely out of touch with the concerns of women at best, or have a "backlash" agenda at worst.

Why didn't that press release, which was released widely, get picked up as the news that it truly was? The Ozer & Bandura study could impact the quality of many women's lives. The marriage crunch story was simply a frivolous exercise in proving how bad "women's lib" was for the well-being of women. Can you discern the decision-makers' bias in the choice of which story would get coverage and which wouldn't?

Much of the "news" is really "olds"; in other words, it's the same old story that gets rehashed and replayed with new characters in the cast. TV news in particular is after the most entertaining, the most visually stimulating news it can get. Since news organizations are in the ratings wars all the time, they must constantly out-do, out-visualize, and out-excite themselves and competing stations and networks.

The images that the media capture are so powerful we almost forget that it's we who create reality not the coverage. But there are serious questions about whether coverage may actually help create reality. We virtually "advertise" that crime does pay or at least it garners a lot of attention. We promote how violent men are, and how weak women are. We reinforce old ideas in words and pictures.

TV also creates reality for children. A friend's daughter watched the President's state of the union address. My friend told her, "Sweetheart, you could be President some day."

Her four-year-old daughter said, "Oh, no, Mommy, no I couldn't."

My friend was taken aback. She's been raising her little girl to have all possibilities available to her. "Why do you say that?"

She said, referring to the cut-aways to Congress and assembled guests, "There aren't many girls there at all. And look at all the boys," (Clinton, Gore, Gingrich, et.al).

How does my friend's daughter feel? What does she think when she sees how easy it is for a man to physically overpower a woman, whether it's in "entertainment" or the news? As they say, "A picture paints a thousand words."

Yes, but, the cameras are only picking up reality, right? Yes and no. Cameras have to be selective. Yes, a wide shot reflects the bigger picture, but the medium and close shots are for details and are highly selective. It's possible to skew news simply by which shots you call. The shots then determine the writing, because TV writing is driven by visuals.

Here's a perfect example of TV propaganda that gets made all the time. I attended the first Tailhook convention after the infamous one in Las Vegas with all of the sexual scandals. I was there in San Diego covering the convention for my weekly column in the *Pasadena Weekly*. There were news crews from local TV stations elbowing each other to get coverage on the march and demonstration outside the convention center where the Tailhook attendees were convening. The demonstration was made up of mostly women, and a few gay men protesting anti-gay military policies.

The women in the crowd of demonstrators were of every shape, size, style, and age. I heard one producer yell to his camera man to "Get that fat, ugly one with her mouth wide open!" The producer could just as easily have had his camera guy "Get that sweet Grandma with her granddaughters," or "Get the yuppie couple," or "the group of college-age girls drinking beer and having a good time."

I have witnessed an anti-feminist bias in most of the media for which I've worked. This bias creates and reinforces a feminist profile that is scary to many mainstream women whose main focus has been on beauty and its pursuit. The women they see in the news identified as feminists tend to be of the "beastly" type, at least by current beauty standards preferred by mainstream men. Many women have seen feminists on the news and surmise that women become feminists because they are not beautiful. Since the idea of being unattractive is threatening to most women in our culture, they run in the other direction if someone thinks they may be associated with a group of unattractive women. Men also decide that women become feminists because they can't "cut it" in the beauty department, and then take it out on men.

In fact, there are as many kinds of feminists as there are people. But many women who are feminists stay "in the closet" about their feminism because of a hostile environment largely generated by the media. The next few times there are stories on women's issues, look at the pictures and see if you don't start to see pattern emerging. The feminist in the picture may be either caught in an unflattering way or be a stereotype.

I had a managing editor once who thought it was clever and funny to send an "anti-feminist" woman to a National Woman's Political Caucus meeting. The anti-feminist reporter called me to interview me as a feminist. Before she started her questions I asked her to tell me what she'd read about the women's movement. One book. She'd read reviews of some books written about women's issues. That's it.

Needless to say, the reporter's "anti-feminist" questions were completely biased. There were no simple answers because the questions were so ignorant; to even begin to give an answer I felt I had to educate her and the reader. If I were a managing editor I wouldn't send an anti-car rally reporter to cover a car rally, *unless* I wanted to ridicule car rallies.

Who Creates News Reality?

Not all coverage is as blatantly biased as my managing editor's assignment to the female anti-feminist reporter. Some is unconsciously biased because of natural human mistakes, ignorance, and a desire to relate to the already familiar. Since there is practically a blackout on women's issues and women in general in education, people tend to be less interested in women and their accomplishments and concerns. A vicious cycle ensues.

I was particularly disheartened by the coverage that the U.N. Conference on Women in Beijing in 1995 didn't receive from the U.S. press. I was there as press, so obviously I couldn't cover the coverage here at home. (A positive exception to the poor coverage was CNN's Judy Woodruff's excellent series on what happened in Beijing.)

Who creates reality? I saw camera crews prowling the fairgrounds where the non-governmental conference was held, "looking" for news. A-hah! One news crew found a demonstration. In no time, all the news crews would be there covering the demonstration. Demonstrations make "good" TV; that is, action, loud noise, and conflict. Peaceful negotiating, talking about solutions, and networking make "bad" TV; that is, little or no action, low talking and conflict resolution.

While this is a generality, crews are made up of men. Many of them have covered sports and wars, "boy" activities. My theory is that they don't know how to cover women's activities. They don't know the issues, they don't know the questions, they don't have the data.

Imagine that I was assigned to cover an American football game. I know nothing, nada, about football. Using what I'd know, I'd probably go to that which I know something about. My piece on football would be interviews with cheerleaders, other women who are clueless about football, the mothers, wives and sisters of football players and perhaps the design of the stadium. Or I'd make my piece about learning the fundamentals. I would simply do my best, but it would short shrift those who know football. Football experts would feel frustrated or bored by my coverage.

Or if I had to cover the game with no preparation, I'd say something like, "They ran out on the grass, they got together in a circle, grunted, yelled and then lined up. One guy threw the ball between his legs and another caught and threw it. Sometimes they kicked and they all ran like crazy knocking each other over. And then it was over, every body cheered on one side, the others weren't happy. And then they all went home."

That is what it's like to send people out to cover stories about women's issues who couldn't care less or know nothing about the topic. They don't know the language, they don't know what the "news" is, they don't know the connections with other issues. On an international level some male crews are, by custom, not even allowed to speak to women. How could they possibly get an objective, informed story even if the desire to do so existed?

I was standing on a walkway in Beijing when a woman from Southeast Asia approached me.

"You are press?" she asked.

"Yes, I am," I replied.

She grabbed my hand and said, "Follow me, please."

I asked her why. She said that her group was having a demonstration *for the press.* (My emphasis.) I asked her if her delegation had planned on demonstrating before they came to China.

"No," she said, "We decided to demonstrate because that's what American journalists like."

That is why the coverage of the U.N. Conference on Women was so sophomoric. The news that came in from the Beijing conference was more or less about the weather, about how some groups didn't get along and who was demonstrating about what. "And then it was over, every body cheered on one side, the others weren't happy. And then they all went home."

There is no news conspiracy. That's the really hard part. There's no trilateral-like commission set up to keep women out of the news. No whispering, plotting, scheming group of white men who don't want to give women's progress its due. We are missing from the news for reasons that are so ingrained, so invisible, so pervasive that it would almost be a relief to discover a conspiracy. Conspiracies can be tracked down and exposed. Newspapers, magazines, and books reinforce the perceived strengths and weaknesses of men and women. It's the same old story. The information and entertainment businesses are controlled predominantly by white males. Now there are fewer and fewer, larger and larger corporations that own all of the news and entertainment outlets. This is a serious threat to democracy in general, and to those who have traditionally been out of the power loop specifically.

I am constantly on the lookout for non-fiction accounts of women's successful defenses, known in the news business as "attempted rapes and murders." I am happy to say I have seen a slight increase in these stories, both in the broadcast and print media, but I'm not sure if it's because I am on the lookout for them or if there actually have been more. Sadly, there's no way to know how many "success" stories are missing. That they are missing doesn't mean there aren't any. It just means someone decided it wasn't news. Not news to whom?

We're still more likely to get a sensational story like that of Lorena Bobbitt, the stereotype of the "castrating bitch" who personifies men's nightmares, than stories about women who fight back in the moment and prevail against a violent attack. Women want to read about other women who successfully, and peacefully, dissuade a would-be assailant. What an inspiration it would be if there were more such stories! What a rip-off that we so rarely read about them or see them on TV. It's up to us as consumers to insist that editors run the pieces that affect our lives. Phone calls and letters do make a difference.

Today's News Is Tomorrow's History

So where does the "history" in this chapter's title come in? History is the news of yesterday. We only know what we know from the past because someone thought it was important, entertaining, or informative enough to warrant passing on to their contemporaries, and then their descendants, and so it was memorized, written about, or recorded. Missing stories in the newspaper affect historical researchers in the future. If the story isn't there, it might as well never have happened. It didn't happen if it's missing, and the vicious cycle continues: future generations will know less about foremothers than they do about forefathers.

Picture our prehistoric ancestors. There's a big fire, everyone's gathered around storytelling, listening and memorizing so they can pass them on and eventually carve them or write them down.

"Tell the one about the Amazons!" Everyone agrees. "Yes, that's a good one, how brave, how valiant, how ferocious those women were." Everyone loves the stories of Amazons, the foremothers who made the world safer for everyone.

At what point did the story elder say, "No, the council decided to not pass on the story of the Amazons anymore. We wouldn't want the women to get the idea that they can defend themselves." If children grew up and heard Amazon stories as frequently as King Arthur stories, do you really think girls would accept victimization as readily as they do now?

There is a body of stories about strong women that have been relegated to shadow legends if they remain at all. We see glimpses of these stories in the wings of the main stage events of men's stories. The women who were bravest, the most defiant, are most likely the ones who are now rejected and ridiculed the most. "Jezebel" or "Amazon" are not usually flattering names when used to describe modern women. Our missing myths are necessary for our full participation in the world. Is it possible that the David and Goliath story was originally a story about a small woman and a large man? It's certainly a story of brain over brawn, about size not being the determining factor in a physical confrontation.

"What you don't know won't hurt you." What a beastly saying. Don't buy it. If women were better armed with stories of our warrior heritage, and were thus inspired to tap our natural drive to defend ourselves, incidents of male violence would harm far fewer of us.

16

The King's Entertainment: Film, TV, Music and Fashion

The only women in my movies are naked or dead.

ATTRIBUTED TO VARIOUS
HOLLYWOOD MOVIE PRODUCERS.

The Ugly Step-Family of "Entertaining" Violence

"On a typical TV drama, male characters outnumber females by three or four to one, but when there's violence, women are more often portrayed as victims. In turn, women perceive the world as fraught with more danger than really exists," says George Gerber, professor emeritus of communications at the Annenberg School for Communication in Philadelphia.

Dr. Gerber coined the term "Mean World Syndrome" which is his term for a person's feeling, more commonly a woman's, that the world is dangerous. It is particularly frightening for women, who usually believe there's nothing they can do in the face of male violence. If you factor in how many times men of color commit violent crimes in our "entertainment," it's easy to see why racism and sexism are so enmeshed and imbedded in our culture. The truth is that there is more intra-racial than inter-racial violence when it comes to male-on-female assaults.

Particularly damaging in film and TV renderings of women and men is how entertainment violence distorts reality. Growing up watching what I've watched, no wonder I used to believe that women can't fight back and that men are invulnerable. How would men like it if the bulk of our entertainment consisted of men being raped, or kicked in the nuts and being saved by women? I don't think they'd like it. Well, boys, we don't like it either.

We have debunked the fiction that women must be helpless financially, so why do we cling to the stories that women are physically incapable of fighting? Because fighting women aren't pretty or romantic. A passive woman is a beautiful and proper woman, dead or alive. She remains a lady even if it costs her her life.

Women are sick and tired of being victims. That is one reason "Thelma & Louise" struck such a deep chord. We thrilled to the cinematic image of "domesticated" women who rebelled — who said essentially, "Give me liberty or give me death." Isn't it interesting that the Patrick Henry quote enacted by women would be perceived by some males as man-hating rather than freedom-loving?

When there are physical fights involving women, what does it communicate to women in the audience that screen women rarely finish or complete the fight? I say that its discouraging and disheartening. Male viewers are given numerous examples of men having to tough it out — of having to fight, literally and figuratively, to make something happen. Sometimes the male protagonists win, sometimes they lose. But most often, the women give up. It's a disheartening message and it's got to be changed. We desperately need more images of more fighting women, not just the "Terminator 2" Linda Hamilton types who have access to weapons only available in fiction, but the smart women who use what they've already got, whether it's a balls-seeking knee, a sharp elbow or very quick wits.

Just in case you are skeptical that movies make a difference in real-life assaults, I'll tell you about a male friend's encounter. He was a bit tipsy and went to the parking lot after having a few happy-hour drinks. All of a sudden his car door was pulled open and a man had a knife at his throat. My friend, a gentle sort, was quiet and asked the man what he wanted. He said, "I want your car but I want some 'fun' first." My buddy, less tipsy yet still under the influence remembers asking himself, "What would James Bond do?" He moved his head away from the knife fast, shoved the man out with both legs, shut the door and drove off.

Who is the female equivalent of James Bond when we're in a pinch? Maybe Xena: Warrior Princess, perhaps Buffy, the Vampire Slayer. No matter who it may be for you, a female warrior image can and does make a difference to women's perception of female defensive ability.

Stories Missing in Action

"Cinderella" was the first movie I remember seeing. What a tough act to follow. Everyone I knew wanted a blue ball gown and handsome prince after that animated lesson in proper femininity. We would never measure up to Cinderella's or any other screen character's beauty. Beauties were in abundance in entertainment when I was growing up. Fighting females were missing. I don't recall seeing any females fighting back, not one. But how do you know if something is missing if you aren't even aware it exists? None of us can harness our fighting spirit until we realize that part of us is missing, or rather, asleep.

One of the most powerful aspects of the recent women's movement has been the search for the missing myths, the missing voices, the under-reported, unpublished and undervalued stories about women. It required a yearning, an awakening, and major sleuthing to realize just how "missing" we all were and are. While many unconsciously assumed that we were missing because we were never there, the more investigative of us found we were missing because we'd been suppressed by a patriarchal structure that was threatened by our presence.

Are women's stories simply men's stories with the gender roles swapped? Not necessarily, although that's a valid style. Gender swapping does tap deeply into the rich mine of women's stories. What if there were once many stories in existence that portrayed women who avenged wrongs, battled for justice and fought off the enemy? It's possible to discover such heroines when one starts to read mythologies, whether Greek or Hebrew, with an eye toward the gender sub-text.

The story of Demeter and Persephone, (or Ceres and Core) an ancient myth of a mother avenging her daughter's rape and kidnapping, is one such surviving story. The lesson there was "It's not nice to fool Mother Nature." The world paid dearly for making Demeter angry. Modern women and men have not had the benefit of Demeter. She's been missing and we need her back.

In our day, the entertainment media reinforces the thinking that women are weak and in need of rescue, and that men are incredibly strong and always the rescuers. Until quite recently, if the women tried to help out in a defense, she was usually incompetent, squeamish, stupid and ineffective. Some man would have to come in and save the day. Or, if she got anything accomplished in the defense of someone, it was by accident, not design. Being helpless was beautiful and desirable. Cinderella longed for her prince to find her and save her from her circumstances.

As a small girl growing up in the glow of the Kennedy New Frontier, I remember falling in love with Arthur, Lady Gweniviere and the Round Table. The whole notion of the knight in shining armor and his helpless lady love was all around me. I ate it with a serving spoon.

From the role models that were apparent, if I couldn't aspire to be President, I certainly could aspire to be a Lady, maybe even a First Lady, by being a beauty to the best of my genetic potential and ability to apply make-up. There were examples and encouragement to that end from all quarters. The message was pretty clear. If I acted like and looked like a lady, I'd be treated like one.

My family and I attended the Huron College production of *Camelot* in Huron, South Dakota, where I swooned at the idea of being a lady burnt at the stake and at the same time of becoming an actress, a lady of the theater and of the world. Little did I know at that time that the two careers had a great deal in common. Why did it not bother us that our greatest romances had a helpless female as their main focus, and that the female character's helplessness was a major shaper of our character? I'm amazed now that the idea of a Gweniviere barbecue was even remotely romantic.

Our cultural images and entertainment are rife with women in peril. In considering the nature of entertainment, I've started in my curmudgeonly way to ask, "Entertaining to whom?" It reminds me of the first time someone pointed out that the Golden Age of Greece was decidedly not "golden" for women. "Golden for whom?" We couldn't do anything; we were virtual if not actual slaves. The Italian Renaissance? "Renaissance for whom?" You get the idea. So, again, I ask the entertainment industry, "Entertaining for whom?" I'm not entertained by watching helpless, co-dependent, stupid women, are you? But such movies continue to be made because there seems to be a whole slew of guys out there who never tire of seeing portrayals of inept yet gorgeous women.

Consider the concept of "chick flicks." It's a relatively new term for movies where the women have character and integrity — where she or maybe even a few she's are integral to the plot and not merely arm decorations and bed accessories for the hero. A chick flick is not noted for the chases, the big boom booms, or T & A, although some chick flicks have some of those things. Women like movies where women aren't stereotyped. Call us nutty for the thrill of seeing variation on the screen.

By the same token, many women are tired of "dick flicks." But that's a problem because more dick flicks get made than chick flicks because the dicks are in charge. The chicks are so few and far between and are under such pressure to succeed that they can't necessarily be counted on to make chick flicks. Understandably so. They have made great strides to even make "entertainment"; they're loathe to be hounded out for not catering to dick flick sensibilities. Besides, one of the greatest sources of revenue for films is the foreign markets. Male action-films with T & A rake in big bucks, because flesh and explosions don't need language skills for understanding. But we also export misogyny with our films. We export ideas that violence is an easy solution and that violence against women is normal. Around the world we reaffirm that women are physically defenseless through our "entertainment."

Listen up men and boys! Women have been putting up with dick flicks since movies started. Be good sports. Put up with chick flicks more often. You'll start to imagine women differently; you may even learn to appreciate them more. You certainly will begin to see beyond limited female stereotyping that dictates that there are only a few "brands" of women.

Wanted: Fairy Godmothers and Godfathers in Entertainment to Show Us How To Rescue Ourselves

Film lags behind television in terms of liberating women from stereotypical roles. Lifetime Television's production of "Shame" a few years back, starring Amanda Donohoe, is a brilliant example of how a woman fighting back can be on the screen. Amanda Donahoe's character is confronted by hostile and criminal teenage yahoos in a small town in Washington state where she has gotten involved with prosecuting the rape of a teenage girl. The alleged rapists begin the attempt to assault her when she nails the leader with a well-placed heel palm to his chin, followed by a strategic knee to his groin. Later, she doesn't boast of her counter-attack; she acknowledges the ugliness of the whole matter without, however, regretting her reaction one bit. She then literally gets in her teenage protege's face and attempts to get her to fight back physically. She exemplifies the outraged and unfrozen woman. She was a fantastic role model and entertaining to boot.

"Shame" and other Lifetime Television made-for-TV movies are inspiring examples of what television can do to portray realistic heroines who fight back. Powerhouse female producers, today's Fairy Godmothers, are more numerous in TV than in films. Women like Linda Bloodworth-Thomason, Roseanne Barr, and others have broken important ground for women. It's not an accident that Ms. Thomason and Ms. Barr both featured Impact Personal Safety in their sit-coms, respectively, "Designing Women" and "Roseanne."

Impact Personal Safety and the Impact Foundation of Los Angeles, and the Chicago Self-Empowerment group were all featured by Oprah Winfrey in the early 1990's. Ms. Terri Treas was the spokeswoman for the full-force community and narrated scenarios while former students demonstrated fighting padded assailants. Oprah reportedly said it was one of her favorite shows. A woman who'd seen the program called to report that she'd saved her own life because she'd learned some self-defense from watching the full-force segment on "Oprah." Oprah Winfrey has been a major Fairy Godmother to women and a leader in showing Americans how to throw off archaic helplessness training. She has been dynamic in her empowerment of women and in her commitment to have women's stories out for everyone to hear, uncensored.

Xena: Warrior Princess and Buffy, the Vampire Slayer are TV characters that are breaking stereotypes, and portray fantasy women that are not wimps but warriors, major warriors. Even though the stories are myth-based, girls, boys, women, and men get to see women heroes in action saving other women, men, and the proverbial day. Hurrah for some new (actually ancient) images that have been missing. Our children need them.

Who is sticking up for girls and fighting sexism in children's programming? Apparently, not enough of us have been Fairy Godmothers and Godfathers. Even the "good" programs, "Sesame Street," for instance, have too few girl characters. The girls notice and it hurts their feelings and self-esteem. They get the message that they're not as desirable as boys unless they have skinny waists and don't give boys any trouble.

"You and your feminist agenda don't belong here."

I once sat on a panel to judge children's programming for a prestigious award that children's producers covet. The judging panel had two women to four men. We viewed six programs. The one I loved was a documentary about Alaskan kids visiting children in Siberia. It was touching, and the girls were just as active as the boys. We nominated our choices and the final vote came down to a tie between the documentary and an animated piece that had one girl character to seven boy characters. The girl character simply was there as set dressing. She always agreed with the boys and if she said anything, she was teased or told to shut up.

We took a vote to break the tie for the award. The Alaskan documentary tied with the sexist one again. I spoke up and told the panel how I felt about the passive sexism in the animated program. One man glared at me like I was a bitch from hell. He hated me for stating my opinion. He snarled,"You and your feminist agenda don't belong here." The other woman quietly agreed with me, but it wasn't until an older man said, "You're right. I wouldn't want my granddaughter to feel like she had to shut up around a group of boys," that we broke the tie and awarded the documentary. What if there had been no Fairy Godparents to stick up for girls on that panel?

How do the heroines presented to today's young girls stack up with regard to self-defense, strength, and courage? Cinderella has been re-released, with all of its 1950's lessons in princess and prince relations. Cinderella is passive. Beauty in "Beauty and the Beast" has terrible boundary skills, the first line of defense. She does have wit and a love of books in the movie version, but it's her beauty, physical and inner, that gets her in trouble in the first place and finally gets her out of her bad situation. All stuff of stereotype. Girls have nothing new to learn from this story. They've been told over and over that if they're pretty enough and nice enough, they'll be fine in life. Yeah, right. And what kind of father barters his daughter to an unknown "monster" or beast?

And what about the film "The Lion King"? In reality, female lions are the mainstay of lion society while male lions are vain sperm donors who lie around all day waiting for the females to work and feed them. But children wouldn't know that from the movie. What about a movie called "The Lion Queen"? No, the experts say; girls will attend movies that feature boys in the lead, but boys won't be attracted to movies with girls in the lead. It's a vicious commercial circle that few dare to break.

Jasmine, Belle, Pocahontas, Ariel, all have unbelievably thin and at the same time, voluptuous and impossible to attain bodies. Their bodies are not designed for defense, but for seduction and rescuing. It really is no wonder that we have girls starving and puking themselves into despair and physical defenselessness.

So, what are we teaching our boys and girls? We're still teaching them: desirable girls are weak and pretty; desirable boys are strong and uncomplaining; a boy's status depends on how much he has and if he has a beautiful princess or lioness on his arm (or paw). Males use a woman's beauty to signify status. A girl's status is still based on how close to looking like a princess she can get. Girls still have to wait for boys to save them physically. The picture hasn't changed much, has it?

The process of including more physically heroic roles for females on TV and in films really begins with writers. If a writer cannot conceive of the possibility of a girl or woman fighting back, or being active, she or he won't write that into a script. I once wrote a short screenplay that was good enough to be nominated in a prestigious screenplay contest I'd entered. I had a scene in it where a woman beats up a man who has attacked her. The most prevalent comment I got was how unrealistic that fight was and that it would have to be re-written. I couldn't re-write the fight scene without re-writing the whole story. The story was about a woman avenging her daughter's abuse by her ex-husband, the "wicked" step-father.

Producers, directors, and actors could all help to change the fact that women don't normally fight back on screen, that they're leered at but not feared. Let's say that Annie Actor gets a scene where she initially defends someone but stops short of actually "saving the day." Let's say she has enough clout to change the scene so that her character just plain saves the day; that she doesn't need the intervention of a man.

First of all, Ms. Actor would have had to have experienced — either first hand or second hand — that women can defend themselves and others, and she'd also have to be convincing enough to the producer and director to get the re-write done. Since there are relatively few female directors and producers, the males would have to be sympathetic to the cause of women not being portrayed simply as sex objects. Since there are so few good women's roles out there, Annie Actor would have to be convincing enough to promote her "cause" and to counter the prejudice within the industry that strong women are "difficult" or "bitches" if they attempt to have a say in the outcome of the endeavor. There are some serious double binds here.

Women are the sleeping giant of the world. When we all wake up, express ourselves and claim our power, we are in for major changes. Women need to empower other women. We each need to empower the women of Hollywood to make the kind of entertainment we want, the kind of films and TV shows that realistically portray all aspects of who we are, including our fighting spirit. We need Hollywood men who are sympathetic to women's world status to stand up too. This requires partnership on a very large scale.

There is no shortage of stories for film and television that portray us as we really are and have been. There are women who have fought in wars, women who have defended their families, women inventors, women composers, women fine artists, you name it, we've done it. Brave, silly, wily, cunning, sweet, stupid, brilliant, cowardly, traitorous, generous, strong, we have embodied every human trait. Women have led families and armies; run husbands and countries; conspired; spied; plotted massacres; judged cases; created laws; officiated at religious ceremonies; saved towns and countries; transformed institutions; muck-raked; written novels, poetry, plays and symphonies; and defended themselves against male violence.

Women have triumphed against terrible odds from time immemorial. If more women knew that via the grapevine, and through accurate portrayals in children's stories, film and TV, we would be less apt to put up with a husband who hits us for dressing the wrong way, with abuse at work, with a bully on the playground, or with an assailant on the street.

The Ugly Step-Brothers of Fashion and Music

Fashion

Fashion is an incredibly powerful device to keep women in their place and is inextricably entwined with entertainment. TV, film, music videos, and magazines are all showcases for what is fashionable. No one wants to be unattractive and no one really relishes sticking out. The desire to conform and belong is a strong one for both genders. Fashion for women, however, is incredibly dangerous to our well-being, both physical and mental. If you buck fashion, you had better hope that you either have a very strong ego or that you can start a trend or a movement.

Archaic dress codes are seemingly minor rules but related to the rampant and growing incidents of violence against women. Modes of dress are related to women being subjected to unwanted male attention, criminal and otherwise. Rigid gender rules, sexual harassment and assault are on the same continuum.

Think about fashion from the point of view of how defenseless so much of our fashion makes women. It constricts, hobbles, binds and exposes. Try running in high heels. Try kicking in a straight skirt. Try anything to defend yourself when moving too quickly hurts. Try staying modest in a trendy "immodest" outfit. Sound absurd? There you go. That's a woman's life.

It's important for girls and women to understand how fashion can be constricting and therefore, hazardous to health. Still, I'm all for women expressing themselves through the decorating process. I happen to think "costuming," which is how I see fashion, is great fun. I wear high heels occasionally as "corporate drag," but I know that I'm at risk for ankle injuries. I also know that I'm prepared to kick them off or rip a skirt if I have to protect myself or someone in need.

I'd love to declare a required cross-dressing week for corporate men. I'd like men to take meetings and try to make important points and maintain credibility while they attempt to keep me and other horny women from staring at their legs or up their kilts. Just a fantasy.

On a more serious note, the most deadly aspect of fashion has to do with the current obsession with extreme thinness. It's bad news. Really bad, bad news that women keep buying into. Let's overthrow the fashion of thinness. Come on gals, let's all say, "Screw it!" at the same time. OK, you first. Right.

Just look at it this way: if a major portion of women's energies are taken up with how they look and how they can maintain or change how they look, how much time do they have left for impacting the world? Could it be that pitting women's bodies in a huge comparison war just keeps us busy enough to keep us from being taken seriously? — from playing on the state, national, global levels? — from learning what we need to know to defend and then forward ourselves?

Small women are frequently told they look like girls as a compliment. I would guess they would fight like an untrained "girl" too if they had to. That's not a problem if only we can get to the small women and girls and show them how to use their size to their best advantage. Hopefully, fighting techniques would get a woman back in touch with her spirit and counteract the poor self-esteem that's at the bottom of her obsession with being skinny. Also, no matter what techniques we teach, if a person is weakened by hunger or eating disorders, she's got to work harder to fight for herself, spiritually and physically.

I have a unique experience of fighting as a light-weight person and a heavier-weight person. After 26 years of smoking, I gave it up and promptly ballooned from a size 6 to a 16. What a reality shift. When I first learned to fight I weighed 145. When I gained over 60 pounds I understood why the prestigious weight classes in men's combat sports are heavy-weights. Wow. The power of a hit with 200 pounds or more behind it was something I had never considered. I'm back down again but I learned more about physical force at a heavier weight. No wonder so many misogynist men want women to stay light-weights.

Music Videos and the Music Industry

"My boyfriend's back, and you're gonna be in trouble." Although I love that song as a nostalgia "girl group" classic, what a message it conveys. It says that the only consequences that a boy will suffer will come from another boy, not the girl. Music is a powerful conveyor of cultural norms and images.

I shudder when I think how I used to play the Beatles' song, "Run for Your Life," with its lyric that describes a man who threatens to kill a woman because of homicidal possessiveness. My girlfriends and I accepted homicidal jealousy as romantic.

MTV is pumping out violent images of male and female relations at an alarming rate. Sut Jhally wrote, directed and narrated a documentary entitled "DreamWorlds 2" that MTV attempted to stop through a lawsuit. Mr. Jhally has done a brilliant analysis of the music video culture and young male violence in his films sponsored by The

Media Education Foundation. Jhally exposes the dehumanizing, systematic objectifying of women in music videos to the point that they become simply playthings, literally dreamed-up objects of desire. He says the women of music videos are the fantasies of old, white men who want young women in utterly compliant, yet wildly sexual, positions. They are strippers, nurses, maids, erotic dancers and always on the prowl to have sex. It's no wonder after seeing "DreamWorlds 2," that boys take rape so lightly. They are being taught that women want it, deserve it and might even benefit from it.

Jhally's films speak eloquently to the importance and power of human story in shaping social attitudes. These attitudes then translate into the environment we live in in terms of what is acceptable and what isn't. The predominant and dangerous story being told is that women are weak yet vicious sex objects, in peril and in need of rescue. They are eager to seduce and be seduced, and are second-class citizens who are easy to victimize, and invite their own victimization. These stories are based on fantasy, but nonetheless shape how people actually think and live. According to Jhally, the main communication in most entertainment created by "adolescent" males, verbal and non-verbal, is that women and girls "want it — they all want it, from any and all men." How can a rape occur if someone really "wants it?" We are living in a rape culture created and maintained by our "entertainment." Entertaining to whom?

We transform culture by taking responsibility for it and reclaiming it as our own. We exclaim, "I'm mad as hell and I'm not going to take it anymore!" We reclaim society and culture by creating or rediscovering stories and myths that are empowering to girls and women. We transform ourselves and our daughters by finding and re-telling stories that make us strong, whether we write songs, novels, screenplays or television scripts. We literally shake ourselves out of a sleep that has kept us down by being invisible to each other and to men. We needn't censor the stories of "Sleeping Beauty," or "Cinderella," but we must balance them with other stories. If we're true to our experience and insist on adding our voices to the culture, one day we'll awaken to find women's full participation in every aspect of life. What a beautiful dawn.

17

The Round Table — Think Globally, Act Locally

Woman's dearest possession is life
and since it is given to her but once
she must live as to feel no torturing regret
for years without purpose,
so live as not to be scarred with the shame of
a cowardly and trivial past
so live that dying she can say:
all my life and all my strength
was given to the finest cause in the world,
the liberation of womankind.

ALICE PAUL, 1885-1977
AMERICAN SUFFRAGE LEADER
AUTHOR OF THE EQUAL RIGHTS
AMENDMENT IN 1923

Take Back the Castles and the Streets

Snooze and we all lose, Beauty. Wake up and the world is our castle, inside and out. Woman is the sleeping giant of the world and we need her to wake up to fight the germs of violence. We need women to be fully expressed. We need women to tap their daring, their courage, their fury, their outrage so we can put the world back into balance. It is difficult to be a citizen of the world if something as mundane as walking to your car at night is a frightening experience. We must begin to look upon all the "vagabonds in the basement," the threatening men, as inspiration rather than allow them to sap our will to change the world. Let them inspire us to fight back, to use our natural fighting spirit to achieve a sense of security and freedom.

We use the language of disease to speak of violence. Violence has carriers who were exposed to violence themselves. In this sense, violence is contagious. Violence spreads through conditions that are prone to creating it: poverty, dreadful mental hygiene and ignorance. Violence injures, maims and kills just as surely as the plagues and fevers of viruses. We face the challenge of the century. Is there a cure for violence? Is there a vaccine?

Yes. Women's self-defense is a vaccine for violence. Vaccination involves using a tiny amount of a contagion to build a person's own natural immune system in order to defend against a full-blown attack of a disease. Traditional western medicine and homeopathy has successfully used the principle of vaccination for years — "like cures like," or *sic parvis magnus*, Latin for "from little comes much."

Physical self-defense is an important factor for a woman in building her own personal immune system, and in preventing physical and psychological damage to her due to violence. By the same token, if a critical mass of women world-wide could become healthy and access their fighting spirit, thus protecting themselves and others from violence — what a vision. We could help to make violence as extinct as smallpox.

Be prepared, however, to listen to anachronistic notions about self-defense similar to the antiquated resistance to vaccination. Amazingly, in 1829, Pope Leo XII declared smallpox immunization to be against the will of God and an interference in the divine plan. Smallpox was thus considered inevitable well into the 19th century. However, with a combination of vaccination, education, and modern notions of sanitation and cleanliness, smallpox was declared to be an extinct disease in the 1970's.

To fully confront violence as an epidemic, we need, as in the battle against smallpox, a combination of methodologies. We need to focus on prosecuting perpetrators, working with prisoners, studying the causes of violence, educating children and parents, and teaching self-defense. Clearly, no single method can eradicate violence. We need the best from everyone.

So far, most violence-prevention discussions have overlooked universal self-defense education for women as a solution to violence. Fighting back does not create more violence; it prevents it. Passivity appears to actually create more violence. Therefore, the learning and practicing of how and when to fight back is literally an effective preventative measure to allay violence — a vaccine.

For a statistics-minded society it's difficult to "prove" that full-force self-defense works. We can't send a control group and a trained group of women out after dark to see who fares better when attacked. But anecdotal evidence has been powerfully convincing. Two Hundred Eighty-six graduates of the Impact Women's Basics (20 hours) self-defense course were asked to review "before" and "after" statements, and then choose a response based on their personal experience. The statements they were to respond to were: a) Prior to taking this course, I think I could have effectively dealt with a physical attack, and b) After graduating from this course, I think I could effectively deal with a physical attack.

Percentage Results from 286 Graduates

	Before Class	*After Class*
Definitely not	30.77%	0%
Probably not	36.71%	0%
Maybe	28.32%	1.75%
Probably	2.45%	23.43%
Definitely	1.75%	74.83%

It's awesome to see what an impact a five- or six-week course can have on a woman who has been scared most of her life.

As I interviewed women for this book, the question, "How would your life be different if you felt safe almost anywhere?" yielded the most poignant answers. I had tapped into a palpable yearning. "I'd travel; I'd feel free; I'd be happy; I'd run; I'd jog; I'd visit places at night; I'd take long walks in the moonlight, by myself." The women exulted in the vision of not being bound by their fear. It's outrageous to think of how many women are frightened needlessly about doing the simplest human activities for fear of harm.

Women of Los Angeles, United

My experience of teaching self-defense in Los Angeles has fired my belief in women's ability to unite beyond ethnic, religious or color barriers. My most ardent dream is to create classes that are racially and ethnically diverse, nationally and internationally. As it is now, white, middle class women make up a large percentage of enrollees, even though they are less apt to be the victims of violent crime than their sisters of color.

Dr. Irene Blea, Chair of the Chicana Studies Program at University of California, Los Angeles, and delegate to the 1995 U.N. Conference on Women in Beijing, believes it's essential to the well-being of the southwest U.S. for Anglo, Chicana, and all Hispanic women to have a way to compare lives and learn how to support one another. She also sees on a day-to-day basis how vital physical self-protection is for the young women she teaches at the university level. They are constantly vigilant, yet feel helpless about male violence.

I had the great fortune to complete my full-force instructor training in Los Angeles working with my own first instructors, Annette Washington and Rondell Dodson, along with the support of Irene van der Zande, Susie Johnson, Terri Treas and the board of directors of the Impact Foundation. The Impact Foundation was created to make full-force self-defense available to high-risk, low-income people through scholarships and scale-priced classes.

We created a basics class at Fairfax High School in Los Angeles, that had an even number of "Anglos," Latinas and African-American women. Predictably, in the first session, everyone sat down with the women in their own ethnic or color group. The staff noticed and predicted that by the end of class all of the women would naturally intermix and interrelate. We were right.

Just as in circles made up of primarily white women, the mixed circles had the same experience of respect, admiration and, dare I say it, love of the other women when they heard about their lives and how violence had affected them. We wept, we laughed, we roared, we growled and we cheered for one another as we vanquished the enemy within, our own fear.

We did more than learn how to fight back during that five-week class. We learned about making Los Angeles work. Women have been largely left out of solving urban problems, much to the detriment of local, state and federal concerns. The women in our diverse class demonstrated how powerful women can be when joined together in a common cause. The world needs us to do that for many problems. We learned that our common concerns were greater than our differences.

Women of the World, United

I found out on my trip to China, on the way to and during the United Nation's Fourth International Women's Conference, that women's hopelessness and fury about personal violence from their menfolk is common to all. Every woman I spoke with about my mission, to make self-defense available to women and girls all over the world, passionately agreed with the need for women to learn how to fight back.

Bowled over by a wave of joy and gratitude, I looked up into the vast seating of the People's Stadium in Beijing and choked up, tears rolling down my face. Utter loneliness as a women's rights activist would be a thing of the past forever. Imagine 30,000 women from all over the world laughing, talking, waiting for the opening ceremonies of the 1995 U.N. Conference on Women to begin. Having dealt with U.S. headlines announcing the untimely and false "Death of Feminism" on and off for twenty years, I needed to see how many other women worldwide had made the same commitment as mine; to get women up to speed as full citizens everywhere. We all had another thing in common. We worked locally, in order to empower all women globally.

These women were leaders — Women of Vision. There were women who had single-handedly brought water to entire regions so that women wouldn't have to walk five miles every day to have potable water. There were women who headed nations. There were rape, incest, and battering survivors, and activists devoted to reparations for war crimes against women. There were women who had brought literacy to thousands upon thousands of women and children. The sheer power and the commitment to empower in that stadium was palpable. And I found that my mission was wanted, needed, and perceived as important by my peers after years of polite nods and suppressed rolled eyes when I told people about my work.

Think globally, act locally. There is nothing more local than self-defense. How can you get more local than your own body? This is good news, because if you are not the type to get involved with "causes," your learning how to defend yourself is an action that helps all of us, with full benefit to your own "local" concern.

Susan Brownmiller's 1975 ground-breaking classic, *Against Our Will: Men, Women and Rape,* opened many an American eye to how pervasive the threat of force against women actually is. Brownmiller has been instrumental in empowering women to rally against unfair practices in evidentiary rules that have been traditionally stacked against women in rape cases. She ushered in an era of prosecutors and police being more sensitized to women who are raped and who bring charges.

She made the necessary connections for women to understand that rape is a social control and not a problem brought on by the behavior of the individual woman. She spoke briefly but favorably about self-defense and martial arts. Now attitudes toward rape have completely shifted so that there's a critical mass of American adults who believe women at least have the right to defend themselves.

Viva Mexicanas

The right and responsibility of a woman to defend herself is not an attitude that is widely shared, even by our next door neighbor, Mexico. But the attitude is growing.

Just released in the spring of 1997, Claudia Rodriguez of Mexico City, languished for more than a year in jail for killing a would-be rapist in self-defense. Within the same period of time, a man who'd shot a thief in Mexico City for stealing his watch was never even charged with a crime.

Charged with homicide, Rodriguez became a feminist icon in Mexico during 1996-97. Her rape self-defense case became one of the first feminist issues that gained national attention, similar to the Hill-Thomas hearings here in the States. Because of the internet, women all over the world knew about Claudia Rodriguez and voiced their strong objections in support of their Mexican sisters. The protests escalated to such a degree that the judge charged and convicted Rodriguez with a lesser crime, "use of excessive force." Not a fair prosecution, it at least was better than a homicide conviction.

Men and boys in Mexico, as in most developing countries all over the world, have not been confronted as steadily and readily about sexism as in more developed countries. Many of their opinions about the Rodriguez attempted rape/self-defense case sound like 19th century reasoning about rape: What was a nice woman doing out late, anyway? Couldn't she have defended her virtue without such force? He was drunk, and didn't know what he was doing; she should have been responsible. He was drunk, she could have escaped easily.

You'd better believe that with AIDS, a woman is not only defending herself from the vicious crime of rape, but also the possibility of a fatal disease. There is not yet a critical mass of decision-makers who believe women have the right to defend themselves in the world, but Mexico has a critical mass of women who believe and demonstrated that they are equal and have the right to be left alone. Viva Mexicanas!

The feministas and their sympathizers simply would not put up with the blatant sexism displayed by their judicial system toward Claudia Rodriguez. The women of Mexico are willing and able to defend themselves, and do. What a self-defense success story.

Everyone Benefits When Women Are Empowered

Why should we care about women all over the world? For one thing, women like and need to travel just as men do. I'd like to alter rape attitudes world-wide, wouldn't you?

Beyond that, universal self-defense is a goal that would benefit everyone, not only business travelers and tourists. We all benefit when we empower a woman to care for herself and her family. The world-wide economy and world-wide peace depend on women transforming their roles from passive to active citizens. Self-defense training is one of the fastest ways available to access a woman's "fighting spirit." Self-defense isn't a substitute for literacy or job skills, but it inspires a woman to become her own person, to take charge of her life. After all, our physical well-being is tied in to everything else we do. Ironically, even anti-violence advocates must access their "fight" in order to accomplish their goals. We need to fight for this planet's health — all of us, with everything we've got.

Full-force self-defense leader and instructor, Judith Roth, of Powerful Choices in Seattle, created the "I Am Your Witness Campaign," for the rape survivors in former Yugoslavia. Because of the tragedy in Bosnia, world opinion has finally shifted to include rape as a crime against humanity. Powerful Choices made a huge difference in a landmark case for women's human rights. For the first time in women's history, the U.S. Court of Appeals for the Second District ruled that women had "standing" to sue for genocidal rape. Serb leader Radovan Karadzic could be sued by Bosnian Muslim and Croat women and children for ethnically-based rape and murder as genocide.

As American women we need to support feminist causes all over the world. Benjamin Franklin said at the signing of the American Declaration of Independence, "We must all hang together or, assuredly, we shall hang separately."

Technology and Space

The internet makes "hanging together" as women more possible than at any other time in history. If you're not on-line, do it. It's a matter of self-defense. It is neither cute nor feminine to be a techno-peasant. Read brilliant thinker and writer Dale Spender's, *Nattering on the Net: Women, Power and Cyberspace,* a must-read, cutting-edge book for women about world-wide web technology. It's not just a guy thing. We need to use and participate in ownership and policy-making on the net or snooze and lose. We will see so much progress in technology during our lifetime that we need to stay in touch with what's happening or find ourselves out of the loop yet again. We need women to be on the cutting edge of technology and space.

Think about women and men in space. For the first time in human history a woman in space can simply bounce a man away from her should he give her unwanted physical attention. Brute force based on muscles will no longer be a factor in gender relations when there's no gravity. That is not to say that some folks won't try to dominate others but muscles will no longer be a "trump" card. Cooperation and teamwork will have to be the way of the future in space; space requires different values and strengths from human beings' gravitational existence.

I want to facilitate a major move on the part of individual women, groups and institutions to train girls and women in full-impact self-defense. This training can take place through schools, corporations, seminars, workshops and of course, through the incredible organizations who are already set up to give excellent training. I'd like this book to inspire studies, scouting merit badges, grants, more books and just plain old walking over to the phone right now and signing up for a class. What are you waiting for?

My commitment is to make self-defense just as accepted, inexpensive and accessible as a vaccination or swimming lessons. Eventually the world will be made up of women who resist being oppressed emotionally, physically and spiritually as a matter of course. And that will be a better world for everyone.

Epilogue

MY HEROINES

Dedicated to Irene, Annette, Lisa, Janice, Kimberlee, Bobi, Elizabeth, Roxanne, Sylvia, Sheryl, Terri, Karin, Heather, Lynn, Melissa, Claudia, Susan, Martha, Donna, Karen, Molly, Mary T., Janet, Kim, Mary B., Carol, Cornelia, Kayla, Susie, Judith, Bridget, Kimiko, Teri, and all other female instructors and defense womenfolk even though I haven't worked with them or know their form of self-defense

These women, my heroines, work with wounds of varying degrees. These wounds range from the bruise that exists like the air we breath simply by virtue of being born female, all the way to the near-fatal injuries inflicted on girls whose fathers stuck cattle prods up their vaginas, and everything in between. We all have survived misogyny. These women know we aren't exaggerating. They don't try to talk us into understanding or excusing the perpetrators. They are the women who are openly outraged at how we've been treated. They know, they've been there.

They are like mid-wives, gently telling us to breathe as we prepare to deliver ourselves, a difficult birth indeed. As they signal their male coaching partner that we are ready for the fight, "No protected areas, Jane is ready," they usher us into our own independence. They are our coaches, cheerleaders, and cheering crowd. Finally, they are the priestesses who witness our emergence from the fear that has kept us prisoners into active members of a community who will not put up with violence against women any longer.

I was always made to feel that feminism is a joke by so many people in my past. Nonetheless, I have been proud to be a feminist since I first heard the word and was told what it meant. It means "an advocate of equal rights for women." Some members of the media and threatened people have made it mean other things.

I have been immersed in feminist theory for awhile, but these self-defense teachers are beyond theory. There's nothing theoretical about a well-placed knee to the groin. As it turns out, the testicles, the biological distinguishers which bestow unearned social privilege on the people who possess them are also the great equalizers. It's no wonder hitting them has been a major taboo.

It is precisely that knee to the groin that will help women take the next step to equality and freedom. These women, my heroines, know we will not form roving bands of gonad-kicking "bitches from hell." But they also know that once we are certain of our ability to protect ourselves from physical attack, we will gain courage to speak up. We will have a character that combines aspects of our own unique personality, the loving mother, the devoted sister, and the ferocious warrior. We've been told that we were "given" the vote. That's not true, we took the vote after 100 years of a bloodless, one-by-one revolution. My heroines are the leaders of another revolution, the women, gentle men and children revolution, the decline of the bully.

I'm in my second childhood now and I want to be just like my female instructors. I want to wear a whistle around my neck and a "Which part of "NO" don't you understand?" t-shirt. I'm finally grateful to be a female in this era because we're going to change the world for good and together.

No protected areas, we are ready.

Appendix

Most commonly-asked questions and expressed concerns about learning self-defense

It doesn't seem fair — why do women have to learn self-defense?

In a fair world it would be a violent man's responsibility to stop being violent, but as we learn over and over as we mature, life is not fair. Also, we cannot change other people; the only person one can change is oneself. I once heard Gloria Steinem say that the definition of "co-dependency" could be a "well-socialized woman." To be free, we must depend on ourselves for our own physical safety.

Violence prevention must begin by stopping attackers from committing violence against us. We can also help stop the cycle of violence in the home by being role models for our daughters and sons. More of our children, sons as well as daughters, need to see that women can handle a violent man, and that violence is not the only solution to problems.

Doesn't fighting back make the situation worse because you make the attacker angrier?

Studies have shown that it's untrue that it's safer or better to mollify a violent person by being passive. Angry rapists have a script that says women are hateful because they are passive and weak. Thus their violence increases when they witness passivity. And as far as anger goes, it's energizing and empowering to use your own anger to fight back if someone has attacked you. Righteous indignation, "How dare you try to hurt me or my loved one," is powerful fuel.

I'm not very strong or athletic.

It doesn't take much force to defend oneself, especially when we realize that human men are not cyborgs or robots, simply flesh and blood like us. Consider how little it takes to hurt an eye; even a hair or piece of sand in the eye is irritating. A poke in the eye with a finger is enough to stop anyone for the precious seconds it can take to then kick a knee or a crotch. Adrenalin also helps strength. Everyone has heard stories of the so-called "weaker" sex performing amazing feats like lifting a car off a baby. It doesn't take an athlete to put up a good fight.

Do I have to take a self-defense class to defend myself?

Absolutely not. People uneducated in self-defense successfully defend themselves all the time. It does take fighting spirit to defend oneself but that is a gift from nature we all have within us. Of course, someone trained in defense will have skills that an untrained person doesn't, and will probably see things in a defensive counter-attack that an untrained person won't.

What if there's a gun or a knife?

One of the most potent aspects of learning full-force, full-contact self-defense is the ability the trained person has to talk to a potential assailant. If there is a knife or gun, ask the person what they want. If they want your property, almost all experts recommend that you give it to them. Property is replaceable. If they want you to get in a vehicle or to tie you up, most experts recommend that you fight then and there. Do not go with anyone even if they promise that they won't harm you. Their word is no good.

If there is a struggle with the armed person, hold on to the knife or gun hand as hard as you can and get the weapon "off line," meaning get it away from your vital organs and head, no matter what. If you can run from a gun, do it with all your might. Very few people can hit a running target especially if the target is zig-zagging.

If you are threatened with a club-type weapon, like a bat, tire iron, or fist, the safest place to be is closest to the person who's got the weapon. (A fist is like a club weapon, the arm is the club.) You are literally safer by being in a bear-hug with someone who's got a bat then at arm's length. There is an old Buddhist saying, "Close to the heart of danger lies safety." That saying often applies to self-defense.

I saw a demonstration of full-force fighting and the women always went for the assailant's eyes or head before they hit his crotch. Why?

Men are very aware of the vulnerability of their testicles and will often protect there first. If you distract an assailant with an eye-strike, it will open the target in his crotch. There's hardly a person on earth who won't protect their eyes if something is coming at them.

I'm thinking about getting a gun instead of learning self-defense. Should I?

Having a gun is not a substitute for knowing how to protect yourself with your body. I don't care how prepared someone is, it's impossible to always have access to a weapon. If you decide to arm yourself with a weapon, please take a fully-accredited course for your weapon of choice, and one that takes into account the socialization of women.

While I am personally anti-hand gun, I would never advise a person to not have a gun, even though I won't. Having a firearm is a tremendously personal decision. But please, don't substitute having a weapon for knowing how to fight with your own body. You always have your own arms, legs and head with you.

I do recommend, however, that a person become aware of the weapon potential of common items. The stereotypical weapons of women, frying pans, hat pins, rolling pins, have usually been used to mock them. However, as my mother used to say, "A rolling pin over the head makes a very big impression."

Look around your house, or even in your purse. What could you use as a weapon if you had to? There's a story in Caignon and Grove's book, *Her Wits About Her: Self-Defense Success Stories by Women,* where a woman fights off an assailant by using a rat-tailed comb from her purse. I heard a story about a woman in Mexico City who was fondled by a man in a movie theater. She took off her high heel and hit him with it, pointy-heel to forehead. That also made an impression on him. He ran away.

I like being feminine and I like the idea of a man protecting me.

How about reframing the notion of femininity to include being a protector? Think of the image of the lioness, or what Dr. Christiane Northrup refers to as "mother bear energy." I like to think of the ferociousness of a female in the wild animal kingdom. As far as the idea of being protected, I think the child within all of us, female or male, likes the idea of being protected by someone. The notion that a man or someone else is going to protect us, however, is dangerous when an actual incident occurs. It would be best to plan for the worst and hope for the best when it comes to people-danger. It's simply not realistic to expect a man to protect us unless we're constantly under guard.

If full-force, full-impact self-defense is so great, why does it cost so much? Why isn't it offered in school or for free?

The costs of classes reflect what it takes a business, profit or non-profit, to stay solvent. The fees for full-impact, full-force self-defense vary widely, depending on the overhead and cost of living in the surrounding area. Most chapters that teach this form of self-defense have flexible payment plans, and/or scholarship programs. They also keep actual costs down by employing extensive volunteer programs. Insurance is expensive and the cost of training female and male instructors is high because of the amount of time they take to become fully competent physically and emotionally.

I attended a demonstration of full-impact self-defense. There were a lot of white women. Where are the minorities?

Unfortunately, the cost of class is often prohibitive to low-income women. Many of us are working very hard to make classes available to the people who need it most. Fortunately, many self-defense providers are extremely accommodating to low-income circumstances, providing scholarships, payment plans, etc. The California Victims Assistance Program covers the cost of full-impact classes which is one way that low-income women can take a class if they have already been the victim of violence, stranger or domestic.

Won't learning self-defense just make me more frightened or maybe too confident?

No. In fact, most women report that learning self-defense gives a woman just the right amount of confidence to realistically assess the situation she is actually in. Some women report that they are able to be more friendly with men than before they learned self-defense because they don't have to indiscriminately reject them simply out of fear.

I am a rape/incest survivor. Wouldn't realistic scenarios hurt me by reminding me too much of the real sexual or violent assault that I experienced?

We always recommend that if the prospective student has a concern about the emotional safety of being in a full-force class, that she check with her mental health care provider. Generally, we find that students who have experienced a violent assault are able to handle classes very well. We also have many therapists who refer clients to full-force, full-contact classes so that they can regain their personal power in a quick, effective, practical manner. Usually, a person's instincts are good about whether they can handle the class or not.

I've already taken martial arts classes. Why should I take a full-force class? Or is self-defense like martial arts?

Full-force classes are not the martial arts. Most people make self-defense and martial arts synonymous. There are many types of martial arts: judo, karate, tae kwon do, aikido, etc. Some full-force classes and some movements borrow directly from traditional martial arts so there's cross-over. Many instructors of full-force are accomplished martial artists. But generally, the martial arts are formal traditions, often from Asia, even from Israel, that are taught by recognized teachers where the students progress from one level of competence to the next. Most people have heard of black belts. That's the highest attainment in karate, for instance, although other Asian arts use the belt system too.

What makes full-force, full-contact classes so valuable for people who have already studied a formal martial art is that they have the opportunity to engage with a padded assailant without having to "pull punches" or be concerned about really hurting a sparring partner.

Most full-force, full-impact instructors actually recommend the martial arts, not instead of full-force, but in addition to full-impact classes. Martial arts can provide on-going exercise, discipline-building, community and on-going study and growth over a long period of time. Full-impact classes are designed to give women the most practical, realistic and intense fighting and learning experience possible in the shortest amount of time.

Many full-force instructors recommend aikido, a relatively new Japanese martial art. Aikido literally teaches "going with the flow" and provides skills for non-violent deflection of violence.

Doesn't it traumatize some women who have been attacked by men to be in a self-defense class with male instructors?

Most women report that their experience with male instructors was a positive one. Many report that they saw men in a different light after witnessing males being empathetic toward women who are worried about male violence. Full-impact, full-force male instructors are specifically trained to be around women who have been traumatized. That's not to state that there's never been an inappropriate male who teaches self-defense. There's a "bad apple" in every barrel, and there are bad female apples sometimes. If you hear stories about abusive people in a self-defense class, follow through and ask questions. Have there been complaints about anyone? How were the complaints resolved?

Generally, the ethics standard is that an instructor of self-defense, female or male, should not get involved with a student on an intimate basis during the class or for an appropriate length of time afterwards. Self-defense classes, while not therapy per se, can be extremely therapeutic and students often idolize their instructors. The instructors should be professional, friendly, and yet keep at arm's length.

How does self-defense work for battered women?

The women who have survived battering husbands and have taken self-defense classes report that the classes are life-changing. Most of the classes, however, deal with mock attacks by strangers even though the statistics are clear: you are more apt to be attacked by someone you know than by a stranger. The betrayal inherent in an attack by a "loved one" is so devastating that most of us find it easier to imagine a stranger and practice what we'd do if a stranger attacks us, verbally or physically. If you can conceive of and then practice fending off a stranger, it makes it easier to be enraged by the assault of an acquaintance, and to fight back in that circumstance.

It's important to know and understand that domestic violence is full of traps that are not present in stranger assaults. Stranger, acquaintance and domestic violence are related like apples, bananas and oranges — are all fruits but one would not mistake one for the other.

There are full-force classes that give the student an opportunity to "customize" an assault scenario. Students can let the instructors know the basics of the scene that they would like to "re-play," but this time with an empowering outcome. For instance, if your brother used to punch you and kick you, the male instructor will re-enact your brother's behavior so that you can react in a way that is not defeating to your dignity or self-esteem. Or the scene can be one of a rape by a trusted person — father, mother, teacher, camp counselor, therapist, clergy.

The success stories that are reported about family members or trusted people are fewer than the accounts of successful stranger assaults or attempts. Most likely that's because people have a desire to protect their own privacy and that of someone they may have to continue to interact with or decide to stay in a relationship with. Although it can be most empowering to be able to say, "I'm leaving," that's not always the choice that a woman wants to make. Statistically, the number of homicides goes up drastically when a battered woman makes a definitive move, like getting a temporary restraining order or moving out of the house.

It's important for the battered woman to know that regardless of how she chooses to continue the relationship, it will be up to her to save herself and her kids. She has the right to never have to be around the person that hurts her, to set her own terms, whatever they may be, no matter what anyone else thinks or says. Somehow we must revolutionize the way we educate women so they learn that they have the right to be left alone or to leave. But we must also educate her to know that no one else can be counted on to protect her. She must be her own protector. Perhaps when there is a critical mass of women who know how to fight, there will be fewer men who will even attempt to batter or physically threaten women.

Whether a woman is defending herself from a stranger or an acquaintance, the key to any effective defense is the determination to hurt the person who is attacking. Frequently battered families have an ambivalence about the batterer. They may love or think they love the person who is hurting them. That's a terrible position to be in when physical violence happens. If a woman isn't willing to "go for it," she will probably give up or stop when the batterer cries or says he's hurt. His retaliation can then escalate once she's stopped. Battered women's concerns are complicated and are for the most part beyond the scope of this book. I have, however, listed several numbers in the Resource section that can be helpful to a woman who needs to escape a violent man.

Resources for Violence Prediction, Prevention, and Healing

For full-force, full-impact classes for adults, and age-appropriate classes for children and teens in your area:

1) FULLPOWER, KIDPOWER and The Impact Foundation: 1-800-467-6997, or visit their Web site, http://www.fullpower.org.
   To order The KidPower Guide for Teaching Self-Protection and Confidence to Young People, *write and send $12.00 to: P.O. Box 1212, Santa Cruz, CA. 95061, or call 1-800: 467-6997 or visit the KIDPOWER web site: safety@kidpower.org.*

2) IMPACT PERSONAL SAFETY and PREPARE, INC. 1-800-345-5425, http://www.PREPAREINC.com

   There are other full-force classes in the nation that I have no personal experience of. When selecting a class, find out if you can visit and observe. Make sure that there is an equal male/female co-instructor team, and that the "armor" that the male instructor uses is safe for him so that you can fight, full-out, with no concern about hurting the man in the suit of armor.

For help in escaping or reporting violence:

National Domestic Violence Hot-Line: 1-800-799-SAFE, referrals for shelters and resources.

National Victim Center, INFOLINK Program: 1-800-FYI-CALL, www.nvc.org, this has a list of all victim assistance programs. Free literature available.

To Heal from Violence:

Eye Movement De-Sensitization Reprocessing (EMDR): National Directory of Practitioners - 408-372-3900 (press 10 for Directory)

EMDR is a relatively new form of therapy which uses eye movement to help survivors of trauma recover. Survivors of sexual or violent assault often suffer from post-traumatic stress disorder. EMDR has been used with great success for survivors of street crime as well as natural disasters and terrorism. Therapists treating victims of the Oklahoma City bombing needed to heal from being around such extensive trauma. Individuals report being able to "let go" of a traumatic event and experience thorough healing.

To Help Change the Culture of Violence:

Victory Over Violence
3175 W. 6th Street
Los Angeles, CA 90020

Victory Over Violence is a non-profit organization that has an advisory board made up of people in business, the entertainment industry and government. V.O.V. is dedicated to increasing public awareness and providing direct support to families fleeing from domestic violence.

To contact the author for workshops or speaking, write:

Ellen Snortland
815 Third Ave., #209
Chula Vista, CA 91911

Or e-mail Ms. Snortland at: 76764.2354@CompuServe.com

Recommended Reading

Aburdene, Patricia, and John Naisbitt. *Megatrends For Women*. New York: Villard Books, 1992.

Bass, Ellen, and Davis, Laura. *The Courage To Heal: A Guide For Women Survivors Of Child Abuse*. New York: Harper & Row Publishers, Inc., 1988.

Bloomfield, Harold H. and Cooper, Robert K. *How to Be Safe in an Unsafe World*. New York: Crown Publishers, Inc., 1997.

Brownmiller, Susan. *Against Our Will: Men, Women and Rape*. New York: Simon & Schuster. 1975

Caignon, Denise, and Groves, Gail. *Her Wits About Her: Self- Defense Success Stories by Women*. New York: Harper & Row, 1987.

Chaiet, Donna, and Russell, Francine. *The Safe Zone: A Kid's Guide to Personal Safety*. New York: Morrow Junior Books, 1998.

Chernin, Kim. *Reinventing Eve: Modern Woman In Search Of Herself.* New York: Random House, 1987.

Cleage, Pearl. *Deals With The Devil, And Other Reasons To Riot.* New York: Ballantine Books, 1993.

Crow Dog, Mary. *Lakota Woman*. New York: HarperCollins Publishers, 1991.

Daly, Mary. *Beyond God The Father: Toward A Philosophy Of Women's Liberation*. Boston: Beacon Press, 1973.

Davis, Angela Y. *Women, Race & Class*. New York: Random House, 1981.

De Beauvoir, Simone. *The Second Sex*. New York: Bantam Books, 1952.

de Becker, Gavin. *The Gift of Fear: Survival Signals That Protect Us From Violence*. Boston: Little, Brown and Company, 1997.

DeEver, Allen and Ellie. *How to Write a Book on Anything In Two Weeks or Less*. Tustin, CA. Educational Awareness Publications, 1993.

DuBois, Ellen C., and Vicki Ruiz, ed. *Unequal Sisters: A Multi- cultural Reader in U.S. Women's History*. New York: Routledge, 1990.

Dworkin, Andrea. *Pornography: Men Possessing Women*. New York: Penguin Books, U.S.A., 1981.

_______ *Woman Hating*. 1st ed. New York: Dutton, 1974.

Estes, Clarissa P. *Women Who Run With The Wolves: Myths And Stories Of The Wild Woman Archetype*. New York: Ballantine Books, 1992.

Faludi, Susan. *Backlash: The Undeclared War Against American Women*. New York: Crown Publishers, Inc., 1991.

Findlen, Barbara, ed. *Listen Up: Voices From The Next Feminist Generation*. Seattle: Seal Press, 1995.

Flexner, Eleanor. *Century of Struggle: The Women's Rights Movement in the United States*. Cambridge: Belknap Press of Harvard University, 1959

French, Marilyn. *Beyond Power: On Women, Men, And Morals*. New York: Ballantine Books, 1985.

Friedan, Betty. *The Feminine Mystique*. New York: Dell Publishing Co., 1983.

Gaeta, Lisa. *Women's Basics Course Workbook*. Self-Published, Van Nuys: Impact Personal Safety, 1994.

Gravdal, Kathryn. *Ravishing Maidens: Writing Rape In Medieval French Literature And Law*. Philadelphia: University of Pennsylvania Press, 1991

Gross, Linden. *To Have Or To Harm: True Stories of Stalkers and Their Victims*. New York: Warner Books, 1994.

Heilbrun, Carolyn G. *Writing a Woman's Life*. New York, Ballantine Books, 1988.

hooks, bell. *killing rage: ending racism*. New York: Henry Holt and Company, 1995.

Ireland, Patricia. *What Women Want*. New York: Dutton, 1996.

Jackson, Donna. *How To Make The World A Better Place For Women In Five Minutes A Day*. New York: Hyperion, 1992.

Krazier, Sherryll K. *The Safe Child Book*. New York: Dell Publishing Co., 1985.

Lerner, Gerda. *The Creation Of Patriarchy*. New York: Oxford University Press, 1986.

Miedzian, Myriam. *Boys Will Be Boys: Breaking The Link Between Masculinity And Violence*. New York: Doubleday, 1991.

Morgan, Robin, ed. *Sisterhood is Global: The International Women's Movement Anthology.* New York: Doubleday, 1984.

_______ *Sisterhood Is Powerful: An Anthology of Writings From The Women's Liberation Movement.* New York: Random House, 1970.

Nelson, Mariah B. *The Stronger Women Get, The More Men Love Football: Sexism And The American Culture Of Sports.* Harcourt Brace & Company, 1994.

Niethammer, Carolyn. *Daughters of the Earth: The Lives and Legends of American Indian Women.* New York: Macmillan Publishing Co., 1977.

Northrup, Christiane. *Women's Bodies, Women's Wisdom: Creating Physical and Emotional Health and Healing.* New York: Bentam Books, 1994.

Pagels, Elaine. *Adam, Eve, and the Serpent.* New York: Vintage Books, 1988.

Quigley, Paxton. *Armed and Female.* New York: Dutton, 1989.

Rainer, Tristine. *The New Diary: How To Use A Journal For Self Guidance And Expanded Creativity.* Los Angeles: Jeremy P. Tarcher, Inc., 1978.

_______ *Your Life as Story: Writing the New Autobiography:* New York: Jeremy P. Tarcher/Putnam Books, 1997.

Rossi, Alice S. *The Feminist Papers: From Adams To De Beauvoir.* Boston: Northeastern University Press, 1973.

Schaef, Anne Wilson. *Women's Reality: An Emerging Female System in the White Male Society.* New ed. San Francisco: Perennial Library, 1985.

Shannon, Jacqueline. *Why It's Great To Be A Girl: 50 Eye-Opening Things You Can Tell Your Daughter To Increase Her Pride In Being Female.* New York: Wagner Books, Inc., 1994.

Snortland, Ellen. *Awakening Beauty.* TBA

Spender, Dale. *Nattering on the Net: Women, Power and Cyberspace.* North Melbourne, Vic.: Spinifex Press, Also, Toronto: Garamond Press, 1996, c1995.

_______ *Women Of Ideas: And What Men Have Done To Them.* London: Pandora, 1982.

Steinem, Gloria. *Outrageous Acts And Everyday Rebellions.* New York: Signet Classic, 1983.

_______ *Revolution From Within: A Book of Self-Esteem.* Boston: Little, Brown and Company, 1992

Stoltenberg, John. *The End of Manhood: A Book for Men of Conscience.* New York: Dutton, 1993.

_______ *Refusing To Be A Man: Essays On Sex And Justice.* New York: Penguin Books, U.S.A, Inc., 1990.

_______ *What Makes Pornography "Sexy"?* Minneapolis: Milkweed Editions, 1994.

Stone, Merlin. *When God Was A Woman.* New York: Harcourt Brace Jovanovich, Publishers, 1976.

Sumrall, Amber C., and Dena Taylor, ed. *Sexual Harassment: Women Speak Out.* Freedom: *The Crossing Press,* 1992.

Tavris, Carol. *The Mismeasure Of Woman: Why Women Are Not The Better Sex, The Inferior Sex, Or The Opposite Sex.* New York: Simon & Schuster, 1992.

Tesoro, Mary. *Options For Avoiding Assault: A Guide To Assertiveness, Boundaries, And De-Escalation For Violent Confrontations.* San Luis Obispo: SDE News, 1994.

van der Zande, Irene. *The KidPower Guide for Teaching Self- Protection and Confidence to Young People.* Santa Cruz: KidPower, 1997.

Warner, Marina. *From the Beast to the Blonde: On Fairy Tales and Their Tellers.* New York: Farrar, Strauss & Giroux, 1995.

Waring, Marilyn. *If Women Counted: A New Feminist Economics.* San Francisco: Harper & Row, Publishers, 1988.

Watkins, Susan A. *Marisa Rueda and Marta Rodriguez. Feminism For Beginners.* Cambridge: Icon Books, Ltd., 1992.

Wolf, Naomi. *The Beauty Myth: How Images of Beauty Are Used Against Women.* New York: W. Morrow, 1991.

Woolf, Virginia. *A Room of One's Own.* New York: Harcourt, Brace & World, Inc., 1957.